Middle-earth and the Return of the Common Good

Middle-earth and the Return of the Common Good

J. R. R. Tolkien and Political Philosophy

JOSHUA HREN

CASCADE *Books* · Eugene, Oregon

MIDDLE-EARTH AND THE RETURN OF THE COMMON GOOD
J. R. R. Tolkien and Political Philosophy

Cascade Books
An Imprint of Wipf and Stock Publishers
199 W. 8th Ave., Suite 3
Eugene, OR 97401

www.wipfandstock.com

PAPERBACK ISBN: 978-1-5326-1119-3
HARDCOVER ISBN: 978-1-5326-5038-3
EBOOK ISBN: 978-1-5326-5039-0

Cataloguing-in-Publication data:

Names: Hren, Joshua, author.

Title: Middle-earth and the return of the common good : J. R. R. Tolkien and political philosophy / Joshua Hren.

Description: Eugene, OR : Cascade Books, 2018 | Includes bibliographical references and index.

Identifiers: ISBN 978-1-5326-1119-3 (paperback) | ISBN 978-1-5326-5038-3 (hardcover) | ISBN 978-1-5326-5039-0 (ebook)

Subjects: LCSH: Tolkien, J. R. R.—(John Ronald Reuel),—1892–1973.—Lord of the rings. | Tolkien, J. R. R.—(John Ronald Reuel),—1892–1973—Political science—Philosophy. | Middle Earth (Imaginary place) | Political science—Philosophy.

Classification: PR6039.O32 H74 2018 (paperback) | PR6039.O32 H74 (ebook)

Manufactured in the U.S.A.   01/23/19

For Peter Y. Paik, my first *Magister*,
with ongoing gratitude

"I'll tell you," I said. "There is, we say, justice of one man; and there is, surely, justice of a whole city too?"

"Certainly," he said.

"Is a city bigger than one man?"

"Yes, it is bigger," he said.

"So then, perhaps there would be more justice in the bigger and it would be easier to observe closely. If you want, first we'll investigate what justice is like in the cities. Then, we'll also go on to consider it in individuals, considering the likeness of the bigger in the idea of the littler?"

"What you say seems fine to me," he said.

—*The Republic*, Plato

For even if the end is the same for a single man and for a state, that of the state seems at all events something greater and more complete whether to attain or to preserve; though it is worthwhile to attain the end merely for one man, it is finer and more godlike to attain it for a nation or for city-states.

— *Nicomachean Ethics*, Aristotle

Socialis est vita sanctorum.

Even the life of the saints is a life together with other men.

—*The City of God*, Augustine

Contents

Acknowledgments

It is difficult, sometimes, to trace causality—as difficult as numbering one's debts. Perhaps this project found its first impetus when I sat at the feet of my Uncle Tom Sanfelippo as he read *The Lord of The Rings* in a manner that left my cousins and me rapt in wonder. For this, and for my parents' provision of Tolkien's books, I remain grateful. I am grateful, also, for the gift of teaching, as it was consideration of my students that led me to dust off Tolkien from the attic box of childhood fantasies where I had placed him. For my students I began teaching Tolkien, and through many of their analyses I forged and reshaped various arguments found throughout this book. My object of study was given greater definition after I read a paper by the late Joseph V. Brogan, professor of political philosophy at La Salle University. I also thank William Fliss, keeper of the J. R. R. Tolkien Collection at Marquette, who guided me through the archives without letting me get lost in the Mines of Moria. Jesse Russell's ardent and intelligent explications of Thomistic philosophy invited an extended study of Aquinas' political thought, and Trevor Cribben Merrill provided indispensable editorial suggestions for the sections concerning Tolkien, René Girard, and mimetic desire. How thankful I am to have had the chance to correspond with Tom Shippey concerning Tolkien, Thomism, and Political philosophy, a correspondence that grew out of my attendance at his "Politics in Tolkien" lecture at Arizona State University. *New Blackfriars* and *Contagion: Journal of Violence, Mimesis, and Culture* published as articles several chapters that appear in this book. My students Jade Becker, Amelia Kumpel, and Kate Weaver all made editorial and formatting contributions that salvaged the manuscript from countless errors. Brian Doak made me keen to the requisites of manuscript submission. Finally, I am deeply indebted to my wife Brittney and my children Anaya, Søren, and Zélie, whose *joie de vivre* prevented this all-too-human author from disappearing into the depths of his cave (office), where, left alone for too long, he surely would have become indistinguishable from Sméagol.

Introduction

Tolkien *and* Political Philosophy

We begin with an *and*. Tolkien *and* political philosophy, rather than Tolkien's political philosophy. In other words, we will seek not first and foremost Tolkien's own political theories, opinions, philosophy—although these will certainly become fundamentally important at various points—but primarily the manifold points of intersection between Tolkien's *legendarium* and the political-philosophical. Further, at times the approach will be more adequately categorized as political science, as political economy, and as ethics, the latter of which Aristotle, in his *Nicomachean Ethics,* includes under the auspices of political science. Given the culminating aim of this book, which is to demonstrate the applicability of Thomas Aquinas' political philosophy to J. R. R. Tolkien's *legendarium,* we would do well to begin building a definition of the political by turning to Thomas Aquinas. If we were to sift into its simplest form our fundamental understanding of the political, its centrality to our existence, and thus its importance for the thorough study of literature, we can rightly turn to Thomas Aquinas' *De Regno,* where he writes:

> If man were intended to live alone, as many animals do, he would require no other guide to his end. Each man would be a king unto himself, under God, the highest King, inasmuch as he would direct himself in his acts by the light of reason given him from on high. Yet it is natural for man, more than for any other animal, to be a social and political animal, to live in a group. This is clearly a necessity of man's nature.[1]

However, it is especially important to note that we will only secondarily concern ourselves with "politics," that is, the transient affairs of politicians

---

1. Aquinas, *De Regno,* 5–6.

in their everydayness. The perpetually controversial Leo Strauss[2] writes that, "political philosophy is nothing other than looking philosophically at things political—philosophically, i.e., *sub specie aeternitatis*."[3] This takes us closer to the heart of our approach, but political theorist Chantal Mouffe brings us even closer when, in her *On the Political*, she makes an illuminative distinction between "politics" and "the political." "Politics," she writes, "refers to the ontic level," the "manifold practices of conventional politics, while the ontological ["the political"] concerns the very way in which a society is instituted."[4] Mouffe acknowledges that her study involves current practices of politics, and is therefore located at the ontic level, even as "it is the lack of understanding of 'the political' in its ontological dimension which is at the origin of our current incapacity to think in a political way."[4] Further, with Mouffe we take as premise the claim that political questions are more than mere technical problems which experts should solve.

If one primary component of political questions is the fact that they require us to made a decision between conflicting alternatives, our inability to think politically is by and large resultant of "the uncontested hegemony of liberalism," liberal thought here understood to be rationalist and individualist and thereby forestalling the problem of facing conflicts unsolvable by means of a rationalist approach. Any contemporary consideration of the political, then, must countenance the problem of liberalism. Like the bourgeois who will occupy a major role in the first third of the following study, liberalism negates the political, because the former demands that the individual be the ultimate point of reference. As Carl Schmitt, yet another controversial political theorist, writes, "The critical distrust of politics . . . is easily explained by the principle of a system whereby the individual must remain *terminus a quo* [the limit from which] and *terminus ad quem* [the limit to which]."[5]

As it exists *outside* of the political, "liberalism not only recognizes with self-evident logic the autonomy of different human realms but drives them toward specialization and even toward complete isolation."[6] In a liberalized world such elements of human life as production and consumption, the market and price formation, cannot be ruled or measured by religious, ethical, or aesthetical categories. The liberal thinker sees freedom, progress, and reason in alliance with economy, industry, and technology as having

2. Whether the real Strauss or not we cannot say.

3. Strauss, "What is Political Theory," 527.

4. Mouffe, *On the Political*, 9.

5. Schmitt, *The Concept of the Political*, 70–71.

6. Schmitt, *The Concept of the Political*, 72.

liberated humanity from feudalism, reaction, and force, which, so the story goes, once held a repressive alliance with kingdom or pre-modern state, war, and politics.

Freedom is in a sense the "queen bee" of liberalism. This is not to scorn freedom *per se*; Tolkien himself did not do so. When anti-liberal communism continued to rise in Russia, he asked, "What of the red Chrysanthemum in the East? And when it is all over, will ordinary people have any freedom left (or right) or will they have to fight for it, or will they be too tired to resist?"[7] Still, we must examine the meaning "freedom" obtains under liberalism. In *The Vocation of Business,* John Medaille defines the liberal understanding of freedom as simply the ability to choose. Whether that choice takes as its object a particular good or not is outside of the parameters of liberalism. In an analysis we will consider at greater length later in this study, according to Aquinas, freedom in its fullest sense can only be adequately described if we consider not merely our *ability* to choose (its formal aspect), but the *object* of our choice (its material aspect). Pope Leo XIII's *Aeterni Patris,* with which Tolkien was almost certainly familiar, beckons all to learn again the meaning of liberty at the feet of the Aquinas, the Angelic Doctor of the Church:

> For the teachings of Thomas on the true meaning of liberty, which at this time is running into license on the divine origin of all authority, on laws and their force, on the paternal and just rule of princes, on obedience to the higher powers, on mutual charity one towards another—on all of these and kindred subjects have very great and invincible force to overturn those principles of the new order which are well known to be dangerous to the peaceful order of things and to public safety.[8]

Middle Earth and *Res Publica*: Tolkien and Political Philosophy

With the 2014 publication of *The Hobbit Party: The Vision of Freedom That Tolkien Got, and The West Forgot,* by Jonathan Witt and Jay W. Richards, we saw the first book-length study devoted to J. R. R. Tolkien and political philosophy. Unfortunately, Witt and Richards, under the magical spell of neoconservative ideology, forget Tolkien's own disillusionment concerning that central value of liberal-democratic political theory: freedom. In a 1944 letter Tolkien sent to his son Christopher he describes the "difficulties of

7. Tolkien et al., *The Letters of J.R.R. Tolkien,* 89.

8. Leo XIII, *Aeterni Patris.*

discovering what common factors if any existed in the notions associated with freedom, as used at present."[9] He concludes that "I don't believe there are any [common factors], for the word has been so abused by propaganda that it has ceased to have any value for reason."[10] *The Hobbit Party* occasions a review of the various analyses of Tolkien and the political, that we may both provide a necessary texture lacking in Witt and Richards' book, but also so that we can see more clearly what work has been done and what work remains to be done on Tolkien and *res publica*.

For Tolkien, Nazi and Communist propaganda were not the only forces that had abused and deformed our understanding of freedom. As Bradley Birzer notes, "Evil [for Tolkien] does not always come in the form of war or totalitarian terror. Tolkien saw in the impersonal, machine-driven capitalism of the twentieth century, and especially in its handmaiden, the democratic bureaucracies of the Western world, a soft form of tyranny almost as oppressive as fascism and communism."[11] Tolkien went further in his criticism of modern or *mass* democracy, that crowning regime of liberalism. For "democracy," a word that had only just become fashionable in England during the war, was "nothing but a sham" that ends in slavery.[12] This is what we find from his schoolboy declarations that democracy meant only "hooliganism and uproar"[13]:

> I am not a "democrat" only because "humility" and equality are spiritual principles corrupted by the attempt to mechanize and formalize them, with the result that we get not universal smallness and humility, but universal greatness and pride, till some orc gets hold of a ring of power—and then we get and are getting slavery.[14]

Liberalism's theory of democracy posits that "there are indeed many perspectives and values and that, owing to empirical limitations, we will never be able to adopt them all, but that, when put together, they constitute a harmonious and non-conflictual ensemble."[15] For thinkers as different as the right-wing Schmitt and "Post-Marxist" Mouffe, however, arriving at a fully rational consensus is impossible, and democracy necessarily demands acts of exclusion. Tolkien enunciates the "humility," "smallness," and

9. Tolkien et al., *Letters*, 93. Witt and Richards, *The Hobbit Party*, 189.

10. Tolkien et al., *Letters*, 93.

11. Birzer, *J.R.R. Tolkien's Sanctifying Myth*, 115.

12. Birzer, *J.R.R. Tolkien's Sanctifying Myth*, 120.

13. Garth, *Tolkien and the Great War*, 21.

14. Tolkien et al., *Letters*, 246.

15. Mouffe, *On the Political*, 10.

"equality" associated with democracy in order to pronounce the impossibility of mechanizing and formalizing them; liberal democratic institutions simply cannot guarantee non-conflictual tolerance. We should not fool ourselves by assuming that modern democracy achieves the formalization of an equal, humble mode of human interaction, a humility that in Mouffe's sense allows for a "neutralization" of conflict and a perpetual possibility for compromise. Certainly this is one of the major projects and aims of modernity. As Pierre Manent writes in *A World Beyond Politics?*, "Modern man, democratic man, wants first to create the framework of his life, the most neutral and even the emptiest framework, in order to live all the more freely."[16] How different the medieval conception of liberty Christopher Dawson explicates in his *Religion and the Rise of Western Culture*: "For the medieval idea of liberty, which finds its highest expression in the life of the free cities, was not the right of the individual to follow his own will, but the privilege of sharing in a highly organized form of corporate life which possessed its own constitution and rights of self-government."[17] As this book aims to contend, Tolkien's *legendarium* returns to us not only the long-awaited king of Gondor, but more broadly the goods that can only come from our participation in a corporate life. Further, to assume that liberalism achieves its purported neutrality and emptiness would be dangerous insofar as it would blind us both to the extraordinary pride and "universal greatness" assumed by the democratic subject and to the very real possibility that a democratic orc (deformed democratic subject) would obtain a ring of power (a means to actualize the *libido dominandi*), which would lead to nothing less than slavery.

We can further understand Tolkien's analysis of democracy by reading his depiction of democracy as the moralization (especially in terms of humility and equality) of politics. In Reinhart Koselleck's unsparing critique of the "moralistic self-decisions of the French bourgeoisie during the time of the Revolution," he spells out the consequences of such a disposition: "the bourgeoisie revolutionaries, claiming themselves to be wholly occupied in the 'non-political' practice of virtue, sought to 'rule indirectly through the moralisation of politics' and thereby ended up taking 'refuge in naked force.'"[18] Insofar as we consider ourselves humble hobbits playing an ever-equal game of gloriously democratic existence filled, at best, with mostly (and gratefully) apolitical aspirations, we should not be surprised if such an existence results in others' or our own ultimate "refuge in naked force" in the face of dilemmas which require the art of compromise. This is all the

16. Manent, *A World Beyond Politics?* 9.

17. Dawson, *Religion and the Rise of Western Culture*, 172–73.

18. Quoted in Paik, *From Utopia to Apocalypse*, 7.

more reason that we need to clear our understanding of the political of all "the drab blur of our triteness and familiarity" with politics. Tolkien's fantasy can help us achieve this clearing out in preparation for "seeing things as they ought to be seen," meaning here that by responding to and deliberating over political things in Tolkien's *legendarium,* we can see the political as not merely a necessary but an elevating aspect of our existence.[19]

Predecessors in the Politics of Middle Earth

If we have established, at least in a preliminary manner, Tolkien's place alongside theorists and critics the political, and especially of liberalism and totalitarianism[20], we have yet to justify our looking to Tolkien's *legendarium—The Hobbit, The Lord of the Rings, The Silmarillion,* etc.—for the political. Certainly others have done so. In "Tolkien the Anti-Totalitarian," Jessica Yates documents a long litany of such criticisms, some that claim Tolkien for the fascists, some for the reactionary but less fierce right wing, some for the left and the "little people," some deeply troubled that his allegedly juvenile and oversimplified portrayal of conflict reduced the world to exaggerated binaries of good and evil. This batch of Tolkien's critics perhaps reaches its apogee in E. P. Thompson's contention that U.S. defense policy in the 1980s, written from an "infantile" and hawkish vantage point, was "derived, I suppose, from too much early reading of Tolkien's *The Lord of the Rings.* The evil kingdom of Mordor lies there . . . while on our side lies the nice republic of Eriador, inhabited by confused liberal hobbits who are rescued from time to time by the genial white wizardry of Gandalf-figures

---

19. Tolkien, "On Fairy Stories," 373.

20 The connection between communism and liberalism is more problematic than is oftentimes admitted. In *A World Beyond Politics?* Pierre Manent points to one of the major tensions of the liberal subject who simultaneously partakes of civil society in a manner that would seem to override politics but lives, nevertheless, under the auspices of the State: "Living at once both in civil society and the state, I am never quite whole anywhere. Half bourgeois, half citizen, I am forever uncomfortable and at times painfully divided. In any case that is the critique voiced by Rousseau and Marx . . . in his critique of the rights of man in *The Jewish Question,* Marx maintains that the separation between the state and civil society must be overcome if modern humanity is to achieve its fulfillment. Communism attempted to do this. The results of the attempt were catastrophic, but seen in its own light the project was understandable. In an extraordinarily primitive and brutal manner, Communism answered a real difficulty of our political regime A regime that is founded on separations, which have in them something abstract and artificial, naturally invites projects aimed at abolishing these very separations. The totalitarian movements of the twentieth century can be considered in this light" (29–30).

such as Henry Kissinger."[21] Yates discovered the first of these political approaches "in the archives of Allen and Unwin, the transcript of the BBC Home Service review of *The Lord of the Rings* by Arthur Calder-Marshall . . . broadcast on 30th October 1955."[22] It is worth quoting the original artifact at length:

> It is possible without fascination to interpret the allegory of *The Lord of the Rings;* its subject is exactly what one would expect a modern magical romance to be, the nature of power. The One Ring is power. Power corrupts and absolute power corrupts absolutely. If you want to make a crude simplification: Sauron, the Lord of Darkness, is the Dictator and the Black Riders his secret police. But that would be an oversimplification. It is rather that in the land of Romance and Faerie, which lies in the magical Department of our mental State, there are enacted dramas which are similar to those of our daily lives in their emotional content. Each age has its contemporary myth, reflecting the dominant moods of the period; and *The Lord of the Rings* is as contemporary in its concern with the nature of power as *Animal Farm* or *Darkness at Noon.* It is a deliberate and successful attempt to use the fairy story as a literary form in order to say something about a contemporary problem without the complication of actual people, places, and political systems.[23]

The next assessment of Tolkienian political realities, "The Politics of Middle Earth," by Malcolm Joel Barnett, appeared in *Polity* in 1969. Like Calder-Marshall, Barnett places *The Lord of the Rings* alongside other 20th Century political novels. Readers' tastes in political novels, he claims, reflect their tastes in politics. Generations who favor the import of the individual read *1984,* whereas eventually "like political scientists, writers of fictions and their . . . readers progress[] to a concern with the problems of groups."[24] Only in this sense, like Golding's *Lord of the Flies,* Tolkien's long

21. Yates, "Tolkien the Anti-Totalitarian," 238.

22. Yates, "Tolkien the Anti-Totalitarian," 232.

23. Yates, "Tolkien the Anti-Totalitarian," 232–33. Calder-Marshall goes on: "There is no attempt at any parallelism between the story and actual events. The parallelism is of a much subtler type; as when Frodo, for example, pursued by the Black Riders, is so frightened that to escape them, he puts on the Ring. But instead of becoming invisible, he becomes plainer to the Black Riders, the Ring having the same nature of evil as they have. I do not think Tolkien himself would object to my concluding that the parallel to this in the modern world is when one nation, convinced of the justice of its cause, employs a weapon of terror against its enemy, and in doing so becomes possessed by the very evil that it is fighting to destroy in the enemy" (233).

24. Barnett, "The Politics of Middle Earth (Book Review)," 383.

tale "focuses on the group as a political unit, on the interaction of political units, as well as on the means and ends of political systems."[25] However, Barnett continues, Tolkien tries to simplify our increasingly incomprehensible and complex political world. As we will see, Barnett's characterization of the Shire as "primitive-democratic" is problematic, but he is largely right to note that the political regimes are sophisticated and centralized in direct proportion to their possession of the Ring of Power. Mordor, over which the One Ring once held sway, is the most sophisticated, the Elven kingdoms next, those of the dwarfs and men next, and the hobbits, who possessed no rings, least."[26] For Barnett, the realms of both Mordor and the Elves are "essentially totalitarian" in that power rests upon the rings of power.[27] In one of his most curious analyses, he claims that one might look at Mordor and Rivendell as "the deep South when seen, alternately, through the eyes of the white liberal and the black community" for both Mordor and Elf communities are tyrannies of fear. "The white liberal in the South, like the Elf in Rivendell, knows that he can do right if only given sufficient time and power. He has some perception of the South as black people see it. He knows that the old world, if not transformed, will erupt into chaos. Yet for him the old world is [gone for himself] even if not for others."[28] Alternately, "only black people in the South" can truly comprehend the depths of Mordor, for they will see Orcs as Rednecks and Ringwraiths as Klansmen, "the manlike allies of Mordor no different from the complacent white community around them."[29] Barnett finds Tolkien's depiction of the political dimensions of Middle-Earth's inhabitants impoverished in that, though we know, for instance, that though Rohan is based upon a patrilineal kingship wherein the primary lords are relatives of the king, and though Gondor, for instance, is basically feudal in character in that those who hold titles are protected by their mother city and in turn support it, "we really know little more about them than the Americans of the middle 1960s know about the Communist world . . . we seldom get any hint of the form of interaction between the rulers and the ruled, though we are aware that this must go on."[30]Although a much more focused and thorough study of Tolkien and feudalism remains possible, for now we can note that for Barnett down the path Tolkien takes "lies not the consideration of real or even desirable communities and political settings,

---

25. Barnett, "The Politics of Middle Earth (Book Review)," 383.
26. Barnett, "The Politics of Middle Earth (Book Review)," 384.
27. Barnett, "The Politics of Middle Earth (Book Review)," 385.
28. Barnett, "The Politics of Middle Earth (Book Review)," 385.
29. Barnett, "The Politics of Middle Earth (Book Review)," 386.
30. Barnett, "The Politics of Middle Earth (Book Review)," 385.

but a mock-fairy. Candy stick worlds may be joyous in appearance, but they are seldom comfortable in practice."[31] Barnett's analysis, if its concern with the problem of simplification in Tolkien is not entirely inaccurate, is bizarre in that his own over-easy allegorical readings—think Rednecks and Orcs, Ringwraights and Klansmen—are themselves inexcusable simplifications.

In *The Politics of Fantasy: C.S. Lewis and J.R.R. Tolkien* (1984), the first major study of Tolkien and politics, Lee D. Rossi situates the work of Lewis and Tolkien within "the literature of political despair," a despair of withdrawal driven by the fact that, as Tolkien writes of the First World War, "By 1918 all but one of my close friends were dead."[32] For Rossi, if Tolkien's work merits a political analysis, it is primarily to situate him as a recent heir "of a long tradition of culturally reactionary fantasists that goes back at least to Scott and includes such figures as George MacDonald, John Ruskin, William Morris, Lord Dunsany, and E.R. Eddison. Taken together, these writers constitute a cultural rearguard of the Middle Ages."[33] However, whereas others who share these authors' critiques seek to overturn or change existing social and political relations immediately, "Tolkien and Lewis ultimately want to withdraw completely from politics."[34] In other words, although purportedly a study of Tolkien's and Lewis's politics, Rossi's overarching thesis is that these two figures, like their fictions, are painfully apolitical, and thus "*The Lord of the Rings* is one of the best expressions of a whole generation's dismay at the modern world" from which magic and splendor provide an imaginative refuge.[35]

Most critics of Tolkien and politics concede Calder-Marshall's claim that "[*The Lord of the Rings*'] subject is exactly what one would expect a modern magical romance to be, the nature of power." Jane Chance hones in on this line of interpretation in her *The Lord of the Rings: The Mythology of Power* (1992), which employs postmodern and feminist theorists to present Tolkien's work as "[a] Voice for the Dispossessed," asserting that "as a theory of power his fiction offers complex solutions to contemporary political, economic, and ideological theoretical problems voiced by Michel Foucault and other thinkers—Tolkien's contemporaries in the 1960s and 1970s."[36] She is right to claim certain affinities between Tolkien and Foucault, exemplified in the almost uncanny similarity between the Eye of Sauron and Foucault's

---

31. Barnett, "The Politics of Middle Earth (Book Review)," 387.

32. Rossi, *The Politics of Fantasy, C.S. Lewis and J.R.R. Tolkien*, 5.

33. Rossi, *The Politics of Fantasy, C.S. Lewis and J.R.R. Tolkien*, 2.

34. Rossi, *The Politics of Fantasy, C.S. Lewis and J.R.R. Tolkien*, 2.

35. Rossi, *The Politics of Fantasy, C.S. Lewis and J.R.R. Tolkien*, 133–34.

36. Chance, *The Lord of the Rings*, 10.

"gaze"—"an inspecting gaze, a gaze which each individual under its weight will end by interiorising to the point that he is his own overseer, each individual thus exercising this surveillance over, and against, himself."[37] However, as Chance traces the "evolution" of "The Political Hobbit" from *The Fellowship of the Ring* through *The Return of the King,* she too often imposes a liberal-democratic framework on Tolkien's fiction, so that the Fellowship of the Ring, this "strange marriage of opposites . . . epitomizes the United Nations, which must eventually allow all different nations to coexist in peace in Middle-earth's coming Fourth Age of man."[38] This line of thought continues when Chance claims that "[p]ower, so Tolkien insists, must be shared with those individuals and peoples who are different, in gender, nature, history, and temperament."[39] Further, as Matthew Scott Winslow observes, "The reader is left scratching his head, trying to figure out what exactly Chance means by 'political.'"[40] Winslow finds the comparison of Tolkien and Foucault "often contrived," this largely because whereas Tolkien saw power as just one dimension of human reality, for Foucault *all* actions are political in nature, so that, for Chance, "*everything* becomes political, and thus *nothing* is political."[41]

Although, as the title of her work suggests, Alison Milbank's book *Chesterton and Tolkien as Theologians* treats them as such, "Fairy Economics" draws forth the importance of political economy in Tolkien's work. The particular form of economy we witness in the *legendarium* is the economy of gift exchange. As a later section of this book will show, Milbank demonstrates that, like Tolkien, Marcel Mauss was influenced by Nordic culture, and thus by a pre-capitalist system of gift exchange that implicates the giver in a thick weave of reciprocity and obligation. Mauss' book *The Gift* finds evidence in the *Edda,* a collection of ancient Nordic literature, and its opening epigraph is the *Eddic* "a gift always looks for recompense."[42] In Nordic culture, however, "the gift" obtains a double meaning as "both positive and negative from the German word for poison," as Germanic gift-exchange was taken to an extreme that included hostage-taking. Georges Baitaille argued that the gift theory "restored life to the gifted object, and opposed the calculated nature of market relations in favor of an economics of excess."[43]

---

37. Chance, *The Lord of the Rings,* 20.

38. Chance, *The Lord of the Rings,* 57.

39. Chance, *The Lord of the Rings,* 62.

40. Winslow, "Two on Tolkien by Jane Chance."

41. Winslow, "Two on Tolkien by Jane Chance."

42. Milbank, *Chesterton and Tolkien as Theologians,* 130–31.

43. Milbank, *Chesterton and Tolkien as Theologians,* 130–31.

Milbank contends that other gift-exchange theorists, in spite of their vaunt-ed postmodernity, are "at once nostalgic and utopian, even when they seek to emphasize the sometimes oppressive power relations that accompany gift-exchange," because the gift-exchange economy belongs to pre-modern cultures far removed from our contemporary atomized individual.[44] These postmoderns, then, find strange currency with the premodern Tolkien, one of whose characteristics is, in the words of Michael Curry, a "radical nostalgia."[45] We see Bilbo's relation to gift-exchange is even more explicit in *The Hobbit*, where, as hired thief for the dwarves' expedition, he "is a kind of scapegoat who will bear prophylactically the transgressive nature of the en-terprise," and he controversially embodies the value of gift exchange when he gives "Thorin's" arkenstone to the lakemen in an attempt to forestall war between men, elves, and dwarves.[46] Milbank finds gift-exchange as "the basis of the [*Lord of the Rings*'] attempt to resist the power of the Ring, just as the Ring itself is the result of gift-exchange gone awry."[47] For, if "to accept a gift is to join a mesh of obligations so strong that the whole state is moved if but one other point of the chain be properly grasped" Sauron, in naming himself "Lord of Gifts" used the rings he gave away as means of control and domination.[48] Milbank goes on to elucidate the far-reaching import of gift-exchange in *The Lord of the Rings*, where, for instance, the gift-giving evinced in Bilbo's birthday party and in Tolkien's letter to A.C. Dunn "had a considerable social importance," one of which might be a "response to the rumour of [the] traumatic murder by Sméagol, so that hobbits . . . give up what was the original object of desire."[49]

Milbank positions Tolkien among the Distributists. Using Pope Leo XIII's encyclical *Rerum Novarum* as the "foundational document" of their movement, Distributists sought a less alienating form of political-econom-ical relations that would restore property to more people, thereby creating the conditions of gift-exchange in that people would be able to exchange *real things*, even things outside of the market. As *Rerum Novarum* pro-claims, "the law, therefore, should favor ownership and its policy should be to induce as many people as possible to become owners . . . If workpeople can be encouraged to look forward to obtaining a share in the land, the

44. Milbank, *Chesterton and Tolkien as Theologians*, 130–31.
45. Curry, *Defending Middle-Earth: Tolkien, Myth and Modernity*, 5.
46. Milbank, *Chesterton and Tolkien as Theologians*, 130–31.
47. Milbank, *Chesterton and Tolkien as Theologians*, 126.
48. Milbank, *Chesterton and Tolkien as Theologians*, 129.
49. Milbank, *Chesterton and Tolkien as Theologians*, 132.

result will be bridged over, and the two orders brought closer together."[50] In spite of the fact that Milbank is primarily concerned with establishing Tolkien as a theologian, her work embodies the Thomistic approach which, while granting each science its rightful object, does not compartmentalize, and in fact preserves the intrinsic relationships between, say, theology and economics, the theological and the political.

Finally, as noted, 2014 saw the publication of Jonathan Witt's and Jay W. Richards' *The Hobbit Party: The Vision of Freedom That Tolkien Got, and the West Forgot*. In their first chapter the pair cite Tolkien scholar Joseph Pearce, who in *Tolkien: Man and Myth*, writes:

> If much has been written on the religious significance of *The Lord of the Rings*, less has been written on its political significance—and the little that has been written is often erroneous in its conclusions and ignorant of Tolkien's intentions . . . Much more work is needed in the area, not least because Tolkien stated, implicitly at least, that the political significance of the work was second only to the religious in its importance.[51]

Strangely, especially considering their consciousness of the fact that "there are no major books dedicated to the subject," Witt and Richards cite none of the aforementioned studies. Instead, they acknowledge as predecessor to their study only one "particularly fine" one: John West's "*The Lord of the Rings* as a Defense of Western Civilization" in *Celebrating Middle Earth*.[52] They do engage with several Marxist criticisms of Tolkien only to—at times rightfully—declaim these authors' "attempt[s] to co-opt him."[53] Early in *The Hobbit Party*, Witt and Richards cite a well-known letter from Tolkien to his son Christopher in which the father shares his politics with the son: "My political opinions lean more and more to Anarchy (philosophically understood, meaning abolition of control not whiskered men with bombs)."[54] It is no accident that these authors leave off the last part of Tolkien's sentence "—or to 'unconstitutional' Monarchy." Conspicuous as this selective citation may be, it provides prime evidence, early on, that the book is by and large an attempt to graft neoconservative political ideals onto Tolkien's masterpiece, "co-opting Tolkien" like the "Others on the left" from whom they claim to save him. For Witt and Richards, because Tolkien was an anti-Totalitarian, he is more or less a *defacto* democrat. But *The Return of the*

---

50. Milbank, *Chesterton and Tolkien as Theologians*, 118–32.

51 Quoted in Witt and Richards, *The Hobbit Party*, 189.

52. Witt and Richards, *The Hobbit Party*, 191.

53. Witt and Richards, *The Hobbit Party*, 17.

54. Quoted in Witt and Richards, *The Hobbit Party*, 16.

Democratically-elected President was not a working title of the third part of *The Lord of the Rings*.

The trouble is, of course, that for Tolkien monarchy was not relegated to the realm of faerie. As Christopher Scarf illustrates in his little-known gem *The Ideal of Kingship in the Writings of Charles Williams, C.S. Lewis, and J.R.R. Tolkien*, the Catholic Inkling describes his ideal King, embodied in the fictional Aragorn, as a "monarch with the power of unquestioned decision in debate."[55] Tolkien biographer Humphrey Carpenter reminds us that the *Beowulf* scholar was "'right wing' in that he honoured his monarch and his country and did not believe in the rule of the people."[56]

If the first problem with *The Hobbit Party* is a neglect of Tolkien's political ideals, the second is a scouring of the economical precepts incarnate in his novels. It is noteworthy that Witt and Richards give public thanks to Fr. Robert Sirico at the start of their book, and that Witt himself is a Fellow of the Acton Institute, Sirico's brainchild. It is often said that the more explicitly unsettling teachings of Machiavelli were made palatable by Rousseau, and yet one can best understand Rousseau's philosophical core by returning to Machiavelli, to whom he is in debt. It is in this spirit that we might find illumination of Witt and Richards by returning to the Sirico, the priest whose Austrian Economics-fueled *Defending the Free Market* promotes as regnant principle "creative destruction," which he defines as "[t]he [goodly economic] phenomenon whereby old skills, companies, and sometimes entire industries are eclipsed as new methods and businesses take their place."[57] Their interpretations involve any number of applications of ideologies imparted by Fr. Sirico and neoconservative Catholic Michael Novak, but Witt and Richards magically make these ideologies palatable.

"In a Hole in the Ground Lived an Enemy of Big Government," quip Richards and Witt (no pun intended), and yet, as is typical for those who bring *a priori* idealization of unfettered capitalism to interpretation of any text, the authors write little to nothing of Tolkien as enemy of Big Business: they treat any textual evidence that smacks of such critiques as forgivable curiosities, but curiosities at best, a fact that finds full force in their treatment of the entire Distributivist economic system as "romantic." This in spite of several glaring examples, from the "Master" of Lake-town in *The Hobbit*, who "may have a good head for business—especially his own business" but who "is no good when anything serious happens" to the banally

55. Quoted in Scarf, *The Ideal of Kingship in the Writings of Charles Williams, C.S. Lewis, and J.R.R. Tolkien*, 114.

56. Scarf, *The Ideal of Kingship*, 115.

57. Fr. Robert A. Sirico, "Creative Destruction."

evil Lotho of "The Scouring of the Shire."[58] Bizarrely, Witt and Richards take time to offer an (admittedly qualified but strangely tangential) appreciation of Walmart, that chain that grows "not by some evil conspiracy but because they enjoy greater economies of scale," so that "if you produce undershirts and Walmart offers to buy ten million of them, you can afford to sell your shirts near your cost of production and still make a handsome profit," all of this fulfilling "our" desire, for "we want lower-income people to be able to buy products that would have once been out of their reach."[59] If Joseph Pearce is right in his appraisal that "the little that has been written" on Tolkien and politics "is often erroneous in its conclusions," regretfully, this, the first book-length study devoted to the subject, is not exempt. Not one of us is entirely freed from ideological interpretations, but too often Witt and Richards bridge the gap between Tolkien's own pre-modern, critical stance toward liberalism and their own wizardly synthesis of neoconservative ideas and Catholic social teaching.

An Excursion into Ethics

We must depart from our linear chronology if we are to escape the conclusion that *The Hobbit Party* signifies "the end of all things" in terms of Tolkien and political philosophy; like Aristotle, perhaps we must begin with a sound grounding in ethics before we can move into politics. In "Tolkien and the Ethical Function of Escape," Lionel Basney observes that "the charge that fantasy is a form of 'escape' is largely an ethical charge. We do in fact expect literature not just to entertain but to instruct . . . not, perhaps, to teach us what we ought to choose and do but to reveal to us some sense of the nature of choosing and doing."[60] While Basney preserves Tolkien's sense of escape as potentially *good*, he asserts a strong limit to the sort of ethical exploration that is possible in fantasy at large and in Tolkien specifically. This being said, ethical discussion in our world at large seems increasingly disconnected from the world of action. For Basney, the interminability of discussions concerning what is good has resulted in a world in which goodness—the center of ethics—"cannot be made active; for the modern world it remains in a sense aesthetic, wasting its fragrance in the desert air."[61] Writing just before 1981, when in *After Virtue* Alasdair MacIntyre undertakes a similar genealogy, Basney contends that the separation of ethics from the

58. Witt and Richards, *The Hobbit Party*, 250.
59. Witt and Richards, *The Hobbit Party*, 151.
60. Basney, "Tolkien and the Ethical Function of Escape," 24.
61. Basney, "Tolkien and the Ethical Function of Escape," 26.

world of action seems to have its historical root in the "ought/is" dilemma, a philosophical problem that stems from David Hume's claim, in *A Treatise of Human Nature,* that "moral standards cannot be derived from the descriptions of facts."[62] An observed fact cannot result in an ethical norm that contains the force of a syllogism. The effect of Hume's "ought/is" conclusion is to drain the ethical meaning from the experiential world. The acting person, even if she considers her decisions *conscientious,* ceases to consider them "ethically significant."[63] But, conceived as such, the world becomes increasingly absurd. For Basney, Tolkien's "simplified ethics is a response to this situation."[64] But *The Lord of the Rings* is not a Sartrean novel, nor is it Heller's *Catch 22.* In simplifying ethics as he does, Basney claims, Tolkien in a sense ensures that ethical absurdity will not triumph—at least in his fiction. Further, the ethics of Middle-earth, which Basney sees as fairly traditional and clear, are urgent in that the story itself is one of crisis and apocalypse. Proclaiming his overarching conclusion one last time, Basney writes:

> Simplicity is, in fact, the requirement of renewed ethical vision as modern fantasy offers it. From the malign and incredible complications of modern society we turn to the fresh, primary-color reassurances of Middle-earth . . . The innocence of mountains and trees, the innocent remoteness of kings and magic mirrors, allow Tolkien to present a simplified ethical vision which works as a refuge for a culture in ethical confusion.[65]

One can detect a characteristic modern hubris in the claim that "kings and magic mirrors" bring with them *innocence*; medieval history, Spenser's *Faerie Queene,* to cite just two obvious reference points, provide evidence contrariwise. Further, even as some ethical dilemmas of modernity are complex enough that *The Lord of the Rings* offers no worthy "applicability," complexity is not always a sign of advanced or even *more realistic* analysis. Martha Nussbaum may be right to suggest that in reading Henry James, that immensely "complex" novelist, one gains a "respect for the irreducibly concrete moral context . . . and a determination to scrutinize all aspects of this particular with intensely focused perception," in a way that invites the reader to pay the same kind of moral attention to life that one deploys toward James's fiction.[66] Nussbaum may be even more correct to note that a Jamesian literary approach will incline the reader toward adoption of an

---

62. Basney, "Tolkien and the Ethical Function of Escape," 26.
63. Basney, "Tolkien and the Ethical Function of Escape," 26.
64. Basney, "Tolkien and the Ethical Function of Escape," 27.
65. Basney, "Tolkien and the Ethical Function of Escape," 34.
66. Quoted in Dadlez, *Mirrors to One Another,* 13.

Aristotelian ethical approach in that it will teach her to "respond at the right times, with reference to the right objects, towards the right people, with the right aim, and in the right way," but *what is right* is as difficult to determine as the definition of *good* which, as Basney notes, is lost in the complexity of modernity. For, as Alasdair MacIntyre argues in *After Virtue,* "James writes of a world in which—the progress of his own novels attest to it—the substance of morality is increasingly elusive."[67] It is my hope that Basney's critique—particularly his allegation that Middle-earth is "primary-colored" in its simplicity—will lose some of its sting once we consult and conduct close readings of Tolkien's texts through the lens of *the political,* and that we will find the paradoxes and even the often impasse-inducing complexity that lies beneath the apparently simple surface. Still more, if Nussbaum champions James's mode of moral complexity, in defending Tolkien we are championing his works' ability to partake of the same tradition of virtue ethics, albeit in another mode and with perhaps radically different conclusions.

However, complexity or simplicity is not the only object of Basney's critique. Behind this critique we can smell a discontent with fantasy itself. Ben Watson traces the dawn of fantasy's disrepute to the "bourgeois revolution and the victory of the experimental method in science."[68] Scorn of fantasy is evident in John Locke's 1689 *Essay Concerning Human Understanding* in which he wrote that use of simile to explain demonstrates that we "rather fancy than know" and the chasm between knowing and fancying only grows under "bourgeois insistence on hard facts."[69] Insofar as study of the political helps us form adequate political judgments, we can find an ally in Theodor Adorno's 1951 claim that "[f]antasy alone, today consigned to the realm of the unconscious and proscribed from knowledge as childish, injudicious rudiment, can establish that relation between objects which is the irrevocable source of all judgment: should fantasy be driven out, judgment too, the real act of knowledge, is exorcised."[70] Adorno here turns to fantasy in order to advance the Frankfurt School's critique of Soviet Marxism and U.S. positivism. While Tolkien and Adorno shared enemies, Tolkien carried no Frankfurt School card. Further, Adorno goes too far when he claims that "fantasy alone" can establish that relation between objects which is the irrevocable source of all judgement. Still, Adorno takes us some distance in defending fantasy from critics who would position it as "exploiting people's need for

67. MacIntyre, *After Virtue,* 243.

68. Watson, "Fantasy and Judgment," 215.

69. Watson, "Fantasy and Judgment," 215.

70. Quoted in Watson, "Fantasy and Judgment," 213.

distraction after mindnumbing labor."[71] On the contrary, for Adorno, as for Tolkien, fantasy is capable of eliminating the numbness of everydayness, is in a sense a "universal necessity, [is] crucial because it dramatizes the difference between thought and reality."[72] Tolkien aims at something similar when he notes that fantasy facilitates "[r]ecovery . . . a re-gaining—regaining of a clear view. I do not say 'seeing things as they are' and involve myself with the philosophers, though I might venture to say 'seeing things as we ought to see them' as things apart from ourselves."[73] Using language that might, strangely, find approval in a Marxist Frankfurt School camp, Tolkien notes that if fantasy needs to free us from the "drab blur of our triteness and familiarity" this triteness is "really the penalty of 'appropriation': the things that are trite, or (in a bad sense) familiar, are the things that we have appropriated, legally or mentally. We say we know them," but once we "laid hands on them, and then locked them in our hoard, acquired them," we "ceased to look at them."[74] Tolkien quickly insists that fairy-stories are not the only means of recovery. Humility, for instance, can accomplish this.

However, we must not lose sight of the particular way in which fantasy and science fiction can achieve recovery of *res publica*. As Peter Paik argues in *From Utopia to Apocalypse*, science fiction—and here we will make the same claims for fantasy—"proves to be eminently constructive for reflecting on these far-reaching [political-philosophical] questions, thanks in considerable measure to its roots in the practice of philosophic speculation."[75] Many works of fantasy and science fiction, distinguished as they are by "the effort to imagine a fundamentally different world, one that, though it might be drastically divergent from the really existing world in its laws, mores, and technologies, nevertheless exhibits the consistency and coherence of actuality."[76] As such, this fiction can serve as a "vital instrument for the investigation of the contingencies governing political life, the forces that structure and dissolve collective existence, by providing the reader with visions in which familiar realities are destabilized and transformed."[77]

71. Watson, "Fantasy and Judgment," 223.

72. Watson, "Fantasy and Judgment," 223.

73. Tolkien, "On Fairy Stories," 373.

74. Tolkien, "On Fairy Stories," 373.

75. Paik, *From Utopia to Apocalypse*, 2.

76. Paik, *From Utopia to Apocalypse*, 2.

77. Paik, *From Utopia to Apocalypse*, 2.

Escaping Fantasy

If Basney's claims about "escape literature" are true as far as they go, we must offer two further rebuttals. Familiar as he was with the general critique of fantasy as "escapist," Tolkien infamously defended "Fairy-Stories" in his 1939 lecture:

> In using Escape in [a derogatory] way the critics . . . are confusing, not always by sincere error, the Escape of the Prisoner with the Flight of the Deserter. Just so a Party-spokesman might have labeled departure from the misery of the Führer's or any other Reich and even criticism of it as treachery. In the same way these critics, to make confusion worse, and so to bring into contempt their opponents, stick their label of scorn not only on to Desertion, but on to real Escape, and what are often its companions, Disgust, Anger, Condemnation, and Revolt.[78]

Secondly, we can question whether Tolkien's *legendarium* can be justly characterized as strict "fantasy" in the sense we have been using, especially given that Tolkien insisted he "much [preferred] history, true or feigned, with its varied applicability to the thought and experience of readers."[79] He takes pains to present himself as "historically minded," one consequence of which is that, for Tolkien,

> Middle-earth is not an imaginary world. The name is the modern form . . . of *midden-erd>middel erd,* an ancient name for the *oikomene,* the abiding place of Men, the objectively real world, in use specifically opposed to imaginary worlds (as Fairyland) or unseen worlds (as Heaven or Hell). The theater of my tale is earth, the one in which we now live, but the historical period is imaginary (though not wholly impossible).[80]

We do not solve the problematic *otherness* of the *legendarium* by situating it more as history than fantasy, even as in so doing we will have "escaped" the ascendancy of bourgeois modernity. In part, this is because Tolkien writes of Middle-earth as existing *in the distant past.* But, secondarily, we have not yet adequately answered the problem of Tolkien's purportedly apolitical approach to the *legendarium.*

Even if the above assessment of our nature as political animals is true, and even if fantasy can help us see political things more clearly, as Joseph

---

78. Tolkien, "On Fairy Stories," 376.
79. Quoted in Shippey, *The Road to Middle-Earth,* 169.
80. Tolkien et al., *Letters,* 239.

Brogan contends, "Any political interpretation" of Tolkien's work "trips upon the threshold" for in the Foreword of the second edition of *The Lord of the Rings*, Tolkien apparently rejects a political meaning to his work.[81] He claims that the mythology was "primarily linguistic in inspiration . . . begun in order to provide the necessary background of the 'history' for Elvish tongues."[82] In a letter to his son, Christopher Tolkien, he claimed that "my long book is an attempt to create a world in which a form of language agreeable to my personal aesthetic might seem real," even as he acknowledges that "I don't know what I mean, because 'aesthetic' is always impossible to catch in a net of words."[83] His use of "aesthetic" here dramatizes the problem of our approach. Tolkien's "apolitical" attitude finds further expression in the Foreword to *The Lord of the Rings*. He was motivated, he insists, by "the desire of a tale-teller to try his hand at a really long story that would hold the attention of readers, amuse them, delight them, and at times maybe excite them or deeply move them . . . As for any inner meaning or 'message,'" he writes, "it has in the intention of the author none. It is neither allegorical nor topical."[84] Tolkien famously denied an allegorical reading, but in so doing he paved the way for a certain "applicability to the thought and experience of the readers."[85] According to Tolkien, then, the *legendarium* would seem to be little more than a long story told in order to create a context for his invented languages. Nevertheless, if we look beyond these somewhat fantastic explanations of the stories' sole purposes, we find that Tolkien's understanding of storytelling was more complex. He articulated this complexity by making a distinction between the story as *vera historia,* which he considered to be the surface meaning of a story, and *mythos,* by which he designated its philosophical, moral, and religious elements. As Joseph Brogan demonstrates, Tolkien knew that "to be even moderately marketable . . . a story must pass muster on its surface value, as a *vera historia.*"[86] Adopting the exoteric/esoteric binary typical of Leo Strauss, Brogan argues that most readers will judge a story for the simple pleasures of its *vera historia,* but "the more intelligent reader" will be drawn deeper into the *mythos.*[87] In

81. Brogan, "Tolkien on Res Publica."

82. Tolkien, *The Lord of the Rings*, 2.

83. Tolkien et al., *Letters,* 264–65.

84. Tolkien, *The Lord of the Rings*, 5.

85. Tolkien, *The Lord of the Rings*, 6.

86. Tolkien et al., *Letters,* 33.

87. Brogan, "Tolkien on Res Publica."

writing a *vera historia*, "one does not escape from the question 'what is it all about?'"[88] For Brogan, then:

> Tolkien's adamant rejection of any allegorical or topical mean-
> ing in *The Lord of the Rings* does not preclude any political inter-
> pretation at the level of transhistorical principles of political life,
> but only an interpretation bounded by the particularity of the
> historical moment. Tolkien is not allegorically describing what
> Winston Churchill did or providing a political commentary on
> his life and times. Tolkien's purpose is the elucidation of truth
> and the encouragement of good morals that is relevant to the
> "human situation (of all periods)."[89]

To the extent that his intention involves a political teaching, however subtle, it will be at the level of the transhistorical, not the particular.[90] Brogan's caution against excessively particular interpretations, historical or otherwise, is appropriate in light of Tolkien's publicized warnings. However, if *vera historia* is superficial, and if the allegorical-historical is to be avoided at all costs, we cannot so readily dismiss the political-historical in the *legendarium*, a conclusion verified by Tolkien's own use of "history" in a manner distinct from *vera historia*.

It would seem that, for Tolkien, as for Frederic Jameson, history, or rather the "political-historical" dimension of a work of fantasy, could foster a recovery of political things, as well. For, "oddly enough, despite their antagonistic political outlooks, conservative writer and radical theorist share a view of literature as solely meaningful within this world and its history rather than as pure fantastic sanctuary."[91] Ishay Landa helpfully problematizes the precise way in which we can understand Tolkien's stories as unfolding historically. For the central conflict in the *legendarium,* the lust for power and domination, is hardly historical: "To say that Middle-earth at the time of the War of the Ring is shaken by struggles over power and domination, though accurate, is as much an historical explanation of that war as it is of the Second World War or the war between Athens and Sparta."[92] Because this theme of the lust for power and its attendant power struggle can be used to explain every war, in a sense it helps us understand no war whatsoever. Although Landa overreaches, egregiously at points, by imposing a Marxist structure and its in-built symbols of "proletariat" and "private property"

---

88. Brogan, "Tolkien on Res Publica."
89. Brogan, "Tolkien on Res Publica."
90. Brogan, "Tolkien on Res Publica."
91. Quoted in Landa, "Slaves of the Ring," 115.
92. Landa, "Slaves of the Ring," 116.

upon Tolkien's fiction, he is correct in arguing that the *legendarium*'s political-historical dimensions are deeply informed by the crises of modernity made especially manifest in the World Wars and the Bolshevik revolution, and not at all wrong—think of *The Hobbit*—to sniff out Tolkien's recurrent engagement with questions of property: "Tolkien, who had taken part in the battle of the Somme, was deeply aware of the calamitous consequences of imperialism, but at the same time was even more alarmed at the prospect of revolution."[93] For Landa, the upshot is that his stories contain a dialectical swing between "a utopian renunciation of private property and its ideological vindication."[94]

Landa insists that the precise historical underpinning informing Tolkien's fiction is the crisis of capitalist property relations that culminates in World War I. This historical-political subtext of Tolkien's aesthetic is not entirely wrong,[95] but we must further probe its ethical-political implications. Toward the beginning of *After Virtue*, MacIntyre brings his analysis upon Kierkegaard's *Either/Or,* that work which plumbs the problem of the choice between the ethical and the aesthetic. Although from behind his many masks Kierkegaard seems to advance the idea that the aesthetic *can* be chosen seriously, MacIntyre disagrees, even as the "burden of choosing it can be as passion ridden as that of choosing the ethical."[96] In order to epitomize such a case, MacIntyre turns to "those young men of [his] father's generation who watched their own earlier ethical principles die along with the deaths of their friends in the trenches in the mass murder of Ypres and the Somme; and who returned determined that nothing was ever going to matter to them again and invented the aesthetic triviality of the nineteen twenties."[97] One of these young men, we can add, was J. R. R. Tolkien, who embarked for France and traveled to the Somme as a second lieutenant in the 11th Lancashire Fusiliers in 1916. There he experienced what thousands of other soldiers had come to know before him: exasperating marches from the billets to the trenches; "a tangled confusion of wires, field-telephones out of order and covered with mud"; and "corpses [that] lay in every corner, horribly torn by the shells."[98] Rescued from the carnage by trench fever, Tolkien began to write "The Book of Lost Tales," which would eventually become *The Silmarillion,* the founding myths and history of the *legendarium*

93. Landa, "Slaves of the Ring," 117.

94. Landa, "Slaves of the Ring," 117.

95. Consider John Garth's *Tolkien and the Great War.*

96. MacIntyre, *After Virtue*, 41.

97. MacIntyre, *After Virtue*, 41.

98. Carpenter, *J.R.R. Tolkien*, 91.

which culminated in his epic narrative *The Lord of the Rings*. Although many have deemed the *legendarium* just the sort of "triviality" which MacIntyre references, we can also see Tolkien's narrative as a profound assertion of the common good against the cynicism and absurd complexity of a modernity that exploded in the Great War. Instead of aesthetic triviality, Tolkien returned from the Somme with a modern mythology.

Tolkien and Res Publica

If many prior studies[99] of Tolkien's politics have been erroneous, it is not always because the authors have either approached Tolkien himself as more ideological than he actually was, nor that the authors themselves have assumed ideological premises and lenses which have led to misreadings. On the contrary, a Marxist or neoconservative reading of Tolkien *can* be fruitful and bring forth good things. Insofar as critics have not made a monstrosity of Tolkien and politics, it is because they have taken as their course of study Tolkien and politics as usual, rather than Middle-earth and the political. Remember Mouffe's contention that political questions are more than mere technical problems which experts should solve. This is especially true concerning Tolkien's work, as this wildly popular corpus, written from the particularly revelatory vantage of a "reactionary monarchist" able to grant us an outside gaze into the mess of modernity. J. Peter Euben advances a similar claim when, in *The Tragedy of Political Theory*, he claims that allegedly nostalgic works such as Plato's *Republic* and More's *Utopia* are uniquely situated to "make the obvious, everyday, natural, necessary, the omnipresently 'modern' seem contrived, absurd, flagrantly unjust, passé, and incomprehensible."[100] In this sense, Tolkien's is a transhistorical teach-

99. Other studies of Tolkien and political reality than those aforementioned do exist: some articles in Marxist journals, such as Ishay Landa's "Slaves of the Ring: Tolkien's Political Unconscious," some postcolonial examinations, such as Elizabeth Massa Hoiem's "World Creation as Colonization: British Imperialism in 'Aldarion and Erendis,'" and, important for our purposes, the illuminative "Political Institutions in J.R.R. Tolkien's Middle-Earth: Or, How I Learned to Stop Worrying About the Lack of Democracy" by Dominic J. Nardi Jr., which won the Alexi Kondratiev Student Paper Award at Mythcon 45 (but, in part because it was published in the specialized fantasy journal *Mythlore*, will likely remain beyond the purview of most readers). Other such analyses have appeared as paragraphs in, for instance, Bradley Birzer's *J.R.R. Tolkien's Sanctifying Myth*, Tom Shippey's *The Road to Middle Earth*, Patrick Curry's *Defending Middle Earth: Tolkien: Myth and Modernity*, Stratford Caldecott's *The Power of the Ring*, and, amid a work primarily focused on ecology, Matthew Dickerson and Jonathan Evans's *Ents, Elves, and Eriador: The Environmental Vision of J.R.R. Tolkien*.

100. Euben, *The Tragedy of Political Theory*, 14.

ing about *res publica* that he understood to be true for all persons at all times because it is rooted in the artistry of human nature and experience, which is nothing if not political. As we will see, Tolkien can cast fantastic light on political and political-theological problems probed by Plato, Hobbes, Hegel, Sombart, Adorno, Voegelin, Foucault and a number of other political theorists and philosophers working at the intersection of the political and the mythical. However, in terms of the political, the premise of this book is that we are "meant to see" political things as intractably bound to a Thomistic understanding of the common good.

The Gift of Death
and the New Magic of Politics

Hegel and Tolkien on Sorcery and Secondary Worlds

The Gift of Death for the Bourgeois World, the Gift Stolen by the Machine

The Doom (or Gift) of Men is mortality," Tolkien writes. Elsewhere he notes that not "even Power or Domination is the real centre of my story. It provides the theme of a War, about something dark and threatening enough to seem at that time of supreme importance, but that is mainly a 'setting' for characters to show themselves. The real theme is . . . Death and Immortality."[1] How important, then, that a reading of *The Lord of the Rings* is able to grant death and immortality their essential place in human life. According to Christianity, death is a door; it marks the end of human life and the beginning of beatific immortality or the banality of damnation. Death, for Christians, does not first and foremost move human life toward a spirited support of the polis Instead, death spurs the soul toward an emulation of the divine by which persons can anticipate the *vita sanctorum*—the life of the saints.

Moderns have lost this sense of death because in modernity death is treated as "neither an ineluctable end that must be courageously confronted, nor the gateway to salvation; it is extrinsic and alien to life and ought to

1. Tolkien et al., *Letters*, 147.

be resisted and overcome."[2] Taken as a whole, the modern project aims to overcome all limitations which nature "imposes" upon human life—most especially suffering and death. Thus the rise of technocracy, by which humanity tries to conquer the natural world and secure prosperity and preservation. In consequence, certain human virtues lose their worth. Consider courage, as important to Aristotle as it is to *Beowulf*. In modernity success comes through the inculcation of the virtues of business, and insofar as *homo economicus* (economic man) eclipses *Zôion politikòn* (man as a political animal), the pertinence of courage wanes. Revolutionary and totalitarian movements, especially since the start of the twentieth century, have sought to disrupt the hegemony of this *bourgeois* world, to end the reign of radical individualism.

Still further, "Modernity's initial premise that death is something to be overcome consequently makes power the crux of human life."[3] Tolkien mythologizes these problems of modernity. As he explains in his letters, the *legendarium* is largely concerned with "Fall, Mortality, and the Machine . . . the will to mere power, seeking to make itself objective by physical force and mechanism, and so inevitably by lies."[4]

For the 19th-century German philosopher G.F.W. Hegel, the unduly private economic interests of the bourgeois world can only be restrained and transcended through war. "War reveals the hard but necessary truth that all possessions, including one's own body and life, are transitory," a truth "obscured in modernity by the success of the liberal state in securing peace and opening up a realm for the proliferation of economic life."[5]

When Tolkien explains that "War" provides his *legendarium* with "something dark and threatening enough to seem at that time of supreme importance," something which allows characters to "show themselves," by which he means demonstrate the classical and Anglo-Saxon virtues, he is thinking in a Hegelian mode.[6] Through war the bourgeois hobbits become political animals. Through the War of the Ring their degenerate understanding of freedom morphs into "the spirited fortitude necessary to maintain free institutions."[7]

And yet "war as restraint and correction" is problematized by the development of modern warfare, which is in part what Tolkien references

2. Gillespie, *Death and Desire*, 155.

3. Gillespie, *Death and Desire*, 155.

4. Tolkien et al., *Letters*, 145.

5. Gillespie, *Death and Desire*, 155.

6. Tolkien et al., *Letters*, 164.

7. Tolkien et al., *Letters*, 165.

when he notes that his tale is concerned with "the Machine."[8] The "Machine" finds its most concentrated mythical expression in the Ring, which represents the "truth that potency (or perhaps rather potentiality) if it is to be exercised, and produce results, has to be externalized and so as it were passes, to a greater or less degree, out of one's direct control."[9] This is not to claim, by the way, that the Ring is an allegory of, say, the nuclear bomb. To such a supposition Tolkien has already responded, stating that "Of course my story is not an allegory of Atomic power, but of *Power* (exerted for Domination)."[10] But we risk no overly-allegorical misapprehension of Tolkien's direct commentary on modern warfare, which comes in a January 1945 letter to his son Christopher. In a quasi-Hegelian note, he accepts that the "diabolic hour" of the current war which spells the "destruction of what should be (indeed is) the common wealth of Europe," "mainly created by Germany" may be "necessary and inevitable." And yet, he continues, "what a gloat! We were supposed to have reached a stage of civilization in which it might still be necessary to execute a criminal, but not to gloat, or to hang his wife and child by him while the orc-crowd hooted."[11] Still, the total destruction of Germany, made possible by modern warfare, Tolkien reads as "one of the most appalling *world-catastrophes*."[12] Well, he concludes:

> The first War of the Machines seems to be drawing to its final inconclusive chapter—leaving, alas, everyone the poorer, many bereaved or maimed and millions dead, and only one thing triumphant: the Machines. As the servants of the Machines are becoming a privileged class, the Machines are going to be enormously more powerful.[13]

Tolkien confirms Gillespie's sense that, in the face of modern war—tyranny of the machines—the individual capitulates to his impotence: "Well, well," he writes to his son, "you and I can do nothing about it. And that shd. be a measure of the amount of guilt that should be assumed to attach to any member of a country who is not a member of its actual Government."[14]

The rise of mechanical, and nuclear, and chemical warfare creates a situation wherein, "since every individual is threatened with annihilation,"

8. Tolkien et al., *Letters*, 165.

9. Tolkien et al., *Letters*, 165.

10. Tolkien et al., *Letters*, 246.

11. Tolkien et al., *Letters*, 111.

12. Italics, which are mine, are meant to enunciate the similarity between Tolkien's language ("world-catastrophe") and Hegel's ("world-historical," etc.).

13. Tolkien et al., *Letters*, 111.

14. Tolkien et al., *Letters*, 111.

and "individual self-sacrifice is meaningless in this situation," modern war "exacerbates the individualism" at the heart of bourgeois life. As Michael Gillespie perceptively contends, "Man is thus plunged into schizophrenia: one moment he forgets death entirely and is concerned only with his present pleasure and advantage; the next moment he recognizes its imminence and dedicates himself to abolishing the weapons that make it possible."[15] Failing to succeed in the latter, he is propelled "into a frenzied accumulation of the means of destruction [he] most want[s] to destroy," eliminating the restraint upon desire that, for Hegel, war is supposed to secure. Gillespie concludes by admitting the disheartening nature of his contentions, but he hopes that "Hegel's analysis is wrong or that he is right on a deeper level, that the same conditions that propel us toward disaster will also give birth to a new way of philosophizing that will yet prove to be our solace and our salvation."[16]

Tolkien's *legendarium* is one such site wherein this philosophizing can occur. I do not mean by this that Tolkien, consciously responding to Hegel, proves him wrong. I do not even mean to say that Hegel *is* wrong, or entirely irrelevant to the world of modern warfare. I do, however, mean that Tolkien provides an important *korrektiv* to Hegel, first by demonstrating the ways in which the bourgeois way of being is restrained through direct engagement in the War of the Ring against Sauron *and* Saruman and by Frodo's pacifistic *kenosis*, a self-emptying which also requires the spirited virtues.

Also, as we will see, Frodo's heroic cultivation of *misericordia* or just-mercy dramatizes, for us, a virtue that corrects and, in a sense, completes various contemporary ethics. In the wake of the pluralism of modernity and, still more, the totalitarian appropriations and distortions of the common good, all of which gave birth to a more-or-less humanist or personalist ethics of "the other," Frodo's *misericordia* returns to us an ethics rooted in the common good rightly understood—something I will explore at length at in the last pages of this study. Further, Frodo's place in the world-events of Middle-earth provides an essential counterpoint to another modern attempt to resolve the tension between morality and political life: Hegel's "World-historical individual."

World-Historical Hobbits?

In his *Elements of the Philosophy of Right,* Hegel contends that world history operates on a plane that surpasses that of morality. Whereas the sphere of

15. Gillespie, *Death and Desire,* 175.
16. Gillespie, *Death and Desire,* 176.

morality "is that of private convictions, the conscience of the individuals," and their particularities, world history "transcends the obligations, liability, and responsibility which attach to individuality by virtue of its ethical existence."[17] "World historical deeds" should not be measured against the "private virtues" of "modesty, humility, charity, liberality."[18] Further, "World-historical individuals" are beyond happiness itself. They choose not happiness but conflict, labour in the service of their end, exertion. Even after they reach their lot, they enjoy no peace or happiness. Instead, "their actions are their entire being, and their whole nature and character are determined by their ruling passion. When their end is attained, they fall aside like empty husks . . . ."[19]

Tolkien's *korrektiv* to Hegel's World-Historical individual is twofold. It is true that Frodo seems to have little happiness at the end of *The Lord of the Rings*. One evening after they have returned to the Shire, Sam finds Frodo pale and estranged in the study. "What's the matter, Mr. Frodo?" he asks, to which Frodo, who has accomplished a "world-historical deed" in destroying the Ring of Power, answers, "I'm wounded . . . wounded; it will never really heal."[20] That he cannot enjoy the fruits of his own end is made even clearer when, just before he departs for the Undying Lands, he tells Sam that he has been "deeply hurt . . . I tried to save the Shire, and it has been saved, but not for me. It must often be, Sam, when things are in danger: someone has to give them up, lose them, so that others may keep them."[21] And yet this is not the end. Aristotelian ethics finds its fruition in contemplation of the truth, as near an approximation of perfect contemplation of *being qua being* as is possible, and Thomistic ethics find their fruition in the theological virtues, which help one to obtain contemplation of the Beatific Vision. In Tolkien, Aristotle and Aquinas kiss; Frodo's ethical actions find their fruition in the Undying Lands, the paradisiac land which in Tolkien's world most embodies *being qua being*.

More importantly, against Hegel's valorization of the World-historical individual who, from a vantage point above ethics, moves the wheels of history, Tolkien gives us a narrative wherein "the great policies of world history, 'the wheels of the world,' are often turned not by the Lords and Governors, even gods, but by the seemingly unknown and weak—owing to the secret life in creation, and the part unknowable, to all wisdom but One," the

---

17. Hegel, *Elements of the Philosophy of Right*, 477.
18. Hegel, *Elements of the Philosophy of Right*, 478.
19. Hegel, *Elements of the Philosophy of Right*, 478.
20. Tolkien, *The Lord of the Rings*, 1025.
21. Tolkien, *The Lord of the Rings*, 1025.

wisdom that these unknown and weak contain in a potency that the common project of the common good will make actual.[22]

However, in order to have eyes to see the way in which, in Tolkien, aesthetical articulations can give birth to ethical-political ones, and the way in which ethical-political articulations find their culmination in contemplative *beatitude,* we will need to increasingly rely on pre-modern philosophers for whom perpetual compartmentalization is foreign. For if we are to discover, as Gillespie hopes, that either Hegel was wrong or he was right on a deeper level, we can only, like Tolkien, look to a way of reading the world that is not defined by separations and compartmentalizations, and increasingly obtuse reorganizations and intensifications of these organizations and separations,[23] an obsession with *difference* and individualism that has in our age emerged as the crown jewel of the bourgeois world. That this crowning obsession with *difference* and the identity politics which comes as its logical outcome are not departures but entirely comfortable with the standard liberal bourgeois world over which their practitioners claim "an enlightened form of moral vigilance" can be seen in two ways.[24] First, the self-proclaimed adherence to Lyotard's logic that in the end "persuasion is also violence and suppression"[25] is merely an extreme outgrowth of the liberal-bourgeois notion of negative freedom, the absence of constraints, and thus practitioners of *difference* will inevitably "[reduce] dissent to a safely foredoomed possibility rather than as a shattering intervention that imposes ineluctable duties and forces choices in clearing the way for the establishment of a new law and the foundation of a new order."[26] To depart from this practice would be to acknowledge the necessity of force against any who understand *difference* differently, should the project of identity politics succeed. Tolkien, on the contrary, while giving full voice to *difference* through manifold species and cultures—Elves and Dwarves, Riders of Rohan and Men of Gondor, hobbits and *istari*—centers his narrative around the need for *difference* to be subjugated to a common project. An "identity politics" reading of Tolkien, such as that which Jane Chance offers in her at times striking study *The Lord of the Rings: The Mythology of Power,* ignores this common good. Turning to the One Ring as enemy of the politics of

---

22. Tolkien et al., *Letters,* 149.

23. One species of which may be Kierkegaard's three levels of existence, but which manifests itself most insidiously in the hyper-specialized efforts of identity politics.

24. Paik, *From Utopia to Apocalypse,* 9.

25. Rosen, *Hermeneutics as Politics,* 192.

26. Paik, *From Utopia to Apocalypse,* 9.

difference, she writes that "the inscription testifies" that "it allows for difference—elves, dwarves, men—but only because there is One Ring intended to align their differences:

> One Ring to Rule them all, One Ring to find them,
> One Ring to bring them all and in the darkness bind them,
> In the Land of Mordor, where the Shadows lie.[27]

For Chance, "Returning the Ring to its origin means refusal of power as domination of the One—of sameness—and acceptance of power as respect for difference and diversity."[28] For Chance, as for most practitioners of identity politics, *difference* is an end-in-itself. For Tolkien, the proper end is a common project that is premised upon a common good. While Chance is correct to note that there is One Ring, she fails to note, at least in this context, the significance of there also being One King.

Further, Tolkien's *legendarium,* if we are to read it in accordance with his own claims concerning fantasy, should help us to "clean our windows," so that we can "'see[] things as we are (or were) meant to see them'—as things apart from ourselves."[29] In contrast to this, a liberal bourgeois hermeneutics aims to "keep the conversation going rather than to find objective truth." Insofar as Richard Rorty is exemplary of this liberal bourgeois mode, its hermeneutics calls for a perpetual continuation of the conversation in perpetual resistance against any claims that we can "see things as we are (or were) meant to see them." Such claims would mark "an attempt[] to close off conversation by proposals for universal commensuration through the hypostatization of some privileged set of descriptions."[30] Or, in plain English, there is no such thing as "things as they are meant to be seen." There is only *how we see them,* in our permanently different ways, none of which should be privileged. A reading of Tolkien that becomes increasingly Thomistic will, I hope, grant us the vision of things apart from ourselves that paves the way for a recovery of the common good, a return of which will remain impossible insofar as we continue to see things and others as mere extensions of ourselves. This return is premised on our need to see things as "apart from ourselves." But this is only the first step, which allows us to see ourselves as always only *parts* of a whole; we are never the autonomous ends-in-and-of-themselves that we often believe ourselves to be.

---

27. Tolkien, quoted in Chance, *The Lord of the Rings: The Mythology of Power,* 32.
28. Chance, *The Lord of the Rings: The Mythology of Power.*
29. Tolkien, "On Fairy Stories," 373.
30. Rorty, quoted in Rosen, *Hermeneutics as Politics,* 185.

Saruman and Hegel: Sorcery, Secondary Worlds, and the New Magic of Politics

We can recover this vision of the common good in manifold ways, but in the case of the *legendarium* the return comes about by means of fantasy. Tolkien posits a notion of fantasy that would "combine[] with its older and higher use as an equivalent of Imagination the derived notions of 'unreality' (that is, of unlikeness to the Primary World), of freedom from the dominion of 'observed fact,' in short of the fantastic."[31] Although Tolkien admits the connotation of fantasy as images of things which are not in fact present, and, still further, which may not be found in the "primary world" at all, he rejects the depreciative tone, stronger in the wake of such Enlightenment masterminds as John Locke, who juxtaposes *mere* fantasy with *actual* knowledge. Tolkien inverts this depreciation, arguing that we should see imagined incarnations of things not present in the primary world as "not a lower but a higher form of Art, indeed the most nearly pure form, and so (when achieved) the most Potent."[32] On the one hand, fantasy has an intrinsic leg up in the world of literary art, in that it contains an "arresting strangeness." However, this strangeness, especially in a bourgeois world bent on hard facts, appears as an unwelcome insurrection against the Primary World: like Bilbo Baggins, people would prefer not to be arrested by anything strange. As a mental prophylactic against fantasy, many *a priori* associate it with dreaming, or even with madness. None of this successfully prevents fantasy from ascending the stairs to the high throne which Tolkien has prepared for it. After all, fantasy, much more than any other literary art, is "difficult to achieve." Surely in a bourgeois world that values hard work, there must be some merit to that which is more difficult? Unfortunately, it is all too possible that fantasy's difficulty, and the attendant proliferation of poorly-written fantastical stories, may have soured still more people to its merit. It is here that Tolkien introduces that which he names "Secondary World." A "Secondary World," which will "command[] Secondary Belief, will probably require labour and thought, and will certainly demand a special skill, a kind of elvish craft. Few attempt such difficult tasks. But when they are attempted and in any degree accomplished then we have a rare achievement of Art: indeed narrative art, story-making in its primary and most potent mode."[33]

Tolkien was not alone in finding the bourgeois world's comfortable reconciliation with the boredom of hard facts problematic. Hegel, like

31. Tolkien, "On Fairy Stories," 362.

32. Tolkien, "On Fairy Stories."

33. Tolkien, "On Fairy Stories," 364.

Tolkien, saw the modern world as a deeply disenchanted age. As culprits who caused this phenomenon, he named those participants in the Reformation who advanced an "undisturbed engagement in the commonness of empirical existence."[34] The "poetry of sacrality" had been expelled from the cosmos, and the empirically-verifiable world which remained bustled with boredom.[35] As Eric Voegelin notes in "On Hegel: A Study in Sorcery," Hegel saw the philosopher as one who was exempt from the spirit of his age, a phenomenon which allowed him to properly diagnose it (if he was not exempt, then how could he, as a patient who has succumbed to the sickness, properly see it for what it was?). Hegel, Voegelin contends, was also heir to the sectarian spirituals of the Middle Ages, magicians and occultists who were able to identify the precise way in which the inner light, or "the Spirit," was manifest in the age. Finally, Hegel grants himself an imaginative superiority which at first glance seems to find common ground with Tolkien the fantasist. In Hegel's case, Voegelin notes, the imaginator "can shift the meaning of existence from life in the presence under God, with its personal and social duties of the day, to the role of a functionary of history; the reality of existence will be eclipsed and replaced by the Secondary Reality of the imaginative project."[36] The key point of distinction is clear from the word "eclipsed." Instead of seeing the imagined Secondary World as something which might *eclipse* the Primary World, Tolkien advocates, as one of fantasy's main functions, *escape*.

Keenly aware of the tone of condescension and scorn which "escape" often connotes, he seeks to transvalue the word and so rescue it from "confusion":

> Why should a man be scorned if, finding himself in prison, he tries to get out and go home? Or if, when he cannot do so, he thinks and talks about other topics than jailers and prison-walls? The world outside has not become less real because the prisoner cannot see it. In using escape in this way the critics have chosen the wrong word, and, what is more, they are confusing, not always by sincere error, the Escape of the Prisoner with the Flight of the Deserter. Just so a Party-spokesman might have labelled departure from the misery of the Führer's or any other Reich and even criticism of it as treachery . . . they would seem to prefer the acquiescence of the "quisling" to the resistance of

---

34. Quoted in Voegelin, "On Hegel," 214.
35. Voegelin, "On Hegel," 214.
36. Voegelin, "On Hegel," 214.

the patriot. To such thinking you have only to say "the land you loved is doomed" to excuse any treachery, indeed to glorify it.[37]

Note how *political* Tolkien's defense of escape is. He makes the bourgeois bent on hard facts and scornful of escape analogous to loyalists who defend the Führer's Reich. The prison of the modern bourgeois world is, it seems, an enemy territory, a land that stands alongside the Nazi Reich as that which we must escape. The bourgeois critic of fantasy will insist that "the land you loved is doomed" to justify and even glorify a treacherous fidelity to a disenchanted world, just as a German patriot will insist that critiques of the Führer are by necessity traitors. We are prisoners in the war on enchantment, and each time, suddenly conscious of our P.O.W. status, we seek sustenance in fairie, the Powers that Be label us deserters.

Escape from the prison of modernity is not meant, as in Hegel's project, to *eclipse* the Primary World. Rather, escape produces "[r]ecovery (which includes return and renewal of health)," a "regaining of a clear view. I do not say 'seeing things as they are' and involve myself with the philosophers, though I might venture to say 'seeing things as we are (or were) meant to see them'—as things apart from ourselves." Escape into fantasy frees us from triteness and excess familiarity, and also "from possessiveness."

Hegel, on the other hand, strives to eclipse the Primary World by replacing the unknown future with the known future. Eras, or ages, must be mapped with scientific certitude. Still more, "it must, finally, conceive the future age in such a manner that the present imaginator becomes its inaugurator and master."[38] Voegelin reads this forceful certitude concerning the meaning of future existence as a symptom of the imaginator's existential anxiousness and diffidence coupled with a fierce *libido dominandi*. Bizarrely, Voegelin observes, we have become accustomed to such megalomaniac madness. The grotesque in such enterprises has lost its capacity to shock: we mistake false messiahs imaginatively constructing "new ages" as run-of-the-mill politicians.

At a central moment in *The Lord of the Rings*, Tolkien's fantasy achieves escape and allows us to see such false messiahs with an arresting strangeness that dilates their grotesqueness. Saruman emerges as a Hegelian sorcerer turned political leader. Tom Shippey articulates an inkling of this in *The Road to Middle Earth*: "What Saruman says encapsulates many of the things the modern world has learnt to dread most: the ditching of allies, the subordination of means to ends, the 'conscious acceptance of guilt in the

---

37. Tolkien, "On Fairy Stories," 364.
38. Voegelin, "On Hegel," 216.

necessary murder.'"[39] Further, Shippey notes, Saruman, more than any other character in the *legendarium,* has mastered the art of balancing phrases against one another so that "incompatibilities are resolved, and none comes out with words as empty as 'deploring' 'ultimate,' worst of all 'real.' What is 'real change'?"

Saruman, Shippey continues, shows signs of being consonant with technology or industrialism. This is evident even on an etymological level. "*Searu* in Old English means 'device, design, contrivance, art.'"[40] For Shippey, Saruman is "learned, but his learning tends to the practical. 'He has a mind of metal and wheels,' says Fangorn. His Orcs use a kind of gunpowder at Helm's Deep; thirty pages later the Ents meet at Isengard, or 'Irontown,' a kind of napalm . . . The implication is that Saruman has been led from ethically neutral researches to the kind of wanton pollution and love of dirt we see in 'The Scouring of the Shire.'"[41]

In Shippey's analysis, Saruman is an imaginative figure "applicable" to any number of twentieth century demagogues. However, Voegelin's reading of Hegel helps us to see Saruman as no mere savvy politician: he is a politicized Hegelian sorcerer. Saruman begins with a conception of history arranged by "ages." The Elder Days, Middle Days, and now "Younger Days." Here, like Joachim of Fiorra and Hegel, he reveals himself to be an imaginator who has systematized history, and who possesses the meaning of an age not yet in existence. Eric Voegelin sees gnostic characteristics in the medieval writings of the deeply-influential, heretical Fiorra, a leading churchman of the 12th century. Joachim divided history into three distinct parts: the Age of the Father, which began with Abraham, the age of the Son, which was led by Christ, and the age of the Spirit, signified by the appearance of the "*Dux e Babylone,* the leader of the third age."[42] In Joachim's conceptualization of the third age, humankind will receive a new descent of the Spirit which will bring gifts necessary for, "a community of the spiritually perfect who can live together without institutional authority."[43] Ellis Sandoz notes that, whereas:

> ancient gnosis as mediated through the sects generally was characterized by the thirst for perfection and radical transformation of evil existence in both personal and cosmic dimensions, the modern gnosis of Joachim [and that which was adopted by his

39. Shippey, *The Road to Middle-Earth,* 119.
40. Shippey, *The Road to Middle-Earth,* 170.
41.. Shippey, *The Road to Middle-Earth,* 171.
42. Quoted in Voegelin, *Science, Politics, and Gnosticism,* 138.
43. Voegelin, *Science, Politics, and Gnosticism,* 139.

political-philosophical successors] transformed gnostic doc-
trine into the speculative reconstruction of the process of history, promising the transfiguration of the world in time."[44]

Further, like Hegel, Saruman makes a clear appeal to "the Wise," the
philosopher as "religious leader" and, in this case, "ruler." The passage, in
which we see Saruman staking his claims before Gandalf, is so poignant that
it would be unjust not to cite it at length:

> He drew himself up then and began to declaim, as if he were
> making a speech long rehearsed. "The Elder Days are gone. The
> Middle Days are passing. The Younger Days are beginning. The
> time of the Elves is over, but our time is at hand: the world of
> Men, which we must rule. But we must have power, power to
> order all things as we will, for that good which only the Wise
> can see." "And listen, Gandalf, my old friend and helper!" he
> said, coming near and speaking now in a softer voice. "I said
> *we*, for *we* it may be, if you will join with me. A new Power is
> rising. Against it the old allies and policies will not avail us at all.
> There is no hope left in Elves or dying Nu´menor. This then is
> one choice before you, before us. We may join with that Power.
> It would be wise, Gandalf. There is hope that way. Its victory is
> at hand; and there will be rich reward for those that aided it.
> As the Power grows, its proved friends will also grow; and the
> Wise, such as you and I, may with patience come at last to di-
> rect its courses, to control it. We can bide our time, we can keep
> our thoughts in our hearts, deploring maybe evils done by the
> way, but approving the high and ultimate purpose: Knowledge,
> Rule, Order; all the things that we have so far striven in vain to
> accomplish, hindered rather than helped by our weak or idle
> friends There need not be, there would not be, any real change
> in our designs, only in our means."[45]

Eric Voegelin writes in "On Hegel: A Study in Sorcery," "As a philosopher Hegel is bound by the tradition of philosophizing from antiquity to the present which he knows superbly well."[46] Hegel would feel
frustrated, however, by a philosopher's existence; "for philosophers, even
of the highest rank, are not historical figures who put their signature on the
millennia."[47] In order to put their signature on the millennia, however, such

44. Voegelin, *Science, Politics, and Gnosticism*, 140.
45. Tolkien, *The Lord of the Rings*, 259.
46. Voegelin, "On Hegel," 218.
47. Voegelin, "On Hegel," 228.

World-Historical individuals need to, Saruman says, "bide [their] time . . . keep [their] thoughts in [their] hearts." Within their esoteric inner circle, they might consider some of the evils committed atrocious, but the ultimate purpose is high enough to excuse all. For the next age will be one defined by Knowledge, Rule, and Order. All that the wise wizards have only known to an especially profound degree must now be conjoined with History itself.[48] Here Saruman's logic finds consonance in Hegel's World-Historical individual, who is "not so unwise as to indulge a variety of wishes to divide his regards. He is devoted to the One Aim, regardless of all else. It is even possible that such men may treat other great, even sacred, interests inconsiderately; conduct which is indeed obnoxious to moral reprehension. But so mighty a force must trample down many an innocent flower—crush to pieces many an object in its path."[49] Here we see that, for Hegel, the World-Historical individual can elevate himself over the chain of absolute necessity which binds the mass of mankind because he knows the direction in which this necessity "wants" to move, and he has learned, from his philosophical studies, to "pronounce the magic words."[50] Voegelin notes that out of the disenchantment of the age, "if not a man, at least a sorcerer . . . can evoke, if not the reality of history, at least its shape."[51] Ultimately, this sorcerer "conjure[s] up an image of history—a shape, a ghost—that is meant to eclipse the history of God's making."[52] Saruman carries himself as a wise-man wizard who has done more than *imagine* the future. He would not be content with the surrealist or even Tolkienian enthronement of imagination as in many respects superior to reason. He is not even, like Gandalf, one whose consciousness of his own capacity for error encourages a self-understanding as a lover, rather than an owner, of wisdom. No, as Voegelin notes of Hegel, Saruman carries himself as having "a final possession of knowledge."[53] But this is not the end. Lest the philosopher be laughed out of court as a "crackpot," he must "tie his messianic ambitions to a reasonably successful-looking political force of his time."[54] Saruman indicates that he ultimately sees the Power as "passing

---

48. Eric Voegelin notes that "Hegel must then develop an imaginative project of immanent history, with a construction of ages that will include an ultimate age to be inaugurated by himself. Voegelin, "On Hegel," 218.

49. Hegel, *Philosophy of Right,* 34.

50. Voegelin, "On Hegel," 221.

51. Voegelin, "On Hegel," 221.

52. Voegelin, "On Hegel," 221.

53. Voegelin, "On Hegel," 218.

54. Voegelin, "On Hegel," 219.

to us," but first it is necessary to ally himself to that Power, the political-theological power of Mordor.[55]

We learn that Saruman's ambitions and vision have come about in part through his study of the arts of the Enemy—that is, *black magic*. His political project is thus deeply theological, insofar as political philosophy, for him as for Hegel, "becomes the *grimoire* of the magician who will evoke for everybody the shape and the reconciliation that for himself he cannot achieve in the reality of his existence."[56] Such a feat can only come about if the imaginator replaces the First Reality of experience with the Second Reality of imaginative construction, "endowing the imaginary reality with the appearance of truth by letting it absorb pieces of first reality."[57]

Here again Voegelin's reading of Hegel brushes against Tolkien, in that Tolkien too hails a Secondary World that passes as a true one, so internally consistent it is, so masterfully textured and wrought. However, Tolkien distinguishes Artistic Enchantment from Secondary Worlds. Magic, Tolkien notes, "produces, or pretends to produce, an alteration in the Primary World."[58] Thus Saruman, for instance, seeks through his imagined ages to alter Middle-earth, and thus Hegel wishes to alter actual History. Magic has as its aim "power in this world, domination of things and wills."[59] Enter Saruman and Hegel, the Sorcerers. Fantasy, on the other hand, comes about when "Enchantment produces a Secondary World into which both designer and spectator can enter, to the satisfaction of their senses while they are inside; but in its purity it is artistic in desire and purpose."[60] Fantasy desires "partners in making and delight, not slaves."[61]

Such an artistic end would not suffice for Hegel's project, nor for Saruman's. Hegel critiques myth as "always a presentation which introduces sensual images, appealing to conception, not to thought; it is an impotence of the thought which cannot yet get hold of itself. In mythical presentation, thought is not yet free."[62]

The darkness of Hegel's project is evident in that he incorporates a dialectical understanding even of the philosopher-magician's relation to negativity, just as Saruman insists that one must directly countenance Saruman

55. Tolkien, *Lord of the Rings*, 260.
56. Voegelin, "On Hegel," 222.
57. Voegelin, "On Hegel," 224.
58. Tolkien, "On Fairy Stories," 368.
59. Tolkien, "On Fairy Stories," 368.
60. Tolkien, "On Fairy Stories," 368.
61. Tolkien, "On Fairy Stories," 369.
62. Voegelin, "On Hegel," 232.

and Mordor in order to usher in a dialectical process by which Power will pass into your hands. The philosopher must "look the negative in the face and dwell with it. This dwelling is the magic force which converts the negative into being."[63]

This darkness is not merely philosophical or political. As Glenn Alexander Magee has exhaustively demonstrated in *Hegel and the Hermetic Tradition,* Hegel's philosophical claims are inseparable from his engagement with the hermetic, occultic traditions. Gandalf recognizes the new voice and logic of Saruman as having a disturbing affinity with the emissaries sent from Mordor. In other words, Saruman could not have conceived of the Secondary Reality which he unveils had he not subjected himself to the influence of Sauron's black magic. Crucially, not all see the Secondary Reality which Saruman constructs within Tolkien's Secondary World as the goodly fruits of the right magic words. Upon hearing of Saruman's theory of the ages, and his claimed mastery over the age to come, Elrond says that "[t]his is grievous news concerning Saruman . . . for we trusted him and he is deep in all our counsels. It is perilous to study too deeply the arts of the Enemy, for good or for ill."[64]

Saruman in his incarnate existence as Lord of Isengard meets with ready resistance, and he becomes increasingly alienated. Like Hegel, though, "his own state of lostness and alienation must be transformed into the absolute position from which he can operate."[65] Pure ego, *des reinen Ichs,* becomes "the immense power of the negative," and is "elevated to the rank of 'absolute power.'"[66] Finally, the subject, this I, becomes the moving force in the *becoming* of the *Geist* or Spirit. In Hegel, the hero or "world spirit" or "World-Historical individual" becomes the concrete universal, and understands himself as the site of this becoming. Saruman understands himself in this way, even though *nature* asserts its force against the reign of his History in the form of the Ents, who thoroughly ruin the sure plans of Isengard, a breeding ground for the sorcerer's Uruk-hai, a creature fit for the New Age in that they are smarter, faster, and stronger. Seemingly, he sees as part of this becoming a new state of disembodiment, a manifestation of himself as "pure voice." For when Gandalf and the Fellowship arrive at Isengard after Treebeard and the Ents have stultified Saruman's plans, the White Wizard speaks:

---

63. Voegelin, "On Hegel," 247.
64. Tolkien, *The Lord of the Rings*, 265.
65. Voegelin, "On Hegel," 246.
66. Voegelin, "On Hegel," 246.

Suddenly another voice spoke, low and melodious, its very sound an enchantment. Those who listened unwarily to that voice could seldom report the words that they heard; and if they did, they wondered, for little power remained in them. Mostly they remembered only that it was a delight to hear the voice speaking, all that it said seemed wise and reasonable, and desire awoke in them by swift agreement to seem wise themselves. When others spoke they seemed harsh and uncouth by contrast; and if they gainsaid the voice, anger was kindled in the hearts of those under the spell. For some the spell lasted only while the voice spoke to them, and when it spoke to another they smiled, as men do who see through a juggler's trick while others gape at it. For many the sound of the voice alone was enough to hold them enthralled; but for those whom it conquered the spell endured when they were far away, and ever they heard that soft voice whispering and urging them. But none were unmoved; none rejected its pleas and its commands without an effort of mind and will, so long as its master had control of it.[67]

The voice is a source of *enchantment*, and a *delight*; Tolkien affiliates both of these with pure art, as opposed to magic. And yet Saruman seems to have achieved unification of thesis and antithesis in that his voice has qualities both of pure art *and* of magic; the voice also manipulates its listeners, in part through its melodious enchantment, in that it *seems* wise, and moves its hearers to *seem* wise themselves. All are moved by it, and though not all are stamped under its spell, urged by its soft whisperings ever after, even those who reject it must steel their wills against its potent control.

Like Hegel, Saruman's voice insists that it alone possesses the key to History. "Much have I desired to see you, mightiest king of western lands," it says, "and especially in these latter years, to save you from the unwise and evil counsels that beset you!"[68] Voegelin notes that Hegel the philosopher posits himself as a savior. Not accidentally does Saruman promise that "still" he will "save you, and deliver you from the ruin that draws nigh inevitably."[69] Gimli, for one, is not fooled. "The words of this wizard stand on their heads," he says.[70] "In the language of Orthanc help means ruin, and saving means slaying, that is plain." Truly Saruman, like Hegel as Voegelin presents him, "forces salvation from the nonreality of his lostness."[71] When

67. Tolkien, *Lord of the Rings*, 578.
68. Tolkien, *Lord of the Rings*, 579.
69. Tolkien, *Lord of the Rings*, 579.
70. Tolkien, *Lord of the Rings*, 579.
71. Voegelin, "On Hegel," 248.

the sorcerer-philosopher realizes that his Secondary Reality results only in the "isolation of the sorcerer from the rest of society, the whole world must be drawn into the imaginary Secondary Reality. The sorcerer becomes the savior of the 'age' by imposing his System of Science as the new revelation of mankind at large. All mankind must join the sorcerer in the hell of his own damnation."[72] Thus Saruman strives to appeal to Gimli and to Theoden and the Riders of Rohan, even, once again, to Gandalf, giving the latter one more chances to enter the wizard's prized hell. Hegel wrote that "the philosophers are closer to the Lord than those who live by the crumbs of the Spirit; they read, or write, the cabinet orders of God in the original."[73] His contempt for those who do not possess wisdom (for remember that for Hegel, the philosopher must not merely *love* wisdom, he must possess it) is plain. Saruman's voice contains the same contempt. He prides himself in bearing no ill will toward Gandalf, even though the latter has returned "in the company of the violent and the ignorant," for they "are both members of a high and ancient order, most excellent in Middle-earth . . . Let us understand one another" he goes on, in order to "heal the disorders of the world."[74] To do this they must "dismiss from thought these lesser folk!" Saruman's words bleed with the Hegelian *libido dominandi*. Yet those listening in on the exchange between Gandalf and Saruman hear the words as though they have been drenched in enchanting wine. They hear Saruman speaking to Gandalf as a kindly king speaking to one of his ministers. The two seem to be of a loftier mold, and surely Gandalf will "ascend into the tower, to discuss deep things beyond their comprehension in the high chambers of Orthanc."[75]

But Gandalf laughs. Tolkien writes that "the fantasy vanished like a puff of smoke."[76] The pure art of Saruman's pure voice is separated from the magician's machinations. Gandalf laughs at him, piercing Saruman's fabricated synthesis between art and magic, and with it the wizard's certainty and superiority. As Voegelin reads the alienated philosopher behind the arrogant sorcerer, so does Gandalf read the alienated wizard behind the condescending wizard. Gandalf tells Saruman that he understands the latter better than the latter does the former. He bids Saruman to come down from the tower, to turn to new things. For a moment the lonely wizard hesitates,

72. Voegelin, "On Hegel," 248.
73. Voegelin, "On Hegel," 255.
74. Tolkien, *Lord of the Rings*, 581.
75. Tolkien, *Lord of the Rings*, 581.
76. Tolkien, *Lord of the Rings*, 582.

and all can see "through the mask the anguish of a mind in doubt, loathing to stay and dreading to leave its refuge."[77]

In the end, though, Saruman's pride and hate decide his fate, and Gandalf, "who has returned from death . . . cast[s] [Saruman] from the order and from the Council."[78] Saruman's staff is broken, and thus he is bereft of the privileges of the order. Gandalf, whose magic, Tolkien notes, is more akin to pure art than Saruman's, and whose mode is one of a true lover of wisdom, ends the History of Saruman's Second Reality.

Or does he? Saruman may be disenchanted, his powers of sorcery taken, but this does not stop him from eking out one last incarnation, albeit a pale echo of his Second Reality. At the same time, his incarnation as Sharkey, Chief of the Shire, is somehow more disturbing than his emergence as the fanatical philosopher-ruler of Isengard. Perhaps this is because the Second Reality of Saruman, in Tolkien's Secondary World of Middle-earth, is more readily read as strange, as arrestingly strange, but as sufficiently estranged from our Primary World, or from what Voegelin calls "First Reality," to be troubling. Rather, although Saruman's original schema is ultimately more dangerous, more demonic, the character of his evil in "The Scouring of the Shire" is arresting not in its strangeness, but in its *merely* political banality. What accounts for this shift?

In Alexandre Kojève's interpretation of Hegel's *Phenomenology of Spirit,* he hones in on the problem of recognition between Napoleon and Hegel. On the day that Jena was occupied by the French, Hegel wrote: "I have seen the emperor—this world soul—riding through the town, and out of it, for a reconnaissance; it is a wondrous feeling indeed to see such an individual who, concentrated in one point, sitting on a horse, reaches over the world and dominates it."[79] It is not hard to see in this interpretation of the World Soul on horseback one who "might have stirred memories of the apocalypse."[80] Kojève contends that, for Hegel, Napoleon is the revealed God of the age, and it is Hegel who reveals him. This dualism, though, this dyad, can only remain unproblematic "if Napoleon 'recognized' Hegel as Hegel has 'recognized' Napoleon. Did Hegel perhaps expect (1806) to be called by Napoleon to Paris, in order to become the philosopher (the sage) of the universal and homogeneous state who would have to explain (justify)," and even direct Napoleon's actions?[81] If when Saruman's *libido dominandi* is at

---

77. Tolkien, *Lord of the Rings,* 582.
78. Tolkien, *Lord of the Rings,* 583.
79. Quoted in Voegelin, "On Hegel," 236.
80. Voegelin, "On Hegel," 236.
81. Strauss, Leo. *On Tyranny,* 153–54.

its height he sees himself as among the World Souls, he nonetheless sees reconciliation with Gandalf as necessary for his own universal and homogenous state. Gandalf had already failed to "recognize" Saruman during their initial conversation at Isengard. But Saruman cannot countenance a second failure of recognition on Gandalf's part when the wizard comes riding on his own horse alongside Theoden and other "such company." How, Saruman might well be thinking, can Gandalf "recognize" Theoden and this rabble, and not recognize Saruman, storehouse of sage counsel? Surely this is due to Gandalf's pride, due to Gandalf's having "misconstr[ued] [his] intentions willfully."[82]

In order to more fully grasp the rivalry between Saruman and Gandalf incited by Saruman's struggle for power, we can momentarily turn to Kojève's response to Leo Strauss' translation of and commentary on Xenophon's *Hiero* or *Tyrannicus*. Assuming a Hegelian mode, Kojève parses out the problem of tyranny with reference to Hegel's *Phenomenology of Spirit*, particularly the section on the Master-Slave dialectic. The Master enters into a "struggle to the death in order to make his adversary recognize his exclusive human dignity. But if his adversary is himself a Master, he will be animated by the same desire for 'recognition,' and will fight to the death: his own or the other's. And if the adversary submits (through fear of death), he reveals that he is not in fact a Master but a Slave."[83] For the Master, however, this revelation means that his victory over his adversary is worthless, for he is victorious only over a Slavish being. The Master's situation is "essentially tragic, since there is no possible way out of it."[84] Kojève pushes this insight to its limit, contending that "the ultimate motive of all *emulation* among men, and hence of all political *struggle,* including the struggle that leads to tyranny," is "recognition."[85] Kojève's totalizing claims do an injustice to Gandalf, on whom many—from Saruman to Denethor—project their own tyrannical motives. However, his analysis helps us to grasp the gravity of Gandalf's "failure" to recognize Saruman's authority and greatness. Power alone is an insufficient motive for Saruman, as it is for most. Recognition by one's subjects, but especially by one's peers, is one of the most compelling *aims* that move a political life bereft of a metaphysics of the common good; desire for recognition replaces the *summum bonum* as the aim of political life.

82. Tolkien, *The Lord of the Rings,* 581.
83. Strauss, Leo. *On Tyranny,* 142.
84. Strauss, Leo. *On Tyranny,* 142.
85. Strauss, Leo. *On Tyranny,* 143.

When Gandalf fails to "come up" to the tower to "consult" with him, not only *not recognizing him*, but in fact *laughing at him*, Saruman, like Hegel, is faced with the impossibility of actualizing his Second Reality, and thus moves toward increasing *negation* for the remainder of the novel.

For Voegelin, although Joachim of Fiora planted the seeds of modern gnosticism, and although others, such as Hobbes, had gnostic proclivities, Hegel is the ultimate philosopher-gnostic. However, it is only with the dawn of the so-called "Left Hegelians" that we see a definitive turn from gnostic philosophical speculation and knowledge to gnostic political action. For Marx, a preeminent proponent of "Left Hegelianism," the truth of *this world* can be established once the *world beyond* empirical truth has been abandoned. Therefore, "the critique of heaven is transformed into the critique of earth; the *critique of religion,* into the *critique of law;* the *critique of theology* into the *critique of politics.*"[86]

In *The Lord of the Rings* Saruman begins with an intensive study of "religion" in the form of the Enemy's dark arts, but after several defeats he abandons the project of a direct alliance with the spiritual power of Sauron and shifts toward a commitment to *this world* of Middle-earth by appearing as the Chief, Sharkey, the gnostic-politician of the Shire. Saruman, the angelic being sent after the creation of the Rings of Power to protect Middle-earth, ends up a banal fascist. Whereas he discovers the existence of the Shire through Gandalf, whose fervent concern is the fruition of the often frustrating but frequently remarkable hobbits, Saruman's interest in the Shire signals a radical counterpoint.

It is important to note, further, that Saruman has engaged in treachery against Sauron. Feigning ignorance concerning the Shire, eventually one of Sauron's servants captures one of Saruman's Shire spies, who exposes the treason of Isengard. After this, Saruman strategizes against Rohan and against the Fellowship, but he fails. Bracketed from the final movements in the War of the Ring, he at last persuades the Ents, through the sorcery of his voice, to let him leave Isengard. Saruman's ambitions shrink with each defeat so that, as noted earlier, his final "frontier" is the Shire.

By the time Saruman arrives in the Shire, Lotho Sackville-Baggins has already secured a monopoly on property and production, and thus has ascended to the position of an industrial baron, a Boss who rules the land. We will examine Lotho, alias "Pimple," elsewhere. Here it is only necessary to note that Saruman exploits Lotho's tyrannical business success; the "private" tyrant Lotho is overtaken by the political tyrant Saruman, who assumes the alias "Sharkey." When Frodo and his friends return home, one of the many

86. Quoted in Voegelin, *Science, Politics, and Gnosticism,* 45.

ruffians who now inhabit the land notes that "This country wants waking up and setting to rights . . . and Sharkey's going to do it."[87] The Boss (Lotho), the ruffian continues, will do what Sharkey says. When Merry later asks Farmer Cotton who Sharkey is, the latter synopsizes the backstory. Around the time of the previous harvest, Sharkey, whom they've "never seen," planted himself at Bag End as "the real Chief now, I guess."[88] Cotton goes on to describe a shift in Saruman that indicates a shift from affinity with Hegel to affinity with Marx. As Cotton relates, the ruffians do what Sharkey says, and "what he says is mostly: hack, burn, and ruin; and now it's come to killing. There's no longer even any bad sense in it. They cut down trees and let 'em lie, they burn houses and build no more."[89] Sharkey, as author of so much annihilation, may well have been spending his evenings reading Marx's "Contribution to the Critique of Hegel's *Philosophy of Right*" in which we encounter the shift from theoretical to practical philosophy: "Its subject is its *enemy*, which it seeks not to refute, but to *annihilate* . . . it no longer acts as an *end in itself*, but only as a *means*. Its essential emotion is *indignation*, its essential task is *denunciation*." Regarding this passage, Voegelin writes that "here speaks the will to murder of the gnostic magician . . . One's fellowman is no longer a partner in being; critique is no longer rational debate. Sentence has been passed; the execution follows."[90] Importantly, the ruffian believes that the same Sharkey whose mode is indignation and whose aim is annihilation is he who will "set things right."

When Frodo at last confronts Saruman, the latter feigns magical power in order to protect himself, but the ringbearer debunks his bluff: "Do not believe him!" he says. "He has lost all power, save his voice that can still daunt you and deceive you, if you let it. But I will not have him slain. It is useless to meet revenge with revenge: it will heal nothing."[91] In spite of this palpable mercy, Saruman tries to stab and kill Frodo, but the latter's mail-coat keeps him safe.

In an apotheosis of annihilation, after Saruman accuses his surrogate Wormtongue of killing Lotho, Wormtongue responds with "a look of wild hatred," insisting that Saruman told him to do it:

> Saruman laughed. 'You do what Sharkey says, always, don't you, Worm? Well, now he says: follow!' He kicked Wormtongue in the face as he grovelled, and turned and made off. But at that

87. Tolkien, *The Lord of the Rings*, 1004.
88. Tolkien, *The Lord of the Rings*, 1012.
89. Tolkien, *The Lord of the Rings*, 1013.
90. Voegelin, *Science, Politics, and Gnosticism*, 46.
91. Tolkien, *Lord of the Rings*, 1019.

something snapped: suddenly Wormtongue rose up, drawing a hidden knife, and then with a snarl like a dog he sprang on Saruman's back, jerked his head back, cut his throat, and with a yell ran off down the lane. Before Frodo could recover or speak a word, three hobbit-bows twanged and Wormtongue fell dead.[92]

Around Saruman's body a grey mist gathers, and it at first moves toward the West, presumably because, as an Ainur, his spirit should be destined for the Undying Lands to receive judgment, but instead "out of the West [comes] a cold wind, and it bent away, and with a sigh dissolved into nothing."[93] Remember that for Hegel the *Geist* can only find its incarnation in the World-Historical individual, the one who, like the late Saruman, has denounced all outside support, if he "looks the negative in the face and dwells with it. This dwelling is the magic force which converts the negative into being."[94] Being can only be brought about in dialectical dwelling with non-being. Though Saruman adheres to this Hegelian belief, the dialectical process never unfolds as it "should"; it is arrested at the point wherein he dwells with the negative. Negation is all that he can accomplish in the Shire, a negation which, he tells Frodo, "you will find . . . hard to mend or undo in your lives."[95] This negation, however, has been absorbed by his surrogate Wormtongue, who brings his master's logic to bear on his master's being. For Tolkien the logical effects of negation triumph over the dialectic effects, and the author of negation is "dissolved into nothing."

The achievement of a Tolkienian "Secondary World" "will certainly demand a special skill, a kind of elvish craft" which, when manifest, will give us a "rare achievement of Art: indeed narrative art, story-making in its primary and most potent mode."[96] Second Reality, on the other hand, is impossible to achieve in actuality, but the philosopher-sorcerer's attempt to bring it about reveals to us something else about the potency of story making. Hegel's disregard for myth and imagination may have its root in the gnawing possibility that what he had tried to give the dignity of actualized knowledge is in truth just one more magician's story. Saruman's Second Reality had for him the inner-consistency of the Primary World, and thus he, like the reader of good fantasy, thought that he was "bodily inside its Secondary World"; he is as one who comes to "experience directly a Secondary World: the potion is too strong, and you give to it Primary Belief,

---

92. Tolkien, *The Lord of the Rings*, 1020.
93. Tolkien, *The Lord of the Rings*, 1020.
94. Voegelin, "On Hegel," 255.
95. Tolkien, *Lord of the Rings*, 1018.
96. Tolkien, "On Fairy Stories," 364.

however marvelous the events. [He is] deluded."[97] In a curious passage from "On Fairy Stories," Tolkien muses over the possibility of introducing into a Secondary World a "further fantasy or magic." To do so "is to demand, as it were, and inner or tertiary world. It is a world too much."[98] Such a world Sauron strives to make. Whereas a Secondary World allows us to be freed from possessiveness, Sauron's attempted Secondary Reality is rooted in the possessive urge. A Secondary World shows us that those things which have "become trite," which we have "appropriated, legally or mentally," those things of which "we say we know," have merely been "locked . . . in our hoard . . . [once we have] acquired them, and acquiring ceased to look at them."[99] A Second Reality, too, is a response to such triteness, such boredom. As Voegelin notes, "in Pascal's language, Hegel's System of Science is a divertissement. The philosopher who wants to heal the disease of society" concocts a false self and an imagined history.[100]

Tolkien sees no intrinsic harm in every maker of a Secondary World hoping that he is drawing on reality, that qualities of the Secondary World are either derived from, or flowing into, Reality; indeed, it is easy to see how this can be insofar as the work contains the "inner consistency of reality."[101] Part of the problem with the stories told by Hegel and Saruman is that they are heretical. Hegel reads great men as Christs. Saruman reads himself as one. Perhaps even more problematic is the fact that both Saruman's and Hegel's visions are progressive, envisioning ages that foster a greater and greater incarnation of the *Geist* as Knowledge, Rule, and Order. As Voegelin notes, they foster a world wherein we witness "violent social and personal catastrophes without the redeeming catharsis of tragedy."[102] For Tolkien, Secondary Worlds of Fantasy may also lack such a catharsis, though they do not "deny the existence of dycatastrophe, of sorrow and failure."[103] What the Secondary World denies is "the universal final defeat"; it does this by giving a "glimpse of Joy" at the very moment when doom seems undeniable. Tolkien's own words tell of this most movingly:

> I would venture to say that approaching the Christian Story
> from this direction, it has long been my feeling (a joyous feeling)
> that God redeemed the corrupt making-creatures, men, in a way

97. Tolkien, "On Fairy Stories," 367.
98. Tolkien, "On Fairy Stories," 366.
99. Tolkien, "On Fairy Stories," 373.
100. Voegelin, "On Hegel," 217.
101. Tolkien, "On Fairy Stories," 361.
102. Voegelin, "On Hegel," 217.
103. Tolkien, "On Fairy Stories," 384.

fitting to this aspect, as to others, of their strange nature. The Gospels contain a fairystory, or a story of a larger kind which embraces all the essence of fairy-stories. They contain many marvels—peculiarly artistic, beautiful, and moving: "mythical" in their perfect, selfcontained significance; and among the marvels is the greatest and most complete conceivable *eucatastrophe*, [or sudden, joyous turn]. But this story has entered History and the primary world; the desire and aspiration of sub-creation has been raised to the fulfillment of Creation. The Birth of Christ is the *eucatastrophe* of Man's history.[104]

Hegel, too, wants "God," or *Geist* to "enter history and the primary world," but *he* wants to be "present at the decision in the innermost sanctuary."[105] The "sorcerer . . . has transmogrified himself into Christ."[106] The birth of Christ is, for Hegel, insufficient, for it did not bring about the End of History; through Christ God merely *entered* History.

Tolkien is content with the fact that the *eucatastrophe* of fairy stories offers a "far off gleam or echo of evangelium in the real world."[107] Hegel, and Saruman, demand that "the reality of existence will be eclipsed and replaced by the Second Reality of the imaginative project."[108] The fairy story, in the end, "looks forward (or backward: the direction in this regard is unimportant) to the Great Eucatastrophe. . . . But this story is supreme; and it is true. Art has been verified. God is the Lord, of angels, and of men—and of elves. Legend and History have met and fused."[109] Secondary Worlds are "verified" insofar as they accord with the Great Eucatastrophe, insofar as they accord with Christ's revelation in History, not insofar as they eclipse or surpass these things.

We live in a world replete with historical lenses that read any number of persons as World-Historical Sorcerer Philosophers, World Soul Politicians. Saruman "talks like a politician," Tom Shippey writes.[110] Many politicians think like Saruman, we may add. Those who have drank from Hegel's stream of *consciousness*, who, like Marx, have concluded that man, "who sought a superman in the imaginary reality of heaven and found only a *reflection* of himself, will no longer be inclined to find just a *semblance* of

104. Tolkien, "On Fairy Stories," 388.
105. Quoted in Voegelin, "On Hegel," 255.
106. Voegelin, "On Hegel," 255.
107. Tolkien, "On Fairy Stories," 385.
108. Voegelin, "On Hegel," 216.
109. Tolkien, "On Fairy Stories," 388–9.
110. Shippey, *The Road to Middle-Earth*, 119.

himself, just a non-man, where he seeks and must seek his true reality."[111] Heaven is excluded from "true reality." True reality replaces heaven. In a world wherein Fantastic Second Realities have been imposed again and again on First Reality, where so many have proffered Secondary Realities whose very Systems exclude and "escape control of the judgment by the criteria of First Reality," in which superman is transposed from comic books into our purported scientific-political capacity,[112] we must perpetually be reminded that:

> in God's kingdom the presence of the greatest does not depress the small. Redeemed Man is still man. Story, fantasy, still go on, and should go on. The Evangelium has not abrogated legends; it has hallowed them, especially the "happy ending." The Christian has still to work, with mind as well as body, to suffer, hope, and die; but he may now perceive that all his bents and faculties have a purpose, which can be redeemed. So great is the bounty with which he has been treated that he may now, perhaps, fairly dare to guess that in Fantasy he may actually assist in the effoliation and multiple enrichment of creation. All tales may come true; and yet, at the last, redeemed, they may be as like and as unlike the forms that we give them as Man, finally redeemed, will be like and unlike the fallen that we know.[113]

Reader, close your proverbial *Phenomenology of Spirit*, and open the phenomenal *legendarium* of Tolkien.

111. Voegelin, *Science, Politics, and Gnosticism*, 44.

112. Voegelin, "On Hegel," 242.

113. Tolkien, "On Fairy Stories," 389.

The Political Theology of Catastrophe

Plato's Athenian Atlantis, Tolkien's Númenoran *Atalantë*, and The Nazi Reich

Although J. R. R. Tolkien never references philosophers by name, a reticence which Franco Manni attributes to his "anti-Classical prejudices,"[1] it is impossible to deny the debt that the Isle of Númenor—also known as Atalantës, or "she that has fallen down"[2]—owes to Plato's story of Atlantis in *Timaeus-Critias*. Tolkien writes that "the particular myth" which lies behind *The Lord of the Rings* is "the Downfall of Númenor: a special variety of the Atlantis tradition. That seems to me so fundamental to 'mythical history' . . . that some version of it would have to come in."[3] The tales of both Tolkien and Plato involve ideal polities that earn divine retribution for acts of profound political arrogance, but, as we shall see, the theological-political backdrop which distinguishes the catastrophe in Tolkien's tale is rooted in the realism of *eucatastrophe*. The "happy ending" of Tolkien is less utopian, though no less concerned with the preservation of Being, than the *kallipolis* of Plato.

In Plato Tolkien found a rich embodiment of the dialectic between high civilization and tyrannical rule, a tension that culminates in cataclysmic destruction. Eric Voegelin contends that the Atlantis Plato constructs in *Timaeus* and *Critias,* although it contains the hallmarks of a conventional Utopia meant to evoke an ideal state, is, rather, meant to evoke "a rival order

---

1. Manni, *Tolkien and Philosophy*, 21.

2. Tolkien, "The Notion Club Papers (Part Two)," 247.

3. Tolkien et al., *Letters*, 196.

to the good polis."[4] Plato does not heap evils upon this rival; instead, we are taken in and invited to become enamored with a prosperous and happy polity and thus the tale, stretched across both dialogues, "is something like the black magic of politics. Most appropriately, therefore, the dream of Atlantis rises in luciferic splendor,"[5] in spite of the fact that Atlantis is the rival order of Athens, whose federated *poleis* is accepted by its subjects, its rulers formed by the gods through philosophy and *philotechnia*. Thus while "the order of Atlantis has its origins in divine lust"—betrayed externally by its expansionist *libido dominandi,* and internally by the fact that the dynasty has to be maintained by bodyguards—"the order of Athens [originates] in divine wisdom."[6] In Plato's enchanted epoch Athenians embody an order of wisdom without decline, while the Atlantians substantiate an order of power and wealth tainted by *hubris* and greed. Yet wisdom is laced with tragedy: both Athens and Atlantis are destroyed, just as both are willed into existence by the gods. Voegelin, reading Atlantis and Athens as cosmic symbols, sees the former as *Nous,* the right order of the polis, and the latter as *Ananke,* sometimes translated as necessity, but here meaning chaos. In *Critias,* Plato posits both as requisite if the cosmos is to take form: "chaos has become co-eternal with the idea,"[7] whereas in Tolkien's retelling of Atlantis, a remnant of *Nous,* carried by the Faithful, outlives the chaos that comes in the wake of Sauron's attempt to coopt permanence.

Whether we are considering Tolkien's Atalantës or Plato's Timaeus-Critias—or, as we shall see toward the end of this chapter—Nazi interest in a Nordic Atlantis, the relation between myth and history is of no small consequence. Tolkien insists that the *legendarium* takes place on this earth, but in an imaginary historical period. The interstices between the tensions evident in Tolkien's interlacing of fantasy and history, and those found in Plato's tale of Atlantis, are striking. In *Timaeus* and *Critias,* Plato gives us a glimpse into Athenian prehistory, a time when the country was populated by a noble, beautiful race of men. As Eric Voegelin notes, "the history of the Athens of old was as distinguished as its order; and the most brilliant of its feats was the victory in the war against Atlantis."[8] Plato is deeply concerned with the status of the ordered polis he evokes in *The Republic*; what consequences follow if this "city in speech" *Kallipolis,* this evoked idea, fails to be incarnate on this earth? Unable to locate such a city in the present, and

4. Voegelin, "*Timaeus* and *Critias,*" 262–63.
5. Voegelin, "*Timaeus* and *Critias,*" 263.
6. Voegelin, "*Timaeus* and *Critias,*" 266–67.
7. Voegelin, "*Timaeus* and *Critias,*" 261.
8. Voegelin, "*Timaeus* and *Critias,*" 227.

unwilling to jettison such a city to the utopic realm of "the future," Plato situates/discovers the existence of a just city in history. The way in which the story of Atlantis surfaces in *Timaeus*, many-layered to the point that it can seem convoluted, is of utmost import in this regard. Socrates' delineation of the "city in speech" in *The Republic* stirs Critias to recollect stories of Atlantis revealed to him by the older Critias, stories related to the Athenian statesman and lawmaker Solon, who was told them by Egyptian priests—all of which culminates in the actual Athens of a prior age, approximately 9,000 years before the time of the dialogue. Tolkien places the events of his *legendarium* at approximately 6,000 years before our present age.

By positioning the myths in history, both Plato and Tolkien seek to ensure that their stories are tied to real historical political events. Critias further elucidates the implications of these interconnections between idea, mythos, and history by insisting that he will deliver a "narrative that is not an invented legend (*mythos*) but a true story (*alethinos logos*)."[9] "We shall now proceed to transfer the citizens and the city you described for us yesterday [in *The Republic*] from your fable into fact and locate that city right here, as Athens; we shall claim that your imaginary citizens are in fact our ancestors."[10] Socrates is satisfied that Critias will give an "adequate eulogy" of the story of Atlantis because, unlike the sophists, whose itineracy leaves them outside of any political rootedness, and unlike poets, who cannot speak truthfully of things beyond their experience, Critias, like Timaeus "share[s] equally in philosophy and politics." Voegelin goes so far as to argue that in this account given in *Critias*, Plato's playfulness of imagination is so abundant that if completed it would have been one of the "most grandiose poems of antiquity." Mention of playfulness that is nevertheless serious and drenched with a "wealth of meaning" reminds us of Tolkien's imaginative power.

In Tolkien's earliest rendering of the Atlantis myth, "The Lost Road," the "present" part of the narrative involves several exchanges—first between young Alboin and his father Oswin, and, later, between Alboin and his son Audoin. Alboin's "return" to antiquity does not take the form of Platonic *anamnesis*. Rather, as is typical in Tolkien, the point of contact is *language itself*. The name Alboin corresponds to the Old English *Ælfwine*, and binds him to a Lombardic legend. Alboin regularly desires "to go back," a desire that we see fulfilled when, on vacation at the seaside with his son, he gazes out upon the roaring waves and says, "The storm is coming upon

---

9. Voegelin, "*Timaeus* and *Critias*," 231.

10. Plato, *Timaeus and Critias*, 15.

Númenor!" which casts him into a "wide shadowy place" in ancient Númenor.[11] Like Plato's *Critias*, Tolkien's "The Lost Road" remains incomplete.
However, in a letter of 1964 Tolkien wrote that "in my tale *we were to come
at last* to Amandil and Elendil leaders of the loyal party in Númenor."[12] Two
things are noteworthy about this passage: first, as with *Critias*, we see the
importance of a direct link—mysterious as it may be—between the present
father and son and the father and son of antiquity. Second, the explicitly
political dimension of the tale, with its protagonists serving as leaders of the
loyal *party*. We find evidence of Elendil's involvement in this party in that
he asserts his loyalty to Manwë, king of the good angels or Ainur. Elendil
strives to maintain loyalty to the king of Númenor, who has come under the
influence of Sauron and his designs. Herendil responds to Elendil's reference to secret building plans that "hath been reported to me by trusty mes-
sengers" by giving voice to his deep filial fear that his father may pay dearly
for this disloyalty to Sauron.[13] In *Critias* one of the few formal laws to which
the kings give their assent is that they should collectively "resist any attempt
to overthrow the royal family in any city."[14] The need for such a law implies
the likelihood of attempted uprisings; we can read Tolkien's "The Lost Road"
as narrated from the vantage point of those who are members of the dis-
senting force. This party, loyal to the ancient traditions, which include an
"orthodox" theology of the Creator God that contradicts Sauron's cynical
theological hermeneutic. Seeing that his son is coming under the sway of
Sauron, Elendil responds by retelling the story of creation. Further, against
the rule of divine lust which Sauron embodies, against the quenchless thirst
for possessed eternality, and, finally, against Sauron's progressive narrative
that presents the present moment as the apex of Númenorian achievement,
Elendil recollects a past wherein "when I was young there was no evil of
mind. Death came late and without other pain than weariness."[15] The tale of
Tolkien, like the myth of Plato, is permeated with political theology. We witness not merely a corrupted ruler whose realm is marred by the reverbera-
tions that result from dictatorial governance, but a king, Tarkalion, whose
wholesale decline is entirely tied to his submission to Sauron, lieutenant
of Morgoth, the fallen angel. Crucially, considering the weight of history
in Plato's Atlantis legend, Elendil's "rebellion" consists of recounting an
element of history "as if long forgotten," a forgetfulness that comes as no

11. Tolkien, *The Lost Road and Other Writings*, 52.
12. Tolkien et al., *Letters*, 62.
13. Tolkien, *The Lost Road*, 76.
14. Plato, *Timaeus and Critias*, 120.
15. Tolkien, *The Lost Road*, 73.

surprise during the reign of one who has supposedly "thrown a new light on history. Sauron knoweth history, all history."[16]

In the "Akallabêth," a later retelling of the Atlantis myth Tolkien gives the crisis of the "Faithful" and those who capitulate to Sauron extensive treatment. Contrary to Plato, where the dividing line is between two distinct realms representing two distinct orders, in Tolkien division comes between two movements within the one land of Númenor, the western land which the Valar, the "angels" of Tolkien's mythology prepare for Men after the end of the First Age. This being said, the conflict that escalates into a crisis emerges because some among the Númenorians begin to compare themselves to the Eldar, or Elves, and this comparison inculcates envy of the Eldar's deathlessness. Men's fixation upon deathlessness begins once the Valar impose upon them a ban against travel to the "lands where all things endure."[17] At first, a contingent of Númenorians called "the King's Men" grow proud, and become estranged from the Valar and the Eldar. This estrangement, and their burgeoning hankering after eternal life, leads them to fear death, which, in turn, brings about a land filled with "tombs in which the thought of death was enshrined in the darkness," even as those who inhabit the land turn toward a pronounced pursuit of "pleasure and revelry."[18] The Valar at first respond by noting that death is not a punishment. Throughout much of The Silmarillion, and "Akallabêth" is no exception, Númenorian mortality is understood as "the gift of death, which comes to men from Ilúvatar."[19] But men are disinclined to believe that deathlessness is to the Eldar "neither reward nor punishment but the fulfillment of their being"; instead of seeing the difference as metaphysical, they grapple with it on the level of reward and punishment, even of virtue, claiming that Men are unjustly required to cultivate "blind trust, and a hope without assurance."[20]

The Númenorians move toward full crisis when the King Ar-Pharazôn, whose "heart was filled with the desire of power unbounded and the sole dominion of his will," assumes the throne at a time when that Sauron, lieutenant of the fallen Valar Melkor, takes the title of "King of Men" and increases his might. Provoked and infuriated by a rival power who might prove himself inferior, Ar-Pharazôn plans to turn Sauron into his vassal and servant, and the king summons the "King of Men" to swear fealty and pay

16. Tolkien, *The Lost Road*, 67.

17. Tolkien, *Silmarillion*, 313.

18. Tolkien, *Silmarillion*, 318–19.

19. Tolkien, *Silmarillion*, 312.

20. Tolkien, *Silmarillion*, 316–17.

him homage.[21] Sauron, capable of gaining by craft what he cannot obtain by force, feigns humble submission and within three years is entwined within the secret counsels of the king. Soon, Sauron critiques all that the Valar had taught, and insists that the ban on sailing into the Blessed Realm is actually an attempt to curb Númenorian expansion into lands filled with "wealth uncounted."[22] More insidious yet, Sauron teaches that the Valar, in "putting forward the name of Eru," appeal to "a phantom devised in the folly of their hearts, seeking to enchain Men in service to themselves."[23] In applying what we can fairly accurately call a Marxian critique of religion, though, Sauron does not aim to turn the Númenorians toward a material advancement of Númenor. Rather, he claims that the Valar themselves are subject to Melkor, "Lord of All, Giver of Freedom," and incites worship of "the Dark." Ar-Pharazôn, first secretly, but soon after openly, leads his people to this worship. Only a remnant of the Faithful—faithful to the Valar, to preservation of the Elven-tongues—remain.

Sauron builds Armenelos the Golden in the city of the Númenorians, a temple reminiscent of the rationally-planned Atlantis in that it has a circular base, with precise measurements enumerated. But it resembles Atlantis even more so in that, like the Atlantean temple, it is crowned with a mighty metal dome. The dome, however, soon blackens, as Sauron burns first the sacred Tree of Nimloth and then, "that [Melkor] should release them from death," fosters human sacrifice—and the victims are most often selected from among the Faithful, on the allegation that these bore hatred for King Ar-Pharazôn, and engaged in plots against their kin.[24]

In Critias, the inhabitants of Atlantis begin to engage in vile actions because "the divine portion within them" fades, "as a result of constantly being diluted by large measures of mortality."[25] Mortality is increasingly felt in Númenor as well. In Akallabêth, for all of these human sacrifices, "Death [does] not depart from the land, rather it [comes] sooner, and more often, and in many dreadful disguises."[26] Sickness and madness abound, and mortal civil conflicts begin with little cause. Like the Atlanteans, who believe that they have achieved happiness at the moment that their corruption is highest, at this dark stage of their history the Númenorians believe that, though they are not happier, they are prosperous, and grow stronger.

21. Tolkien, *Silmarillion*, 323.

22. Tolkien, *Silmarillion*, 325.

23. Tolkien, *Silmarillion*, 325.

24. Tolkien, *Silmarillion*, 328.

25. Plato, *Timaeus and Critias*, 121.

26. Tolkien, *The Silmarillion*, 328.

Fixating on and furthering this advance in strength, they slaughter many on altars, which they build, it seems, to slake their thirst for violence. Though the human sacrifices do not bring them immortality, they do at least contribute to the Númenoreans' power, just as the ritual bull sacrifice, if it does not increase any rational embodiment of justice in Atlantis, congeals the Atlantean kings' power.

At this point in "Akallabêth," the structure of the conflict more closely parallels the external conflict of Plato's Atlantis myth in that, near to death, Ar-Pharazôn plots a war against the Valar. Whereas in *Timaeus-Critias* the Atlantean "decision" to invade Athens is at least in part a punishment meted out by Zeus, in Akallabêth Ar-Pharazôn's willed rebellion is the cause. Still, his decision to war against the Valar, and, simultaneously, Sauron's declaration of himself as god over Ilúvatar, leads to the cataclysmic Númenorian demise. While Sauron inhabits the innermost circle of the Temple, goading an orgy of human sacrifice, Ar-Pharazôn leads his archipelago of ships into the Blessed Realm, and there he and his men claim the land from which the Eldar flee. At this crucial point, the Valar "[lay] down their government of Arda," but Ilúvatar intervenes directly, literally changing the fashion of the world, opening a chasm between Númenor and the Deathless Lands, diminishing the world by removing the Blessed Realm.[27] But this rift is not the final divine punishment. "Akallabêth" tells us that "in an hour unlooked for by Men"—and it is this entirely unsuspected aspect that adds to the tragic sense of this story—a great doom befalls them: fire bursts from the high Númenorian mountain, and Númenor itself sinks into the sea, sinks there "with all its children and its wives and its maidens and its ladies proud," all of its mirth and music, its painted things and its wisdom and lore.[28]

The story makes clear that Eru/Ilúvatar is the author of the doom that drowns and severs the sea and the land, but Sauron adds his own share—his own share of absence, if we can conceive of absence being "added"—to the cataclysm. Importantly, he laughs when he hears Ar-Pharazôn's trumpets sounding the battle with the Valar. He laughs even as his seat in the Temple lowers into the abyss. The symbolism of the scene is thick, especially if we remember that Sauron's master Melkor's fall from blessedness comes in large part because to him "it seemed . . . that Ilúvatar took no thought for the void, and he was impatient of its emptiness."[29] Master of disordered affection, Melkor loves the Void. Sauron extends this disordered existence even

27. Tolkien, *Silmarillion*, 334.
28. Tolkien, *Silmarillion*, 335.
29. Tolkien, *Silmarillion*, 5.

further when he laughs amid the abyss; at the pinpoint of tragedy, Sauron turns grotesquely comic.

In *The Gay Science,* Nietzsche expresses his sorrow that "the comedy of existence has not yet 'become conscious' of itself . . . [that we therefore] . . . still live in the age of tragedy, the age of moralities and religions."[30] For Nietzsche, those who set forth reasons according to which life is worth living, that life should be treated with great solemnity, "want[] to make sure that we do not laugh at existence, or at ourselves—or at him."[31] We are perpetually proclaiming, Nietzsche writes, new things at which it is forbidden to laugh. Perhaps Sauron, like Nietzsche, laughs at the inadequacy of the human, laughs because he alone has both the desire and capacity of the overlord: to live driven by a creative will to power. And yet, unlike Nietzsche's dreamed overman, Sauron is unable to create. In *Metaphysics of Faerie,* Jonathan McIntosh argues that

> In his effort to go beyond the boundaries established by the beautiful rhythms of Ilúvatar's original theme, Melkor succeeds not, as is his intent, in discovering or creating hitherto unrealized musical possibilities, so much as he does in nihilistically negating or distorting those possibilities provided for by the infinite perfection of Ilúvatar's own being."[32]

Sauron, Melkor's lieutenant, likewise does not create, but rather, as Tolkien's *legendarium* unfolds, becomes more and more of an absence. He returns to Middle-earth, to Mordor, as a "shadow" rather than under the guise of something fair, and is only able to emerge as a terrible eye—"malice and hatred made visible."

Plato's Atlantis myth is also tragic in that, although Atlantis itself is the object of Zeus's punishment in the form of an Athenian victory, sometime after Athens erects its trophy, "appalling earthquakes and floods occurred, and in the course of a single, terrible day and night, the whole fighting-force of your city sank all at once beneath the earth, and the island of Atlantis likewise sank beneath the sea and vanished."[33] Why Athens should be "punished" or at least woefully sunk along with Atlantis remains unexplained. However, in the context of *Timaeus-Critias,* even if Atlantis was willed by the gods and therefore not easily bracketed as an "evil" force pitted against a good, and even if Athens sinks just like its enemy, ancient Athens is the object of praise—ancient Athens is the historical evidence of extraordinary

30. Nietzsche, *The Gay Science,* 28.

31. Nietzsche, *The Gay Science,* 28.

32. McIntosh, "The Flame Imperishable," 172.

33. Plato, *Timaeus and Critias,* 13.

existence. In the words of the Egyptian priest to Solon, "the noblest and most heroic race in human history once existed in your land," a land "outstandingly well governed in all respects . . . The noblest achievements and the finest political institutions we've ever heard of on earth are attributed to it."[34] What is the aim of this recollection of such historical greatness? To shame the present Athens? To imply that if Athens once achieved such superiority, it can again? The tragic fate of a once-great civilization hangs over these dialogues.

Tolkien's tale, though it has a tragic tenor, is not defined by tragedy. The nature of its ending comes into greater relief when read with the author's lecture on "eucatastrophe" in mind:

> It does not deny the existence of *dyscatastrophe*, of sorrow and failure: the possibility of these is necessary to the joy of deliverance; it denies (in the face of much evidence, if you will) universal final defeat and in so far is *evangelium*, giving a fleeting glimpse of Joy, Joy beyond the walls of the world, poignant as grief.[35]

Númenor's decadence and corruption as well as its eventually being swallowed by the sea; the removal of the land of Aman and Eressa beyond the reach of Men forever: these things are drenched in sorrow and failure.

However, amidst this, Tolkien preserves the story of Amandil and his son Elendil, carriers of the eucatastrophic seed. Once Amandil, a holy one among the Faithful, learns of Ar-Pharazôn's plans to make war on the Valar, he is moved to undertake a journey the logic of which parallels Christ's substitution. Although Númenorians are banned from sailing into the West, Erendil will sail there anyway, not to try and commandeer or plead for longevity or deathlessness, but to plead for "mercy upon Men and their deliverance from Sauron the Deceiver . . . since some at least have remained faithful. And as for the Ban, I will suffer in myself the penalty, lest all my people should become guilty."[36] Before departing, Amandil instructs his son Elendil to gather those among the Faithful who are "still known to be true."[37] This last qualification implies that the Faithful have reached a point of considerable caution, testing even those who are formally of their number to be sure that their fidelity is intact. On the other hand, Amandil also warns his son not to let it be seen that he intends to take many men, or Ar-Pharazôn may be troubled in that he needs bodies to serve as soldiers in

34. Plato, *Timaeus and Critias*, 11.
35. Tolkien, "On Fairy Stories," 384.
36. Tolkien, *Silmarillion*, 330.
37. Tolkien, *Silmarillion*, 330.

his war. Along with this carefully chosen band of Faithful, Elendil is to pack ships with "all such things as your hearts cannot bear to part with," and hide in the haven of Rómenna along the western shores.[38] Elendil obeys; he and the Faithful preserve many things the Númenorians "had contrived in the days of their wisdom, vessels and jewels, and scrolls of lore written in scarlet and black."[39] Above all these things they brought with them the young tree, scion of Nimloth the Fair; Sauron had burned the latter as the first fruits of his unquenchable sacrifice. Watching with yearning for some sign of his father, he descries only the growing fleets of Ar-Pharazôn. As Númenor begins to sink under the weight of the king and his prized counsellor Sauron, Elendil resists the summons of the king bidding him to war, and evades Sauron's soldiers who at last come to drag him into the Temple fires. In spite of this narrow escape, the fate of the Faithful seems doomed when the very elements of the earth, the sea churning and beating with wrath and wild winds, "rent their sails and snapped their masts, hunting the unhappy men like straws upon the water."[40] Just as final defeat seems inevitable, as they sail "out of the twilight of doom into the darkness of the world," this section of the narrative breaks off, leaving us with more descriptions of earthly cataclysm.[41]

At the very start of the next section, however, we are taken away from the foundering sea and told in an undescriptive manner reminiscent of a detached chronicle that Elendil and his sons founded kingdoms in Middle-earth, that the wild men of the world consider their lore and craft tremendous, even though it is a mere trace of that which had existed before Sauron infiltrated Númenor. Though we do not know "whether or no it were that Amandil came indeed to Valinor and Manwë hearkened to his prayer," the story states quite clearly that "by the grace of the Valar Elendil and his people were spared from the ruin of that day."[42] The narrative remains somewhat obscure concerning the nature of this grace which spared the heirs of Amandil from the three waves of doom: the summons of the king; the soldiers of Sauron; and the tossing elements. However, the exceptional nature of their delivery points to the likelihood that the Valar were responding directly to Amandil's substitutionary journey. In "On Fairy Stories," Tolkien contends that "in the 'eucatastrophe' we see in a brief vision that the answer may be

38. Tolkien, *Silmarillion*, 330.
39. Tolkien, *Silmarillion*, 331.
40. Tolkien, *Silmarillion*, 335.
41. Tolkien, *Silmarillion*, 336.
42. Tolkien, *Silmarillion*, 335.

greater—it may be a far off gleam or echo of *evangelium* in the real world."[43] It is worth noting that in "Akallabêth" this eucatastrophe is in part political: the buoyant escape of the heirs of Amandil does not end with only a note of their survival. Rather, they *found kingdoms*, and this political organization allows them to continue war with Sauron; their committed resistance to Sauron is possible through political rootedness and manifest in action that is very much of this world. And yet it also has philosophical and theological dimensions insofar as they may well be driven in part by their hereditary memory of the Deathless Land.

At first glance, it seems that this memory has no political implications, that the belief in and memory of the deathless lands is no more than a pique which sends Men seeking, often haplessly, in search of a world without death. Many among the Faithful believe that even after the island sunk, "the summit of the Meneltarma, the Pillar of Heaven, was not drowned forever, but rose again above the waves, a lonely island lost in the great waters."[44] The argument of these Faithful is metaphysical: if the Deathless Land has been taken away, nevertheless, "once they were, and therefore they still are, in true being and in the whole shape of the world as at first it was devised."[45] This belief in *true being* leads great mariners to search empty seas, longing to locate the Ilse of Meneltarma. Most return to proclaim that "[a]ll roads are now bent," but since the Eldar are permitted to depart for Ancient West, the loremasters insist that a "Straight Road must still be," an invisible bridge that, according to subsequent rumors, some blessed mariners were given to travel, beholding the White Mountain before death.[46]

We may gain insight into the significance of the Dunedains' description of the Deathless Land as *true being* when we consider the manifestation of being in Plato's myth. In Eric Voegelin's reading:

> Being is Athens, Becoming is Atlantis . . . The drama of incarnation assumes the form of the war between the two poleis of Being and Becoming, and in this mythical struggle Being remains victorious over Becoming. The victory, however, is not final, for in the realm of history, decline and disembodiment is the fate of every incarnation.[47]

In *The Silmarillion*, "being" never assumes a definitive association with Númenor's established political order. Rather, it remains distinct, and

43. Tolkien, "On Fairy Stories," 387.

44. Tolkien, "On Fairy Stories," 337.

45. Tolkien, "On Fairy Stories," 337.

46. Tolkien, "On Fairy Stories," 338.

47. Voegelin, "*Timaeus and Critias*," 260.

eventually severed, from Númenor and Middle-earth. Still the *Akallabêth* does contain a "mythical struggle" between Being and Becoming, especially when Ar-Pharazôn and his men attempt a conquest of the Deathless Land. Metaphysically speaking, this is Becoming's attempt to *become* Being. Being—The Valar and their land—remains victorious over Becoming, which is enunciated in that Sauron once again shifts shapes and forms upon his defeat. However, though decline and disembodiment define the subsequent history which is evident in that even the Faithful's lore and craft is "but an echo of that which had been" before the collapse, in Tolkien the preservation of at least a remnant of the Faithful defies total decline.

Against this eucatastrophic mythical tale, Plato's dialogues, though rich with images and narrative, is ridden with unrestrained rationality. As Voegelin notes, in Atlantis "the system of communication, and the financial and military organization of the country, Plato has indulged in an orgy of rational planning."[48] Part of the dark side of Atlantis emerges from the fact that this "orgy of rational planning" is undertaken to the exclusion of the teleological aim of justice, or whether rationality and justice perfectly meet Atlantis. We learn that Atlantis is divided into ten cities, and that each of the ten kings is "more powerful than most of the laws, in the sense that he could punish and kill at whim."[49] At first glance, this passage points to a social order in which the will or whim of the ruler, being above the law, leads to a regime organized around arbitrary dictates of power rather than justice. However, the kings themselves are "governed by the regulations of Poseidon" whose shrine—set precisely in the middle of the island—serves as a meeting ground in which the kings test one another according to Poseidon's principles, trying offenders as necessary.[50] Justice, however, insofar as it is upheld on the island, depends upon a sacrificial ritual wherein the kings slaughter a choice, consecrated bull and, pouring libations of bull blood into fire, swear to "adjudicate in conformity with the regulations inscribed on the stele . . . and would neither rule nor obey any ruler unless his injunctions accorded with their father's regulations."[51] Only after the ritual do the kings give and receive judgments, which they inscribe on a golden tablet that is subsequently dedicated in the shrine. The text goes on to enumerate several of the "many other rules and customs" pertaining to the rule of kings.[52]

48. Voegelin, "*Timaeus and Critias*," 260.
49. Plato, *Timaeus and Critias*, 119.
50. Plato, *Timaeus and Critias*, 119.
51. Plato, *Timaeus and Critias*, 120.
52. Plato, *Timaeus and Critias*, 120.

While it is true that, after his admission that the kings of Atlantis are more powerful than most laws, Critias goes on to give us a fairly detailed description of the rites and procedures affiliated with justice; in speaking of Atlantis as a whole, he concludes by calling it a "mighty power," a "force that the god mustered and brought against these regions here."[53] This emphasis on force and power seem to suggest that in the case of Atlantis we are, as Voegelin contends, dealing with an order which has its origins in divine lust, rather than an order concerned with justice. A close reading of the text reveals that, though words like "rule," "regulations," "infringements," and "injunctions" are of considerable concern in Atlantis, we do not come across the word "justice." In place of justice, we have the "regulations of Poseidon, as bequeathed to them by tradition and by a stele of orichalc inscribed by their first ancestors," under which was found an inscribed oath which "called down terrible curses on anyone who disobeyed the regulations."[54] That we are never given an exact account of the regulations seems to enforce the sense that Poseidon is defined by power more than *phroenesis*, and a realm bereft of wisdom and practical reason is a world without justice.

Such a terrible curse Zeus metes out to the Atlanteans by driving them into conflict with the ancient Athenians. However, if something of the nature of their infraction is made clear, Plato's depiction of it lacks precision, thereby enforcing the sense that the obscurity of Poseidon's "regulations" or requisites is not entirely absent from Zeus's punishment. The kings can kill their citizens at whim, whereas there is a special law among the kings which stipulates that kings "should never take up arms against one another." Another law among the kings requires that each come to the other's aid in case of an uprising, which suggests a restlessness among a repressed populace. In the final pages of *Critias* we find a depiction of inhabitants who do not at all seem defined by their being formed by divine lust. Kin of the gods, the Atlanteans "looked down on everything except virtue," held principles that were "true and perfectly high-minded," were not intoxicated by the luxuries their wealth allowed them, and they saw that wealth declines and friendship is undone when a people seeks purely materialistic ambitions and aims.[55] Such reasoning, combined with the divine element within them, led to a remarkably flourishing island.

Over time, however, the inhabitants of Atlantis engage in vile actions, "the divine portion within them" fading "as a result of constantly being

53. Plato, *Timaeus and Critias*, 120.

54. Plato, *Timaeus and Critias*, 119.

55. Plato, *Timaeus and Critias*, 119.

diluted by large measures of mortality."[56] Again, this corruption is difficult
to assess. We are told of their having reached the tragic pinnacle of believing
that they have "finally attained the most desirable and enviable life possible"
at the very moment that they are "infected with immoral greed and power."[57]
That which causes their divine nature to be diluted with mortality, however,
is unclear, in that the text itself seems to suggest that the Atlanteans only
become vile once their "mortality" increases, rather than vice versa. The am-
biguous reasons for Atlantean decline, coupled with the clear divine origins
of Atlantean ascendancy suggest that when Plato ends his myth tragically
he is sinking a political theological problem that Tolkien solves by locating
the source of Númenor's fall in free will; though he is seduced by Sauron,
Ar-Pharazôn is the author of his evil acts.

The starkest contrast between Plato's and Tolkien's myths of Atlantis,
Plato's tragedy and Tolkien's eucatastrophe, has profound political implications. The Athenians' origins in and participation in divine wisdom does
not prevent them from being destroyed along with the Atlanteans. In spite
of its troubling character, Voegelin insists that Atlantis is "by no means con-
temptible"; its "order is willed by the gods"; even though, "characterized as
wealthy and powerful, as barbarian and perhaps sinister," it is the "counter-
polis to the Athenian polis of the idea."[58] Athens, whose federated poleis is
accepted by its subjects, its rulers formed by the gods through philosophy
and philotechnia. Thus while "the order of Atlantis has its origins in divine
lust"—betrayed externally by its expansionist libido dominandi, and internally by the fact that the dynasty has to be maintained by bodyguards—"the
order of Athens [originates] in divine wisdom."[59] Though Tolkien is often
criticized for creating overly simplified conflicts between good and evil, in
"Akallabêth" even though the "Enemy" is distinct from the Númenoreans,
the enemy, Ar-Pharazôn, emerges from within. Both the resisting Faithful and the corrupted and corrupting ruler are Númenorean, children of
Iluvatar.

Given the Atlantis myth's compartmentalization of good and evil, it
is no accident that the Nazis sought in myth justification for their political
program. Tolkien himself observed this appropriation, noting that Hitler
had corrupted the imagination of Europe by "[r]uining, perverting, misap-
plying, and making forever accursed, that noble northern spirit, a supreme
contribution to Europe, which I have ever loved, and tried to present in its

56. Plato, *Timaeus and Critias*, 119.

57. Plato, *Timaeus and Critias*, 119.

58. Voegelin, *"Timaeus and Critias,"* 261.

59. Plato, *Timaeus and Critias*, 266–67.

true light."[60] However, the Nazis reached beyond the northern myths to the heart of mythologized Greece—the lost race of Atlantis. While the Atlantis story entered the Nazi racial theories of Julius Evola[61] and Alfred Rosenberg, who understood pure Germans to be a race of "Nordic-Atlantean"[62] Übermenschen, Tolkien's retelling of the Atlantis myth is in part an implicit critique of Nazism. Around a year before Heinrich Himmler organized a search in Tibet for a remnant of white Atlanteans, Tolkien was writing the Third Reich into his Atlantis myth. As Christopher Tolkien notes in The Lost Road and Other Writings, at the end of the fall of Númenor, there emerges, among other things:

> a sinister picture: the withdrawal of the besotted and aging king from the public view, the unexplained disappearance of people unpopular with the 'government', informers, prisons, torture, secrecy, fear of the night; propaganda in the form of the 'rewriting of history' (as exemplified by Herendil's words concerning what was now said about Earendel, p. 66); the multiplication of weapons of war, the purpose of which is concealed but guessed at.[63]

When Tolkien "reached back to the world of the first man to bear the name 'Elf-friend' he found there an image of what he most condemned and feared in his own."[64] Plato portrays utopian political order in a tragic key, implying that the ideal political order will, incarnate in history, collapse in a catastrophe. The Nazis narrate their link to the Atlanteans in a triumphalist justification for their crimes, tracing their purity to a source in history even as their project culminates in a historical catastrophe. When Tolkien re-mythologized the West—be it the northern myths or that of the classical Greek Atlantis— he, like Plato, moves from utopia to apocalypse. Like Plato in The Republic, he resists the temptation which would suggest that the ideal city can be established on earth; or, rather, his narrative contends that political projects that overreach in their quest for immortality conclude with a cult of death characterized by human sacrifice disturbingly reminiscent of the Nazi Reich, And yet, if he resists the temptation of permanent Númenorean political splendor, through eucatastrophe, a remnant remains—a remnant that fosters resistance to the regimes that unfold in the sinister, shifting shapes of Becoming, even as they proclaim mythical ties to purity and a permanence

---

60. Quoted in Caldecott, The Power of the Ring, 123.

61. Evola, Revolt Against the Modern World.

62. Rosenberg, The Myth of the 20th Century.

63. Tolkien, The Lost Road and Other Writings, 84.

64. Tolkien, The Lost Road and Other Writings, 84.

of Being. By preserving Being through a remnant rather than pinning Being down in a polis, Tolkien sets the stage for a people who preserve in Middle-earth a political theology that embodies the Biblical principle of the saving remnant more than a Classical paradigm of the perfect polis.

Burglar *and* Bourgeois?

Bilbo Baggins' Dialectical Ethics

Backstory of the Bourgeois

Tolkien is filled with dialectical riddles. For all of his characterizations and creations of fantasy, he insists that he is "historically minded. Middle-earth is not an imaginary world. The name is the modern form . . . of *midden-erd* >middel-erd, an ancient name for *olkoument,* the abiding place of Men, the objectively real world, in use specifically opposed to imaginary worlds . . ."[1] He goes on to clarify that the *legendarium* takes place on *this earth,* but in an imaginary historical period. Curiously, some of the *dramatis personae* in Tolkien's "ancient history" are, in the words of Nicholas Boyle, "Tolkien's vision, or fantasy, of the people of England."[2] Tolkien does not hesitate to note this himself: "The hobbits are just rustic English people [and] the Shire is based on rural England . . . I lived for my early years in 'the Shire' in a pre-mechanical age."[3]

Given this depiction of the Shire, when we have Escaped into Tolkien have we, then, escaped from the bourgeois environs? Yes, if by bourgeois culture we understand that which, in the words of Christopher Dawson, "turns the peasant into a minder of machines and the yeoman into a shopkeeper, until ultimately rural life becomes impossible and the very face of nature

---

1. Tolkien et al., *Letters,* 239.
2. Boyle, *Sacred and Secular Scriptures,* 250.
3. Quoted in Boyle, *Sacred and Secular Scriptures,* 250.

is changed by the destruction of the countryside and the pollution of the earth and the air and the waters."[4] In the Prologue to *The Lord of the Rings* we read that hobbits love "good tilled earth: a well-ordered and well-farmed countryside was their favorite haunt," so that it is no surprise that they "did not understand or like machines more complicated than a forge-bellows, a water-mill, or a hand-loom . . . Growing food and eating it occupied most of their time."[5] But we have not escaped if we mean by bourgeois that shrunken insistence on hard facts and comfort, for Tolkien explains that the hobbits were "made small in size because it reflects the generally small reach of their imagination."[6] Further, not all hobbits devoted most of their days to eating and growing their food. Bilbo, for instance, occupies the position of the early propertied creature, analogous to the medieval bourgeoisie. Contra the farming peasant and manservant Sam, Bilbo was "free to lead his own life, to mind his own business."[7] Further, as the historian E.J. Hobsbawn observes, "The home was the quintessential bourgeois world, for in it, and only in it, could the problems and contradictions of society be forgotten or artificially eliminated."[8] Tolkien teaches us the centrality of *home* for Bilbo in the very first lines of the novel:

> In a hole in the ground there lived a hobbit. Not a nasty, dirty, wet hole, filled with the ends of worms and an oozy smell, nor yet a dry, bare, sandy hole with nothing in it to sit down on or to eat: it was a hobbit-hole, and that means comfort.
> It had a perfectly round door like a porthole, painted green, with a shiny yellow brass knob in the exact middle. The door opened on to a tube shaped hall like a tunnel: a very comfortable tunnel without smoke, with panelled walls, and floors tiled and carpeted, provided with polished chairs, and lots and lots of pegs for hats and coats—the hobbit was fond of visitors.[9]

His bourgeois disposition is pressed into greater relief when Gandalf and the dwarves come to hire him as their burglar. As Tom Shippey notes, "trying to be business-like" he "flees to abstractions, only to have the narrator expose them."[10] In a comical moment, Bilbo demands knowledge of the

---

4. Dawson, "Catholicism and the Bourgeois Mind."
5. Tolkien, *The Lord of the Rings*, 9.
6. Quoted in Boyle, *Sacred and Secular Scriptures*, 250.
7. Dawson, "Catholicism and the Bourgeois Mind."
8. Hobsbawm, "The Bourgeois World," 230–31.
9. Tolkien, *The Hobbit*, 1.
10. Shippey, *The Road to Middle Earth*, 73.

out-of-pocket expenses, the risks, the time required and remuneration, and so on. Here, he is paradigmatically bourgeois.

Again, the modern English bourgeoisie did not exist in the ancient past during which the events of *The Hobbit* and *The Lord of the Rings* take place. However, the prominent placement of the bourgeoisie's hobbit-corollary at the commencement of the story communicates the circuitous way by which the contents of Middle-Earth can have a "certain applicability" to the events and personages of earth.

Having established the significance of a bourgeoisie at the beginning of the *legendarium*, we should now turn to the significance of the bourgeoisie's emergence at the beginning of the modern world—especially in England—as well as its ascendancy. In doing so, we will be able to better *see* the way in which modernity seeps into the myth. This is especially necessary in that the only full-length study of the political dimensions of Tolkien's work engages in a grave and inexcusable misreading facilitated by the author's own imposition of bourgeois values on the text. In the "Adventure, Inc." chapter of *The Hobbit Party*, Jonathan Witt and Jay W. Richards claim that "there's something almost ostentatiously capitalist sitting in plain sight in the opening pages of *The Hobbit*."[11] Although we seem to be witnessing a wizard and a troupe of dwarves speaking of dragons and lost treasure, if we shake ourselves free from these fantastical elements we see "something right out there in the open: a business consultant [Gandalf] bringing together two parties [Bilbo and the dwarves] to create a formal contract."[12] The upshot of Gandalf's "contract negotiation" is a "legal document":

> Thorin and Company to Burglar Bilbo greetings! . . . Terms: cash on delivery, up to and not exceeding one fourteenth of total profits (if any); all traveling expenses guaranteed in any event; funeral expenses to be defrayed by us or our representatives, if occasion arises and the matter is not otherwise arranged for.[13]

For Witt and Richards, "the central plot element of the novel" is "launched by a commercial bargain complete with shareholders, two scheduled meetings, a modest life insurance provision, a signed contract and—in good businesslike fashion—an emphasis on punctuality."[14] The contract, they go on to note, would not have been possible without customs of hospitality, propriety, property rights, and the rule of law, all "elements economic

11. Witt and Richards, *The Hobbit Party*, 32.
12. Witt and Richards, *The Hobbit Party*, 33.
13. Tolkien, *The Hobbit*, 29.
14. Witt and Richards, *Hobbit Party*, 33.

historians have highlighted as crucial to wealth creation and the rise of enterprise economies, beginning in the monasteries and the city-states of Northern Italy in the Middle Ages."[15]

Not surprisingly, Witt and Richards contrast Bilbo the goodly bourgeois to Smaug the aristocrat. The pair finds support for their claims in Tom Shippey's observation that Smaug "talks like a twentieth-century Englishman, but one very definitely from the upper class, not the bourgeoisie at all" for he speaks with "a kind of elaborate politeness, even circumlocution, of course totally insincere (as is often the case with upper-class English), but insidious and hard to counter."[16] In this way, Smaug becomes an aristocratic snob who recalls Michael Novak's "historical analysis of the rise of capitalism," important elements of which include property rights, stable financial institutions, rule of law, and economic freedom.[17] According to Novak's narrative, outlined in *The Spirit of Democratic Capitalism,* we learn that in the Middle Ages the bourgeois started to heroically overturn the aristocratic class' monopoly of wealth, which provoked disdain toward the upstart capitalists:

> A beautiful, beautiful wood work, or cutlery, or a millinery— ladies' hats, and great wines, great cheeses—all of these are produced by the bourgeois, but the aristocrats had no respect for them and neither did the artist. Western literature is filled with putting down the bourgeois, and the artist tends to think of herself or himself as an aristocrat, an aristocrat of the spirit if not by birth, and they dislike unaesthetic quality of work, and sweat, and discipline that is required to produce a really good wine, a really good cheese, a really good anything.[18]

Witt and Richards conjoin Shippey's characterization of Smaug as upper-class Englishman and Novak's sympathetic portrait of the bourgeois and in turn condemn the dragon as an *anti*-capitalist who is to be faulted not on his exorbitant amount of gold, but on the fact that he hoards it instead of risking it in a business enterprise or other investment.[19] Again, against this aristocratic dragon Tolkien pits Bilbo the bourgeois burglar, whom Gandalf rescues from insularity and moves to "the dynamic, diligent, and open— recovering, in essence, the bourgeois virtues of exertion, competitiveness, and entrepreneurial daring that allowed them to join and grow the middle

15. Witt and Richards, *The Hobbit Party*, 34.

16. Shippey, *Author of the Century*, 37.

17. Novak, *The Spirit of Democratic Capitalism*, 150.

18. Novak, *The Spirit of Democratic Capitalism*, 150–55.

19. Witt and Richards, *Hobbit Party*, 56.

class in the Middle Ages."[20] In this impositional interpretation—one that borders on magic—the bourgeois "virtues" emerge as fancy fireworks that overpower *The Hobbit*'s more obvious exploration of the virtue of courage extolled in the sagas and epics of the ancient North[21]: Tolkien's satire of the social contract becomes an enshrinement of the same. Through his brave actions along the way—whether in the presence of trolls, Gollum, goblins, spiders, or elves—Bilbo habitually acquires not a courage that allows him to partake of the company of heroes but a "competitiveness and entrepreneurial daring" that allows him to purchase his place in the flourishing middle-class. Such an interpretation goes beyond reflecting Christopher Dawson's contention that "we are all more or less bourgeois and our civilization is bourgeois from top to bottom"[22] in that it does not merely mirror bourgeois prejudices and virtues: it aggressively advances them. While it is imperative that we avoid "treating the bourgeois in the orthodox communist fashion as a gang of antisocial reptiles who can be exterminated summarily by the proletariat," it is equally important that we avoid a mythologization of the aristocracy as reptilian dragons.[23] We must proceed, then, along two paths less taken in order to both bring Witt, Richards and Novak's revisionist history of the middle-class into conversation with other studies of the bourgeois. In so doing, we will be better able to excavate the gift economy that undergirds Middle-earth, and prepare the way for a reading which brings the tradition of "aristocratic" virtue ethics to bear upon the *legendarium*.

In a central and forceful passage of the *Communist Manifesto,* Karl Marx observes that

> the *bourgeois,* wherever it got the upper hand, put an end to all feudal, patriarchal, idyllic relations, pitilessly tore asunder the motley feudal ties that bound man to his 'natural superiors,' and left remaining no other bond between man and man than naked self interest and callous cash payment . . . Constant revolutionizing of production, uninterrupted disturbance of all social conditions, everlasting uncertainty and agitation distinguish the bourgeois epoch from all earlier ones. All fixed, fast-frozen relations, with their train of ancient and venerable prejudices and opinions, are swept away, all new-formed ones become antiquated before they can ossify. All that is solid melts into the air, all that is holy is profaned, and man is at last compelled to face

20. Witt and Richards, *Hobbit Party*, 58.
21. Shippey, *The Road to Middle Earth*, 79.
22. Dawson, "Catholicism and the Bourgeois Mind."
23. Dawson, "Catholicism and the Bourgeois Mind."

with sober senses, his real conditions of life, and his relations with his kind.[24]

Here Marx proclaims the *revolutionary* ethos of the bourgeois, an ethos as revolutionary as its socialist rivals: Marx the revolutionary signals his own fear of the revolutionary spirit of capitalism. In *Capitalism, Socialism, and Democracy* Joseph Schumpeter goes so far as to claim that here and elsewhere throughout *The Communist Manifesto* Marx gives evidence of "his broad-mindedness," an appreciation "nothing short of glowing of the achievements of capitalism"[25]: "The bourgeoisie . . . draws all nations . . . into civilization . . . It has created enormous cities . . . and thus rescued a considerable part of the population from the idiocy [sic!] of rural life . . . The bourgeoisie, during its rule of scarce one hundred years, has created more massive and more colossal productive forces than have all preceding generations together."[26] Here, in spite of their dramatically different affiliations and premises, the radical Marx and neoconservative Michael Novak would seem to mesh, for in *The Spirit of Democratic Capitalism,* the latter praises the *bourgeois* for growing industry, inventing new technologies, constructing skyscrapers, building roads and serving as architects of all the transformations of modern life. Novak cites the historian John Lukacs, who in *The Passing of the Modern Age* attributes "the mathematicability of reality, the cult of reason, free trade, liberalism, the abolition of slavery, of censorship, the contractual idea of the state, constitutionalism, individualism, socialism, nationalism, internationalism" to the bourgeois.[27] For Lukacs, again channeling Marx, what characterizes the bourgeois is the fact that they are perpetually changing. Were the aristocracies to have had their way, so his story goes, we would have seen little change. Novak notes that in spite of these "accomplishments," and at times because of them, Catholic writers—and we can seemingly include Tolkien in their ranks—have been palpably hostile to the bourgeois ideal. As noted earlier, the Austrian Catholic economist Joseph Schumpeter was not one of these hostile critics. His appraisal of the bourgeois is by-and-large favorable, even as, importantly, he points to the *limits* of the bourgeois mode of being, limits which may help us to comprehend Catholic writers' generally anti-bourgeois stances.

In Schumpeter's chronology, capitalism first made the world safe for the bourgeois, not vice versa. It destroyed or nearly destroyed the feudal world's institutional arrangements. The capitalist entrepreneur's competitive

24 Marx, *The Communist Manifesto,* 61–63.

25. Schumpeter, *Capitalism, Socialism, and Democracy,* 7.

26. Quoted in Schumpeter, *Capitalism, Socialism, and Democracy,* 8.

27. Lukacs, quoted in Novak, *The Spirit of Democratic Capitalism,* 143.

force destroyed the world of the artisan, in part through corollary political action that removed atrophic regulations and ridded those arrangements privy to the lord and the peasant. Perhaps more importantly, with the new economic organization the economic privileges of the landed nobility, gentry, and clergy disappeared: "Economically all this meant for the bourgeois the breaking of so many fetters and the removal of so many barriers. Politically it meant the replacement of an order in which the bourgeois was a humble subject by another that was more congenial to his rationalist mind and to his immediate interests."[28] Schumpeter calls this "creative destruction." Notable as the *bourgeois* might be as far as he goes, Schumpeter does not hesitate to call him "rationalist and unheroic."[29] The stock exchange, he quips—and this is important for our reading of Tolkien—is no surrogate for the Holy Grail. Economic leadership does not, as did the medieval lord's, easily expand into the leadership of whole peoples; whereas cost calculation and the ledger confine and absorb, care of the common weal expands, demands magnanimity. The bourgeois' habits of life are not the sort that promote personal fascination: "A genius in the business office may be, and often is, utterly unable outside of it to say boo to a goose—both in the drawing room and on the platform. Knowing this he wants to be left alone and to leave politics alone."[30] In terms of confined genius, *The Hobbit's* Master of Lake-town is *persona par excellance.*

Witt and Richards rightfully characterize the Master of Lake-town, which lies at the base of the Lonely Mountain, as "shrewd but imaginatively stunted, a small-souled individual who cares only about profit and loss."[31] When Smaug takes vengeance upon Lake-town, and "there [is] mourning and weeping" as the populace tries desperately to escape the flames, "The Master himself was turning to his great gilded boat, hoping to row away in the confusion and save himself."[32] After Bard summons his knightly leadership and kills the dragon, the townspeople arrange their ire toward the Master, complaining that "[h]e may have a good head for business—especially his own business . . . but he is no good when anything serious happens!"[33] When the people call for his deposition, venting that they have "had enough of . . . the money counters!" "Up the Bowman, and down with Money-bags," we learn that "the Master had not gotten his position for nothing," as he

28. Schumpeter, *Capitalism, Socialism, and Democracy,* 135.

29. Schumpeter, *Capitalism, Socialism, and Democracy,* 137.

30. Schumpeter, *Capitalism, Socialism, and Democracy,* 138.

31. Witt and Richards, *Hobbit Party,* 54.

32. Tolkien, *The Hobbit,* 248.

33. Tolkien, *The Hobbit,* 250.

suavely reroutes their fury toward the dwarves, who are truly to blame, for it is they who awoke the dragon from his slumber.[34] On the novel's last page we learn that the Master "had come to a bad end. Bard had given him much gold for the help of the Lake-people, but being of the kind that easily catches such disease he fell under the dragon-sickness, and took most of the gold and fled with it, and died of starvation in the Waste, deserted by his companions."[35]

Although the Master seems to epitomize Schumpeter's characterization, Witt and Richards generously apply their neoconservative reading when they argue that the real problem with the Master is that he was both mayor and businessman, and "when an economy is marked by an overly cozy relationship between politicians and capitalists, we call this cronyism," which is detrimental in that it "diminish[es] economic freedom."[36] In the Master, the capitalist and the mayor are not merely cronies: they are the same person. The trouble with this reading is that it valorizes the small-minded, unheroic economic virtues, touts freedom for its own sake, and implies—whether intentionally or not—that the problem with the Master is not his myopic money-mindedness, but simply that he was cronyism incarnate. If he was not the mayor, we may assume, all would have been well. This is of course a problematic argument.

The bourgeois' desire to both maintain their political privileges and leave politics alone is not stoked by economic or material factors alone. In "Locke's Law of Private Censure and its Significance for the Emergence of the Bourgeoisie," Reinhardt Koselleck posits that John Locke, author of "the Holy Scriptures of the modern bourgeoisie" [*Essay Concerning Human Understanding, Of Civil Government*], in locating the origins of judgments concerning virtues and valuations in the human conscience, "gave a political charge to the interior of the human conscience which Hobbes had subordinated to State policy."[37] By essentially demanding that citizens "proclaim their private opinions to be generally binding laws" because "it is only in their independent judgment that the power of society is constituted," Locke "furnished the justification for the English form of government as it had come to prevail since 1688, with the rise of the economically determined Whig bourgeoisie."[38] Koselleck contends that, as private spheres became center of moral authority, and, by extension, models for political society,

34. Tolkien, *The Hobbit*, 251.
35. Tolkien, *The Hobbit*, 303.
36. Witt and Richards, *Hobbit Party*, 67.
37. Koselleck, *Critique and Crisis*, 58.
38. Koselleck, *Critique and Crisis*, 54–59.

these same private spheres allowed no notice of the contingencies and con-straints under which political leaders inevitably operated.

The bourgeois class is ill equipped, then, to countenance social and political problems of any importance, and for this reason the bourgeois can-not be left alone, even to take care of its personal interest, unless protected by some non-bourgeois group. It may be thus that explains Gandalf's recur-rent rescues throughout *The Hobbit*. In the capitalist order, however, there exists no Gandalf. As Schumpeter demonstrates, the capitalist process and its attendant psycho-social effects abolished all "protecting masters."[39] That is, capitalism eliminated not merely the king but all political structures that the village and guild would have formed. These things were not tenable at the time capitalism and its bourgeois character made their appearances, but capitalist policies incited destruction that overturned far more than that which was already crumbling. Thus the bourgeois cosmos "forced upon the peasant all the blessings of early liberalism—the free and unsheltered hold-ing and all the individualist rope he needed in order to hang himself."[40] Novak does not see this. For him, the bourgeois—an almost mythical, he-roic figure—delivers serfs from the windowless mud huts of feudalism, in-adequate sanitation, and lack of warmth.[41] And surely here Novak is right? But Schumpeter asks us to consider the position into which the bourgeois delivered the peasant.

As Christopher Dawson, Catholic writer, Englishman, and contempo-rary of Tolkien wrote in his essay "New Leviathan," though the European peasant's existence was indubitably "harsh and narrow," he yet possessed "the liberty to be himself—a liberty which flowered in a rich diversity and an intense vitality of character and personality."[42] For Dawson, there is no question that for the ordinary, bourgeois man, life is more enjoyable and filled with more opportunities than ever before: an entire culture of amusement everywhere awaits him. And yet, if a man is to reap the material benefits of this mass civilization, he has to "put off his individuality and conform himself to standardized types of thought and conduct."[43] He who would escape the pressures of this position must, Dawson notes, "undergo a kind of penance."[44]

39. Schumpeter, *Capitalism, Socialism, and Democracy*, 139.

40. Schumpeter, *Capitalism, Socialism, and Democracy*, 139.

41. Novak, *Spirit of Democratic Capitalism*, 153.

42. Dawson, "New Leviathan," 5.

43. Dawson, "New Leviathan," 6.

44. Dawson, "New Leviathan," 6.

This use of religious language is not what Novak means when he writes that those who critique the bourgeois class also "appeal to the ideals of the middle class, and specifically to its religious and moral ideals. The ideas and ideals brought into historical actuality by a bourgeois civilization, inspired by the yeast of Christian, Jewish, and humanistic wisdom, are required even in the act of pointing to injustices and inequalities."[45] Here Novak's argument wanes flimsy on several counts. First, the ideals and virtues incarnated by, formative for, and furthered by the *bourgeois* order are not intrinsically Christian. Indeed, many of them are hardly compatible with the cardinal virtues and ideals of Christianity. One must strain in order to reconcile distinctly bourgeois virtues such as thrift, comfort, punctuality, risk-taking, etc with either the classical or theological virtues. Of the mercantilist origins of such virtues, Reinhart Koselleck writes "it is no longer the sovereign who decides; it is the citizens who constitute the moral laws by their judgments, just as merchants determine a trade value."[46] Further, as Amintore Fanfani demonstrates in *Catholicism, Protestantism, and Capitalism,* his careful critique of Max Weber's *The Protestant Ethic and the Spirit of Capitalism,* Christianity—namely Protestant Christianity—furthered the capitalist spirit and practice not primarily in a positive sense, but in a negative sense. For, insofar as it "denied the relation between earthly action and eternal recompense," thereby rendering invalid "any supernatural morality, hence also the economic ethics of Catholicism," it paved the way for the "action of innumerable impulses, which—like the risks entailed by distant markets, in the pre-Reformation period, the price revolution at the time of the Reformation, and the industrial revolution in the period following—led man to direct his action by purely economic criteria."[47] Catholic tradition, on the contrary, opposes and restrains capitalism by chastening these impulses via the classical and theological virtues, and by striving to bring the various spheres of life into harmony.

Bilbo Baggins' Dialectical Ethics

The stunning success of Peter Jackson's film adaptations of Tolkien's *legendarium,* besides being a glowing instantiation of the culture industry, prompts us to consider the question of why a narrative so seemingly drenched in medieval lore, Nordic treasure tales, and lauded monarchs would find so many viewers and readers in a liberal democracy. At the beginning of J. R. R.

45. Novak, *Spirit of Democratic Capitalism,* 154.
46. Koselleck, *Critique and Crisis,* 56.
47. Fanfani, *Catholicism, Protestantism, and Capitalism,* 205–6.

Tolkien's *The Hobbit*, Bilbo Baggins is more than a mere everyman anti-hero whose quotidian existence calls out for the antidote of adventure. We can more precisely diagnose his quiet crisis as a near-absolute habituation to bourgeois existence. By "bourgeois" I mean in large part that shrunken insistence on hard facts and comfort, a description echoed in Tolkien's depiction of hobbits as "made small in size because it reflects the generally small reach of their imagination,"[48] a smallness emphasized in Tolkien's note that "you could tell what a Baggins would say on any question without bother of asking him."[49] Tolkien's contemporary and Catholic fellow traveler Christopher Dawson contends that "we are all more or less bourgeois and our civilization is bourgeois from top to bottom," and this goes a long way toward explaining the contemporary fascination with Tolkien's fantasy.[50] But if this is our first clue, this initial explanation is complicated by Tom Shippey's insistence that it is *because* Bilbo is "a bourgeois . . . [that] Gandalf turns him into a burglar."[51] If the Baggins side of Bilbo's family, the side most clearly emblematic of the modern bourgeoisie, is "considered . . . very respectable" both because they were rich and because they evaded adventures, but perhaps more so because they never "did anything unexpected, the Tookish side is notorious for an adventurousness that makes Shire inhabitants conclude that there is something "not entirely hobbitlike about them."[52] We can begin to make sense of Bilbo's dialectical-familial heritage by turning to *Der Bourgeois*, translated into English as *The Quintessence of Capitalism*, in which Werner Sombart posits piracy, magic, and scheming as means of wealth acquisition characteristic of those that preceded and morphed into modern bourgeois culture; the comfort-loving Bilbo's participation in all three of these categories reveals him as the site of the dialectic that haunts the bourgeois ethos.[53]

48. Quoted in Boyle, *Sacred and Secular Scriptures*, 250.

49. Tolkien, *The Hobbit*, 2.

50. Dawson, "Catholicism and the Bourgeois Mind."

51. Shippey, *The Road to Middle-Earth*, 72. In his poetics Aristotle argues that a work of dramatic art is made more powerful by the presence of *peripeteia*, or a reversal, and certainly the movement from bourgeois to burglar fulfills this poetic device. But if this reversal produces *anagnorisis* (recognition) in Bilbo, it is the audience's own *anagorisis* concerning the dialectical relationship between bourgeois ethics and the burglar's ethos that illuminates the action and adventure of *The Hobbit*.

52. Tolkien, *The Hobbit*, 3. Not insignificantly, we are told that the Tooks are richer than the Bagginses.

53. In *Dialectic of Enlightenment*, Horkheimer and Adorno expose a similar dynamic to that which we are here tracking when they write of a "merchant who returns home with untold wealth because has once, against tradition, stepped outside the confines of the domestic economy and 'put to sea' The adventurous element in his undertaking is,

Shippey sees Bilbo at the narrative's start as Tolkien's satire of modern English society, which is full of nonsense. Bilbo "takes pride in being 'prosy,' pooh-poohs anything out of the ordinary and is almost aggressively *middle* middle-class in being more respectable than the Tooks . . . He is admittedly a bourgeois."[54] His bourgeois disposition is pressed into greater relief when Gandalf and the dwarves come to hire him as their burglar. As Tom Shippey notes, "trying to be business-like" he "flees to abstractions, only to have the narrator expose them."[55] In a comical moment, Bilbo demands knowledge of the out-of-pocket expenses, the risks, the time required and remuneration, and so on. In this satire, we see the aptness of Adorno and Horkheimer's insistence, in *Dialectic of Enlightenment,* that "Bourgeois society is ruled by equivalence. It makes dissimilar things comparable by reducing them to abstract quantities. For the Enlightenment, anything which cannot be resolved into numbers" is suspect.[56] Horkheimer and Adorno argue that "all bourgeois enlightenment is agreed in its demand for sobriety, respect for facts, a correct appraisal of relative strength. Wishful thinking is banned."[57] In the aforementioned scene, we behold a hobbit who has banished all wishful thinking. As the wizard and dwarves arrive and lay out their plan to retrieve their stolen treasure from a dragon, Bilbo instinctively tries to resolve the forces that such a fairy-story connotes by immediately taking refuge in the abstract.

In this we are able to better see the remarkable strands that bind the historical bourgeois to the burgling hobbit, and the fantastical bourgeois to historical burglary. To do so, we turn to Werner Sombart's classic study *Der Bourgeois.* Sombart begins his examination of "The Spirit of Enterprise" with the *Völuspá,* a Nordic myth from which Tolkien took the dwarf-names of "Thorin and Company."[58] Tom Shippey insists that though the litany of dwarf names has been called a "rigamarole," a meaningless list, "*The Hobbit* implies . . . that the meaningless list is the last faded memento of something once great and important, an Odyssey of the dwarves."[59] The nature of the odyssey is absolutely consequential for our purposes. In the *Völuspá* we learn that all crime and conflict entered the world through the union of

---

in economic terms, nothing other than the irrational aspect his reason takes on in face of the prevailing traditional forms" (48).

54. Shippey, *The Road to Middle-Earth,* 72.

55. Shippey, *The Road to Middle-Earth,* 73.

56. Horkheimer and Adorno, *Dialectic of Enlightenment,* 44.

57. Horkheimer and Adorno, *Dialectic of Enlightenment,* 44.

58. Shippey, *The Road to Middle-Earth,* 70.

59. Shippey, *The Road to Middle-Earth,* 70.

the Kingdom of Light, populated by the Anses, and the primeval kingdom of Water, populated by the Wanes. Yellow metal belonged to the realm of Water, but the dwarves, "who lived in the deep caverns of the Earth, enjoying the reputation of gold-thieves and goldsmiths," helped the Anses obtain the gold.[60] In the Edda (of which the *Völuspá* is a part), gold is the central symbol of envy and strife, pomp and power—that which all covet, or can be enchanted into coveting. Bilbo's initial hesitation at the dwarves' arrival gives way when Thorin strikes up music that is "so sudden and so sweet that Bilbo forg[ets] everything else, and [is] swept away into dark lands under strange moons."[61] The song begins with nothing other than an Eddic gold-hunt:

> *Far over the misty mountains cold*
> *To dungeons deep and caverns old*
> *We must away ere break of day*
> *To seek the pale enchanted gold*

The lay initiates Bilbo into the history of "hoards," "goblets" of yellow metal which "we must away, ere break of day,/To win our harps and gold from [Smaug, the dragon]!"[62] It would seem that Bilbo Baggins departs from his comfortable existence only to embark upon a journey that epitomizes the mythic origins of "the spirit of enterprise" which, for Sombart, moves from the pleasure of adornment, to the desire to possess glittering things, to the joy of possession to, finally, the delight in owning much gold, in no matter what form. We see evidence of each of these stages in the dwarves' songs, if not in the precise order Sombart outlines, and Thorin further appeals to the bourgeois Bilbo's questions—"I should like to know about risks, out-of-pocket expenses, time required and remuneration . . . by which he meant 'What am I going to get out of it?'"—with a story of his ancestor Thror who had led his people in mining and tunneling, in the making of magnificent halls and workshops so that "they grew immensely rich and famous."[63] Bilbo, if he burgles well, will receive "cash upon delivery, up to and not exceeding one fourteenth of all total profits"—no small portion of the gilded hoard, and not just any gold, but that once owned by "the King under the Mountain" whom the mortal men treated with "great reverence."[64]

60. Sombart, *The Quintessence of Capitalism*, 25.

61. Tolkien, *The Hobbit*, 13.

62. Tolkien, *The Hobbit*, 15.

63. Tolkien, *The Hobbit*, 23.

64. Tolkien, *The Hobbit*, 29.

Sombart contends that those peoples who operated outside of a money economy—especially early historical Germans upon their contact with the Romans—were attracted to gold not because they could use it as coin, but because they desired vessels and ornaments. "To the overlord treasures spelt power," in part because "his largess was sure to be praised at the minstrel's board,"[65] a practice which, in *The Hobbit,* earns Thror esteem even through the generations. Further, like the early Germans, in listening to the dwarf lays Bilbo is swayed by "the love of beautiful things made by hands and by cunning and magic moving through him, a fierce and jealous love, the desire of the hearts of the dwarves."[66] Shippey reads this as the "first clash between ancient and modern," in which "'ancient wins easily; in an entirely proper sense (*res* = 'thing') it seems much realer."[67] A modern bourgeois, Bilbo, if landed and wealthy, has lost contact with the material sources of wealth. Is it the dwarves "fierce and jealous love" of *things* in particular by which he encounters the echoes of his bourgeois origins, therein finding an unspoken affinity?

This leads us to ask what greed for gold has to do with *Der Bourgeois.* Sombart shows that greed for gold gave way to the love of money, the frenzied desire of gain: *lucri rabies.* From the twelfth through the fourteenth centuries we witness increasing complaints across Europe that *pecuniae obediunt omnia*: everything is subject to money. In his *Descriptions of Florence* (1339), Dante's contemporary Beato Dominici complains that

> money is much beloved of high and low, of the laity and the clergy, of rich and poor, of monks and prelates . . . The cursed gold hunger leads the crazy souls to all manner of evil; it dims the intellect, blots out the conscience, weakens the memory, misguides the will, knows no friendship, has no fear of God nor shame before man.[68]

By the fifteenth and sixteenth centuries, gold had obtained a position of preeminence in all of Western Europe, and the jeremiads against desire of gain continued, but it was only in the early decades of the eighteenth century that the English went through for the first time what others on the Continent had experienced in 1634: "a feverish, greedy money madness."[69] Sombart is perhaps right that Alberti "may be said to have been dominated by the capitalist spirit," as evinced in his fourteenth century writings on the

---

65. Sombart, *The Quintessence of Capitalism,* 26.

66. Quoted in Shippey, *The Road to Middle-Earth,* 73.

67. Shippey, *The Road to Middle-Earth,* 73.

68. Quoted in Sombart, *The Quintessence of Capitalism,* 33.

69. Sombart, *The Quintessence of Capitalism,* 32.

four ways to acquire money: "to seek for treasure-trove; to ingratiate your-self with rich folk with a view of becoming their legatee; . . . usury; and to let out pastures or horses and the like."[70] Still, we lack sufficient correlation between his fourteenth-century advice and the seeds of the modern capital-ist enterprise—and thus the *weltanschauung* of the bourgeois. Sombart sifts through ways and means of money-getting in order to separate those that aided the rise of capitalist economic order and those that contributed no such influence. In the former category he includes force, magic, scheming/invention.

Acquisition via Force

By acquisition via force he means in part "highway robbery," a form of economic activity familiar to barons and knights everywhere, no mere oc-casional adventure of the Middle-Age gentry, but a veritable social institu-tion. A young poet advises young noblemen to earn their living by prowling about the forest where one can "lie in wait for the burgher with his well-lined purse."[71] Highway robbery, as a trade, was learned in the same way as weaving or shoemaking.

When merchants engaged in business and came up short, theft took the place of fair transaction, as they frequently became corsairs, and often received political and cultural sanction to claim what we can call, without undue exaggeration, their "stolen treasure." Pertinent for our purposes, "the real corsairs were difficult to distinguish from the burghers who took part in the raids and battles for their own profit under the supervision of the state."[72] The two were, in a sense, types of a single species. We find etymo-logical evidence of this in that "it is not easy to explain the different shades of meaning in the terms *cursales, praedones* [robbers] and *pyrate*. Moreover, the term *corsar* . . . had nothing blameworthy or discreditable about it," so that there was nothing "dishonorable in the calling itself, in the *pyraticam artem exercens.*"[73]

Wrestling with Mr. Baggins' name, characterization, and condition as "the bourgeois burglar," Tom Shippey notes that Bilbo's "heart is in the right place . . . He likes flowers . . . is ample, generous, substantial of undeniably plain and old-fashioned" and thus has "not entirely lost his passport into the ancient world, and can function in it as our representative, without heroic

70. Sombart, *The Quintessence of Capitalism,* 34.

71. Sombart, *The Quintessence of Capitalism,* 37.

72. Sombart, *The Quintessence of Capitalism,* 67.

73. Sombart, *The Quintessence of Capitalism,* 67.

pretensions but also without cynical ironies."[74] In a passage that serves as a touchstone for our examination, Shippey goes on to note that Bilbo "is admittedly a bourgeois. That is why Gandalf turns him into a Burglar."[75] But *why* the somewhat whimsical "that is why"? What *is* the connection between the two? Both words, burglar and bourgeois, are derived from the same root, "(*burh* = 'town' or 'stockaded house') and while they are eternal opposites, they are opposites on the same level."[76] Thus we see that the same striking affinity between *burghers* and pirates exists between bourgeois and burglars. Venting his doubts as to Bilbo's capacity, the dwarf Gloin tells his company that Bilbo "looks more like a grocer than a burglar."[77] Overhearing this, Bilbo's Tookish (adventurous) side wins, and he appeals to his ancestor Bullroarer Took who was swift as a dragon in a pinch—thereby assuring them that he will do what the dwarves want: Bilbo himself emerges as the site of binary streams of blood—the bourgeois Bagginses and the adventurer-Tooks. Gloin continues to give voice to his concerns, emphasizing the chasm of time and habituated mores that separate Bilbo from Bullroarer. Still, Gloin does acknowledge that the hobbit's door had the "usual [mark] in the trade . . . *Burglar wants a good job, plenty of Excitement, and reasonable Reward.*"[78] Perhaps the bourgeois side would prefer to give greater respectability to his trade: "You can say *Expert Treasure-hunter* instead of *Burglar* if you like. Some of them do. It's all the same to us."[79] Here, then, Bilbo exhibits what Ishay Landa considers to be a further characteristic of the bourgeois psyche: "they are eager to conceal, even from themselves, the violent way by which they have come to own their riches and contrive mendacious rationalizations to justify it."[80] Eventually, once he has stolen Gollum's ring, Bilbo lies to the dwarves about the means of acquisition and eventually "come[s] to believe [his] own yarns about the legitimate origins of [his] private property."[81]

In *After Virtue* Alasdair MacIntyre corroborates this point when he contends that the modern world's property owners, far from being Lockean

74. Shippey, *The Road to Middle-Earth*, 72.

75. Shippey, *The Road to Middle-Earth*, 72.

76. Shippey, *The Road to Middle-Earth*. As Jacques Derrida posits in his *Positions*, every binary has another by which it defines itself. Derrida famously defines the relationship between the two binary terms as being part of a "violent hierarchy" in which one term "governs the other." Derrida, *Positions*, 41.

77. Tolkien, *The Hobbit*, 18.

78. Tolkien, *The Hobbit*, 18.

79. Tolkien, *The Hobbit*, 18.

80. Landa, "Slaves of the Ring," 127.

81. Landa, "Slaves of the Ring," 127.

individualists who have legitimately acquired their property, are "the inheritors of those who, for example, stole, and used violence to steal the common lands of England from the common people, vast tracts of North America from the American Indian, much of Ireland from the Irish, and Prussia from the original non-German Prussians."[82] Sombart's observation concerning the affinity between the bourgeois and piracy, then, is revealed to be central to *The Hobbit,* for in being the "missing link" between the ancient and the modern, Bilbo is also the link between modes of respectable acquisition.[83] In other words, while he at first distances himself from the label of "burglar," soon enough he begins to assume a burglar's psyche, and this—crucially—of his own volition.

Early along their journey to the Misty Mountains, the troupe sees a red light through the trees. The dwarves insist that the burglar investigate, and he finds several trolls sitting around a fire. Although he has not been asked to do so, and though he "wished himself a hundred miles away," yet somehow Bilbo cannot return. He has read of professional burglars, and thus knows that "A really first class and legendary burglar would at this point have picked the trolls' pockets . . . [and] Others more practical but with less professional pride would perhaps have stuck a dagger into each of them before they observed it."[84] Further, "of the various burglarious proceedings he had heard of picking the trolls' pockets seemed the least difficult," and thus he sneaks up behind William.[85] He does in fact find a nice-sized purse in William's enormous pocket, but just before the thief can claim his wealth, the troll snatches him up and shows the little creature to his fellows. Together the trolls entertain the possibility of having him for dinner. As the dwarves make their presence known in an attempt to rescue their burglar, soon the trolls capture nearly the entire company. In a *deus ex machina* drenched in guile, Gandalf appears, interjecting arguments in a voice that sounds like one of the trolls and thus provoking an internal ordeal that distracts the creatures from recognizing the dawn, and "trolls, as you probably know, must be underground before dawn, or they go back to the stuff of the mountains they are made of, and never move again."[86] After the failed theft, Bombur scolds Bilbo for his imprudent pocket-pinching, but not for thieving proper; he simply wishes Bilbo would have tried to steal food. In turn, Gandalf makes clear his own protective and leaderly role, and we are

82. MacIntyre, *After Virtue: A Study in Moral Theory,* 251.

83. Quoted in Shippey, *The Road to Middle-Earth,* 73.

84. Tolkien, *The Hobbit,* 36.

85. Tolkien, *The Hobbit,* 36.

86. Tolkien, *The Hobbit,* 41.

thus reminded of Reinhart Koselleck's contention[87] that the bourgeois cannot countenance social and political problems of any importance alone, but must be protected by some non-bourgeois group.

Remember that Koselleck asserts that as private spheres became the centers of moral authority, and by extension models for political society, these same private spheres allowed no notice of the contingencies and constraints under which political leaders inevitably operate. The bourgeois class is ill equipped, then, to countenance social and political problems of any importance, and for this reason the bourgeois cannot be left alone, even to take care of its personal interest, unless protected by some non-bourgeois group. It may be thus that explains Gandalf's recurrent rescues throughout *The Hobbit*. In the capitalist order outside of Tolkien's Secondary World, however, there exists no Gandalf. As Joseph Schumpeter elucidates in *Capitalism, Socialism, and Democracy*, the capitalist process and its attendant psycho-social effects abolished all "protecting masters."[88] Thus the burgeoning burglar is pathetically vulnerable without the wizard's wardship.

Gandalf in a sense redirects and educates the burglar-instinct, asking, "Don't you realize that the trolls must have a cave or a hole dug somewhere near to hide from the sun in? We must look into it."[89] Bilbo holds up a key, which he found on the ground during the troll fight, and Gandalf uses it to open the cave. Inside, amidst jumbled food and bones, the company finds "an untidy litter of plunder, of all sorts from brass buttons to pots full of gold coins standing in a corner."[90] Swords, in particular, catch their eye, largely— and here we can hear Sombart—"because of their beautiful scabbards and jewelled hilts."[91] Later, the company learns that they have been plunderers of plunderers, for when the goblins take them captive and the Great Goblin, on seeing the swords, proclaims them "[m]urderers and elf-friends!" for the sword taken from the trolls "had killed hundreds of goblins in its

---

87. In Koselleck, *Critique and Crisis.*

88. Schumpeter, *Capitalism, Socialism, and Democracy*, 139. Schumpeter does not hesitate to call the bourgeois "rationalist and unheroic" (137). The stock exchange, he quips—and this is important for our reading of Tolkien—is no surrogate for the Holy Grail. Economic leadership does not, as did the medieval lord's, easily expand into the leadership of whole peoples, for cost calculation and the ledger confine and absorb. Further, and here Bilbo is in the wings, while the Master of Lake-town is *persona par excellence*, the bourgeois' habits of life are not the sort that promote personal fascination: "A genius in the business office may be, and often is, utterly unable outside of it to say boo to a goose—both in the drawing room and on the platform. Knowing this he wants to be left alone and to leave politics alone" (138).

89. Tolkien, *The Hobbit*, 42.

90. Tolkien, *The Hobbit*, 42.

91. Tolkien, *The Hobbit*, 43.

time, when the fair elves of Gondolin hunted them in the hills or did battle before their walls. They had called it Orcrist, Goblin-cleaver, but the goblins called it simply Biter. They hated it and hated worse anyone that carried it."[92] Here Tolkien allows us to trace the trail of forceful acquisition across several "owners."

Bilbo's acquisition of the ring itself, which is central to the story, is muted and anti-climactic. After crawling along the ground, the hobbit's hand suddenly "met what felt like a tiny ring of cold metal lying on the floor of the tunnel. It was a turning point in his career, but he did not know it. He put the ring in his pocket almost without thinking."[93] His pocketing the ring at first seems "fair enough." Soon after, however, he discovers the owner. Shortly we will return to the significance of Bilbo "winning" or at least maintaining the ring in part through a "competition" which he wins by scheming and inventing. For now we can simply note that Gollum screams out for his "birthday present!"[94] Bilbo begins to put the pieces together; at last he sees that the "birthday present" is the ring which he pocketed with such initial nonchalance. Even though Bilbo, provoked by a sudden understanding, begins to look on Gollum with "a pity mixed with horror" he nevertheless steals it and uses it to escape.

We will address the Arkenstone in the next chapter. In this context suffice it to say that acquisition by theft reaches its pinnacle when Bilbo steals "the fairest of all [gems, the] Heart of the Mountain, the Arkenstone of Thrain."[95] Here too burglary and legitimate payment coincide. Bilbo pockets the stone for himself as his "one fourteenth" share of the profits which his contract promises; although in so doing he employs no outright force against another, his act contains a kind of quiet violence.

Last in our list of thefts, we come to the teleological end of the burglar's trip: the dragon and his gold. Remember that Witt and Richards consider "the aristocratic dragon [. . .] a plundering miser, not an investing and enterprising capitalist."[96] Considering this, it is noteworthy that Smaug and his fellow dragons "usually have a good notion of the current market value."[97] Yet, unlike the enterprising middle class capitalist whose investing those goods in the market would be dovetailed by invention, "they can't make a

92. Tolkien, *The Hobbit*, 64.

93. Tolkien, *The Hobbit*, 68.

94. Tolkien, *The Hobbit*, 80.

95. Tolkien, *The Hobbit*, 229.

96. Witt and Richards, *The Hobbit Party*, 196.

97. Tolkien, *The Hobbit*, 23.

thing for themselves, not even mend a little loose scale of their armour."[98] Like the aforementioned Lockean individuals of whom MacIntyre speaks, Smaug steals property in several senses (land, gold, jewels) and ultimately "[takes] all [the dwarves'] wealth for himself."[99] In other words, he engages in an unrespectable form of burglary in that rather than stealing what is, according to some measure of justice, his, he merely plunders.

After establishing the connection between *burghers* and *burglars*, Sombart acknowledges that one might ask why he should bring "conquerors and robbers into connection with capitalism? The answer is simple enough. Not so much because they themselves were a sort of capitalist undertaker, but principally because the spirit within them was identical. The two were equally expeditious of adventure and conquest."[100] From adventurer to sea-robber to merchant we see, Sombart suggests, "three imperceptible stages in development."[101] We see strong strands of this "progression" in the movement from Smaug's outright plunder to Bilbo's expert treasure-hunting.[102]

Acquisition by Magic

Sombart's second category of money-getting that contributed to the rise of the capitalist economic order is acquisition by magic. Men pined for gold,

98. Tolkien, *The Hobbit*, 23.

99. Tolkien, *The Hobbit*, 23.

100. Sombart, *The Quintessence of Capitalism*, 71.

101. Sombart, *The Quintessence of Capitalism*, 71.

102. The dwarves are not mere stand-in for ancient virtues, for they bring with them the modern virtues of the bourgeois: "dwarves are not heroes, but calculating folk with a great idea of the value of money" (211). The dwarves' ties to *Der Bourgeois* deepen in that the source of their enmity with their other enemies, the elves, has its origins in a theft that could be taken directly from the pages of Sombart. In the ancient days the elves had warred with the dwarves, "whom they accused of stealing their treasure. It is only fair to say that the dwarves gave a different account, and said that they only took what was their due, for the elf-king had bargained with them to shape his raw gold and silver, and had afterwards refused to give them pay" (167). The elf-king's prime weakness was "for treasure, especially for silver and white gems; and though his hoard was rich, he was ever eager for more, since he had not yet as great a treasure as other elf-lords of old" (167). In exchange for the dwarves' purported theft, the elves take the former prisoners, as though their "persons" can at least make some reparation. Of course, in turn Bilbo burgles these same persons back, smuggling them into barrels and rolling them down the river while the Elves droop with wine. The narrative never allows us to definitively determine who legitimately owes repayment to whom, but we do learn that the acquisitive spirit is central to the conflict, as Thorin's lust for gold finds parallel in the elf-king who "had a weakness . . . for treasure, especially for silver and white gems, and though his hoard was rich, he was ever eager for more, since he had not yet as great a treasure as other elf-lords of old" (167).

and could obtain it either by finding it or by making it: alchemy. Sombart notes that over the course of fifteen centuries of Nordic history we witness "the finding of treasure-trove among their secret desires."[103] Persons who worked to unearth or discover hidden treasure were not looked upon as foolish. Rather, the common imagination posited in the earth large sums of gold and silver ornaments, coin, and jewelry. Magic formulae which would locate the desired spot proliferated. Ever the sober modern, Sombart quips that "Possibly we are calmer in the [present age]. Fairy tales of wondrous golden princes, or of the Sun's golden palace, no longer attract the gold-digger; but the inwardness of our present-day efforts differs in no wise from those of long ago."[104]

Inward as our present-day efforts may be, *The Hobbit* is certainly one such tale wherein magical means of gaining gold are central to the events. Toward the beginning of the novel, Gandalf takes out a map made by Thror, Thorin's grandfather, a "plan of the Mountain" that houses the dragon and his bed of gold.[105] Thorin glances at it and scoffs, vocalizing his already-solid knowledge of the land's layout. Balin joins the chorus of scoffs, noting that there is a dragon marked in red on the map, but that one does not need a map to locate a dragon. Gandalf points to a portion of the map they have not noticed, "the secret entrance. You see that rune on the West side, and the hand pointing to it from the other runes/ That marks a hidden passage to the Lower Halls."[106] Thorin's incredulity surfaces again, and he asks why they should trust that the entrance yet remains secret. Gandalf explains that the door is small: five feet tall, a width that would cover three walking abreast. Therefore, Smaug could not use it, and couldn't have even as a young dragon. Bilbo gives voice to his own doubts and asks how such a large door could have escaped the notice of everyone else outside. Gandalf cannot offer a full answer, but according to the runes on the map "[he] should guess there is a closed door which has been made to look exactly like the side of the Mountain. That is the usual dwarves' method—I think that is right, isn't it"?[107] Thorin gives his assent. Gandalf admits that he also forgot to mention that a small and curious key, which he bestows upon Thorin, came with the map.

The map is more magical than the company originally anticipated. In Rivendell, the noble elf Elrond, who "knew all about runes of every kind,"

103. Sombart, *The Quintessence of Capitalism*, 38.

104. Sombart, *The Quintessence of Capitalism*, 38.

105. Tolkien, *The Hobbit*, 19.

106. Tolkien, *The Hobbit*, 19.

107. Tolkien, *The Hobbit*, 20.

offers to help them read the map, "for even if he did not altogether approve of dwarves and their love of gold, he hated dragons and their wickedness."[108] As he holds up the map the white light of the moon shines through it, and reveals "moon-letters," which are "rune-letters, but you cannot see them, not when you look straight at them. They can only be seen when the moon shines behind them, and what is more, with the more cunning sort it must be a moon of the same shape and season as the day when they were written."[109] The dwarves who invented them wrote the letters with silver pens, and as it happens these particular letters were written on a summer's eve, during a crescent moon, and thus Elrond is able to read them. They say "five feet high the door and three may walk abreast," which Gandalf already knew, but Elrond also reveals that they instruct the prospective Mountain-guest to "stand by the grey stone when the thrush knocks, and the setting sun with the last light of Durin's Day will shine upon the key-hole."[110] Exhilarated, Thorin explains that he is Durin's heir, and that Durin's day is the first day of the dwarves' New Year, the first day of Autumn's last moon.[111]

When at last they find themselves on the outside of the Lonely Mountain, Bilbo borrows Thorin's map and ruminates over the runes and Elrond's exposition of their meaning. He orders the dwarves to search the western slopes for the secret door. After days of fruitless jaunts, Bilbo at last stumbles across a stone that looks like a pillar with rough steps ascending upward. At the ascent's end they come across a glassy floor atop a steep-walled bay, a spot that could not be seen from beneath because the cliff's overhang blocked it. Further, the door itself was so miniscule that it looked like little more than a crack. But, if they had discovered the secret passage, still more magic was needed to bridge them toward their gold, for "they beat on it, they thrust and pushed at it, they implored it to move, they spoke fragments of broken spells of opening, and nothing stirred."[112] As they camp outside and continued to try and pry their way in, they find that "mining work . . . was clearly no good against the magic that had shut this door."[113] In their dejection, which is stoked by their concurrent eagerness to and inability to enter, the dwarves aim their frustration toward Bilbo. The degree of "magic" requisite for entrance is unnerving.

108. Tolkien, *The Hobbit*, 53.

109. Tolkien, *The Hobbit*, 53

110. Tolkien, *The Hobbit*, 53.

111. Tolkien, *The Hobbit*, 54.

112. Tolkien, *The Hobbit*, 205.

113. Tolkien, *The Hobbit*, 206.

Fortunately, after a particularly miserable night, Bilbo hears a sharp crack, and he turns to see "an enormous thrush, nearly coal black, its pale yellow breast freckled with dark spots."[114] The bird was cracking a snail on a stone. At once an epiphany overcomes him, and Bilbo hails the dwarves, who come tumbling toward him (except Bombur, who is of course asleep). And then the necessary pieces align. The little moon dips into the horizon as a red ray of sun pierces a cloud like a finger, so that "a gleam of light came straight through the opening into the bay and fell on the smooth rock-face."[115] The thrush gives a trill as a rock flake falls from the wall. A hole appears three feet from the ground and Thorin inserts the key as the gleam goes out, the sun sinks, the moon disappears. The company collectively pushes against the door until a door appears, five feet high and three broad. The magical alignment of events, the secret codes and ancient runes: all has prepared the way for the burglar to do his bidding.

Acquisition by Scheming and Invention

Especially as we link it to a narrative text, Sombart's third category of money-getting, "Acquisition by Scheming and Invention," reminds one of Horkheimer and Adorno's analysis of Odysseus' cunning and its relation to transaction[116]:

> Cunning as a means of exchange, in which everything is done correctly, the contract is fulfilled yet the other party is cheated, points back to a form of economic activity which is found, if not in mythical prehistory, at least in early antiquity: the ancient practice of "occasional exchange" between self-sufficient households . . . The behavior of the adventurer Odysseus recalls that of the parties to the occasional exchange. Even in the pathetic guise of the beggar the feudal lord bears features of the oriental merchant who returns home with untold wealth because he has once, against tradition, stepped outside the confines of the domestic economy and "put to sea."[117]

114. Tolkien, *The Hobbit*, 208.

115. Tolkien, *The Hobbit*, 209.

116. Horkheimer and Adorno also make connections between adventure and economics that are pertinent to our study: "The adventurous element in his undertaking is, in economic terms, nothing other than the irrational aspect his reason takes on in face of the prevailing traditional forms" (48).

117. Horkheimer and Adorno. *Dialectic of Enlightenment*, 48.

Though the correlation here is imperfect we can, especially in terms of the regulated riddle game between the hobbit and Gollum, see "cunning as a means of exchange." After he and his company are assailed by Orcs, Bilbo slides down into the "black orc-mines deep under the mountain."[118] As he crawls along, his hand feels a ring, which he pockets. Soon after Bilbo encounters Gollum, who, we read in the Prologue to *The Lord of the Rings,* would likely have attacked Bilbo "had the ring been on him when they met; but it was not, and the hobbit held in his hand an Elvish knife . . . So to gain time Gollum challenged Bilbo to the Riddle-game, saying that if he asked a riddle which Bilbo could not guess, then he would kill him and eat him, but if Bilbo defeated him, then he would do as Bilbo wished."[119] In the Prologue we further learn that the riddle game was one of the hobbits' ancient means of settling disputes, and its rules were established by "Authorities" whose exact identity we do not learn. The first several riddles fall within the provinces of the game's rules, but "[t]he Authorities, it is true, differ whether this last question was a mere 'question' and not a 'riddle' according to the strict rules of the game" even as "all agree that, after accepting it and trying to guess the answer, Gollum was bound by his promise."[120]

Before we examine the controversial final riddle/question, it is important to note that in tracing the bourgeois' predecessor culture, Sombart writes of "scores of people whose calling it was to live by their wits. Scheming, as we may term it, became a business; the man with the ideas was ready to sell them to whomsoever chose to pay his price."[121] Such men, Sombart goes on, were ancestors of "company-promoters," even as "they were not in business" themselves, for "theirs were the ideas that were to generate capitalism, a consummation which came about so soon as the ideas were united with enterprise."[122] Those who acquire by means of scheming and invention are, and here Sombart cites Daniel Defoe's *Essays on Projects,* "masters of more cunning than their neighbours," who "turn their thoughts to private methods of trick and cheat, a modern way of thieving."[123] Defoe links this sort of cunning and thieving to the figure he calls the "mere projector," who, seeking a fortune, beats "his brain for some such miracle in vain," finding "no remedy but to paint up some bauble or other, as players make puppets

---

118. Tolkien, *The Lord of the* Rings, 11.
119. Tolkien, *The Lord of the* Rings, 11.
120. Tolkien, *The Lord of the* Rings, 12.
121. Sombart, *The Quintessence of Capitalism,* 40.
122. Sombart, *The Quintessence of Capitalism,* 44.
123. Quoted in Sombart, *The Quintessence of Capitalism,* 41.

talk big" then gains a patent for this new invention, and swells this new whim into a magnitude.[124]

The connotations of the riddle-game are complex, and are by no means reducible to a sort of nascent capitalist acquisition by scheming and haggling. Erin Sebo notes that "[r]iddles in English folklore 'appeal to a process of thought not an inventory of knowledge,' as Taylor and Auden put it. Such riddles are about seeing through disguises, asking if things are really as they seem and seeing things as they really are."[125] Sebo goes on to observe that, because the hobbit lacks strength, his jousting by means of riddles is most appropriate. After all, if Gollum uses the riddle game because he is threatened by Bilbo's possession of an Elvish blade, Bilbo, "not daring to disagree" over Gollum's suggested "competition," is afraid for his own life as well.[126] At least on the surface, the very terms of the contest favor Gollum, for while Bilbo's win merely grants him Gollum's guidance out of the cave, his loss—and Gollum's win—spells his death. Sebo writes that the archetypal riddle contest is "not a fair fight in which both take the same risk, rather [it is] a true corollary of life in which the odds always favour the powerful."[127] There is no question that, in Tolkien's construction, Bilbo's conundrum is primarily an outgrowth of the Icelandic/Germanic stories that involve riddle games. Still, if the riddle game has other connotations, and we cannot *reduce* the riddle game to its correlation with skills typical of nascent capitalist acquisition, neither should we dismiss the correlation's significance. Although he first uses his wit to cook up legitimate riddles, the crowning of his scheming wittiness comes when he develops a question which "trick[s] and cheat[s]."[128]

Like Defoe's "projector" who "beat[s] his brain for some such miracle"[129] of invention that will bring him profit, Bilbo first finds himself

---

124. Sombart, *The Quintessence of Capitalism*. Again, Horkheimer and Adorno's analysis of *The Odyssey,* which also turns to Defoe, contains germane echoes to our own: "This irrationality of reason has been precipitated in cunning, as the adaptation of bourgeois reason to any unreason which confronts it as a stronger power. The lone voyager armed with cunning is already *homo oeconomicus*, whom all reasonable people will one day resemble: for this reason the *Odyssey* is already a Robinsondale" (48).

125. Erin Sebo, "'Sacred and of Immense Antiquity': Tolkien's Use of Riddles in the Hobbit," 137.

126. Tolkien, *The Hobbit,* 73.

127. Sebo, "'Sacred and of Immense Antiquity,'" 137.

128. Quoted in Sombart, *The Quintessence of Capitalism,* 41.

129. Sombart, *The Quintessence of Capitalism,* 41.

"nearly bursting his brain to think of riddles that could save him from being eaten."[130] Unable to think clearly, he says:

> *Thirty white horses on a red hill,*
> *First they champ*
> *Then they stamp*
> *Then they stand still.*[131]

Gollum knows "the answer as well as you do . . . 'Chestnuts, chestnuts,' he hissed," and the contest continues.[132] Eventually, Gollum asks something "horrible":

> *The thing all things devours:*
> *Birds, beasts, trees, flowers;*
> *Gnaws iron, bites steel;*
> *Grinds hard stones to meal;*
> *Slays king, ruins town,*
> *And beats high mountain down.*[133]

Bilbo plumbs his mind but, failing to procure an answer, he begins to grow fearful. He desires more time, and thus calls out "Time! Time!,"[134] thereby giving the answer by pure luck. Bilbo's creative wit begins to suffer, and though it is his turn, he cannot come up with a question. Reaching into his pocket he fingers the ring, and says aloud, "What have I got in my pocket?"[135] Although initially he is merely musing aloud, Gollum takes it for the next riddle and hisses, "It wasn't a fair question . . . Not a riddle, precious no"; nevertheless, Bilbo, thinking his life is threatened, thieves the ring and uses it to escape.[136]

Bilbo's decision to break the sacred rules of the riddle game is morally nuanced in the sense that he did so in order to preserve his life. Nevertheless,

---

130. Tolkien, *The Hobbit*, 74.

131. Tolkien, *The Hobbit*, 74.

132. Tolkien, *The Hobbit*, 74.

133. Tolkien, *The Hobbit*, 77.

134. Tolkien, *The Hobbit*, 78.

135. Tolkien, *The Hobbit*, 78.

136. Tolkien, *The Hobbit*, 82–83. If Bilbo's initial musing lacks volition, he now assumes culpability for the unfair question, as he repeats, louder, "What have I got in my pocket?" Gollum is dreadfully disadvantaged, and his guesses fall wide of the mark. Bilbo rationalizes his willful question. Although "[h]e knew, of course, that the riddle-game was sacred and of immense antiquity; and even wicked creatures were afraid to cheat when they played at it," and even though "that last question had not been a genuine riddle according to the ancient laws," he justifies his injustice on the grounds that he cannot trust Gollum.

Gollum is right when he cries out "Thief, thief, thief, Baggins!" and when he says "it's [Bilbo is] tricksy. It doesn't say what it means."[137] Excuses standing, the hobbit exhibits the capacity to "live by [his] wits," which Sombart identifies with the bourgeoisie's predecessor culture and practices.[138] However, it is also important to note that the "ring he had was a magic ring: it made you invisible."[139] Although he uses the invisible ring for many and varied purposes, without question he would not have been able to thieve the dragon's gold without it; riddle the dragon with wit he may, but the ring engenders courage to enter Smaug's lair in the first place, and allows him the invisibility needed to steal the chalice. In this way, Bilbo's case embodies acquisition by magic and scheming at once.

For Sombart, the capitalist economic system does not produce the bourgeois, even as it certainly sustains, satiates, and proliferates him. Does Bilbo, in entering on a journey to the pre-capitalist *welt,* in which he is called upon to do things that chafe against the middle-class English ethos, reverse the "progression" Sombart outlines? What *is* his relationship to those traits and attributes extant in the pre-capitalist era which prepared the way for the modern bourgeoisie? In "The Bourgeois Burglar," Tom Shippey writes that in creating Bilbo Tolkien "did not want to be ironic about heroes," and his response to this difficulty is "Bilbo Baggins, the hobbit, the anachronism whose initial role at least is very strongly that of mediator. He represents and often voices modern opinions, modern incapacities."[140] And yet the hobbit goes far beyond this. Sombart shows us the degree to which bourgeois and burglar are *on the same level.* Acquisition by force, magic, scheming, and invention all provide a foundation for the bourgeois "undertaker" who first obtained gains through the aforementioned piracy. Again, Sombart makes it clear that he is not claiming that pirates themselves were capitalist undertakers. Instead, he contends that the spirit within each is identical: the spirit of trade and colony planting on the one hand, and piracy and burglary on the other, is the same. Nevertheless, when we attempt to situate Bilbo in the ranks of the pirates of Sombart's study, "strong, healthy adventurers, sure of victory, brutal and greedy, conquering all before them," we come up short.[141] This seems in part to be because Bilbo acquires also by scheming and by magic. However, our coming up short may also be due to the fact that in witnessing and even participating in what for Sombart would be the seeds

---

137. Tolkien, *The Hobbit,* 84.

138. Sombart, *The Quintessence of Capitalism,* 30.

139. Tolkien, *The Hobbit,* 85.

140. Shippey, *The Road to Middle-Earth,* 71.

141. Sombart, *The Quintessence of Capitalism,* 70.

of the capitalist spirit, Bilbo is repulsed, and by the end of the novel he goes a long way toward rejecting or at least moderating it, as the next chapter will demonstrate. His rejection of the seeds of the bourgeois spirit in its rudimentary forms is even more astounding in that the modern bourgeois spirit itself, of which at the novel's start Bilbo is a blooming exemplification, seems a flimsy moral structure by which to chasten one's acquisitive urges or even establish an ethics worth its name. As Christopher Dawson notes, "The ideal of the [modern] bourgeois culture is to maintain a respectable average standard. Its maxims are: 'Honesty is the best policy,' 'Do as you would have done by,' 'The greatest happiness of the greatest number.'"[142] We can add frugality and moderation, but these things undertaken predominantly to increase one's acquired monies and property and comfort. As Sombart illustrates, according to the "business morality" of the bourgeois, one need not by any means "*be* respectable. [One] must be regarded as such."[143] Thus we have Bilbo's qualms over being called "burglar," and the dwarves' offer to proffer the more respectable title of "expert treasure hunter." By the end, however, such titles are dross, for above all else Bilbo's very respectability is thieved from him, even as he receives gifts from unexpected quarters.

Acquisitive Imitation and the Gift-Economy: Escaping Reciprocity in J. R. R. Tolkien's *The Hobbit*

Thirteen dwarves and a wizard invade the quiet abode of Bilbo Baggins in an effort to recruit him for an expedition, the purported purpose of which is to recover stolen treasure and exact vengeance on Smaug the dragon, the robber who had killed a large portion of Thorin's family and friends. Although most readers and critics approach J. R. R. Tolkien's *The Hobbit* as a children's story, an unserious dress-rehearsal-sketch of *The Lord of the Rings*, *The Hobbit*, with its "Secondary World" of fantastical creatures, may yet come bearing gifts of insight into, of all things, human nature itself, especially the mimetic nature of much desire. Tolkien's story dramatizes in narrative form René Girard's claim that our desires are not our own. Rather, they originate in models and obstacles whom we imitate in hopes of possessing their being. Of course, as in Virgil's *Aeneid* when Laocoön, priest of Troy, tells his countrymen to *Timeo Danaos et dona ferentes* ("beware of Greeks bearing gifts"), we too may yet be suspicious of that bourgeois burglar Bilbo Baggins, for the gift he bears—though not a Trojan horse—is stolen. Tolkien's enduring appeal involves, in part, the universality of mimetic desire.

142. Dawson, "Catholicism and the Bourgeois Mind."
143. Sombart, *The Quintessence of Capitalism*, 124.

However, Bilbo's draw extends beyond his mere "relatability" as mediocre-made-heroic in the fact that he is simultaneously enchanted-insider tangled into the web of mimetic desire and scapegoated-outsider—and therefore able to reveal the mechanisms and monstrosities of mimesis, especially as it pertains to possessiveness and exchange. Perhaps more importantly, Bilbo's quest also points to the possibility of Escape from an economy of mimesis and gives us the economy of gift.

It has taken a Marxist critic to seriously examine the problem of theft in *The Hobbit*. In "Slaves of the Ring: Tolkien's Political Unconscious," Ishay Landa argues that "Bilbo begins his inveighing against private property by stealing from the trolls, then from Gollum, then from Smaug the dragon, and, finally and most importantly, from the dwarves."[144] How could a children's story be so rife with what at first glance might seem a case of kleptomania made heroic? In the tales that most deeply inform Tolkien's work—Sigurd and Fafnir in the saga of the *Völsungs*, or Beowulf and Grendel's mother in *Beowulf*—thieving from the hoard is typically dangerous. However, in *The Hobbit* we witness a greater ambivalence toward theft. Tom Shippey sees this movement toward burgling as a departure from bourgeois existence. Bilbo's "heart is in the right place . . . He likes flowers . . . is ample, generous . . . undeniably plain and old-fashioned" and thus has "not entirely lost his passport into the ancient world, and can function in it as our representative, without heroic pretensions but also without cynical ironies. He is admittedly a bourgeois. That is why Gandalf turns him into a Burglar."[145] However, the problems raised by Bilbo's burgling cannot be resolved by our seeing it as merely a counterpoint to his initial comfort-loving malaise. Tolkien is not working beneath the Marxist dictum that "private property is produced by theft" so much as he is working within the Girardian dictum of "prized property is preceded by desire." To this end, the origins of Bilbo's desire to burgle and his "reason" for becoming a thief are especially important for our investigation.

In order to examine this, it is first necessary to determine whether dwarves themselves are primarily motivated by reciprocity or something else entirely. In "The Ambivalence of Scarcity," Paul Dumouchel develops a Girardian critique of modern economics. He contends that desire precedes the object of desire. If mimesis eventually escalates to make people violently clash around a single object, mimesis "emerges before the object, and even, at the limit, creates the object, it is inseparable from the illusion that the

---

144. Landa, "Slaves of the Ring: Tolkien's Political Unconscious," 113–33.
145. Shippey, *The Road to Middle Earth*, 72.

object came first."[146] According to Thorin, during a period of exile his family brought "all their wealth and their tools" to the Lonely Mountain, where "they mined and tunneled and they made huger halls and greater workshops—and in addition I believe they found a good deal of gold and a great many jewels too."[147] They "grew immensely rich and famous" and mortal men began to treat the King, Thorin's grandfather, with great reverence.[148] During this time of abundance, even the poorest among the dwarves had money to lend and spend, and the halls "became full of armour and jewels and carvings and cups," which "undoubtedly" brought the dragon.[149] The dragon's desire is mimetic insofar as Thorin is right to conclude that when the dragon "took all their wealth for himself" he was driven by the fact that King Thror's halls were "the wonder of the North."[150] Significantly, dragons steal jewels and gold even though they "never enjoy a brass ring of it."[151] As Dumouchel notes, because the object receives its value from the other, "If the subject succeeds in obtaining the desired object, he or she will soon see the victory transformed into failure," for "since the object is no longer mediated by the model, it loses the value that made it so desirable."[152] For Smaug, though, even if the object has lost the value that made it *desirable,* he nevertheless settles in to guard his plunder as long as he lives, piling it up into a great heap and sleeping on it for a bed. One is reminded of the fable of the manger dog, who guards the hay greedily even as he cannot eat any of it.

In seeking to retrieve the gold, Thorin acknowledges that the motive is not sheer necessity, as it once may have been during the initial period of exile, because the dwarves "'have a good bit laid by and are not so badly off'—here Thorin stroked the gold chain round his neck—'we still mean to get it back, and to bring our curses home to Smaug—if we can.'"[153] Revenge, then, is mingled with the desire for beautiful things, even as the dragon does not share this desire. Though the dragon's "motives" cannot, in a Girardian sense, precede the object, Thorin and Company are caught up in mimetic desire insofar as their desire for revenge (recovery of wealth) is coupled with their longing for former prestige, an influence, power, and presence in the land which now only the dragon owns. Again, they have no true rational

146. Paul Dumouchel, *The Ambivalence of Scarcity and Other Essays,* 25.

147. Tolkien, *The Hobbit,* 22.

148. Tolkien, *The Hobbit,* 22.

149. Tolkien, *The Hobbit,* 22–23.

150. Tolkien, *The Hobbit,* 22.

151. Tolkien, *The Hobbit,* 23.

152. Dumouchel, *The Ambivalence of Scarcity and Other Essays,* 26.

153. Tolkien, *The Hobbit,* 24.

need for the hoard, and thus Tolkien demonstrates yet again the manner in which desire is intertwined with our relationships, even conditioned by them.

Bilbo's initial hesitance concerning the dwarves' arrival and aims gives way when Thorin strikes up music that is "so sudden and so sweet that Bilbo forg[ets] everything else, and [is] swept away into dark lands under strange moons."[154] The song begins with nothing other than an Eddic gold-hunt:

> Far over the misty mountains cold
> To dungeons deep and caverns old
> We must away ere break of day
> To seek the pale enchanted gold[155]

The song initiates Bilbo into the history of "hoards," "goblets," "harps" of yellow metal which "we must away, ere break of day, / To win our harps and gold from [Smaug, the dragon]!"[156] Listening to the dwarf lays, Bilbo is swayed by "the love of beautiful things made by hands and by cunning and magic moving through him, a fierce and jealous love, the desire of the hearts of the dwarves."[157]

In *To Double Business Bound*, René Girard argues that "desire chooses its objects through the mediation of a model . . . The model designates the desirable while at the same time desiring it."[158] In the beginning Bilbo had no desire to depart from Bag End, let alone to obtain the "pale enchanted gold." The sung songs of stolen treasure incite not a desire to help the dwarves regain their just due, but a "love of beautiful things," the "desire of the hearts of the dwarves." The dwarves designate what is desirable while simultaneously desiring it.

Later, Bilbo's rather petty theft of the goblet stirs the dwarves' desires, and they sit outside of the mountain reminiscing about specific parts of the "great hoard" that Balin and Thorin remembered. After a long litany of treasures, we learn that "the fairest of all was the great white gem, which the dwarves had found beneath the roots of the Mountain, the Heart of the Mountain, the Arkenstone of Thrain."[159] Thorin, half-dreaming in the dark, his chin upon his knees, murmurs, "The Arkenstone! The Arkenstone! . . . It was like a globe with a thousand facets; it shone like silver in the firelight,

---

154. Tolkien, *The Hobbit*, 13.
155. Tolkien, *The Hobbit*, 13.
156. Tolkien, *The Hobbit*, 15.
157. Quoted in Shippey, *The Road to Middle Earth*, 73.
158. René Girard, *To Double Business Bound*, 39.
159. Tolkien, *The Hobbit*, 229.

like water in the sun, like snow under the stars, like rain upon the Moon."[160] Bilbo, though, having encountered the tremendous dragon, sits uncomfortably nearby in anticipation of foreign sounds, half listening to the dwarves: "the enchanted desire of the hoard had fallen from [him]."[161] Not long after, though, as Bilbo once again returns to the Mountain's heart, that fallen desire is resurrected. As usual, the dwarves employ Bilbo to face the dangers of their quest. Allison Milbank contends that, as hired thief for the dwarves' expedition, Bilbo "is a kind of scapegoat who will bear prophylactically the transgressive nature of the enterprise."[162] Nevertheless, in consequence of his being sent ahead of the others, he is the first to find "the Arkenstone, the Heart of the Mountain."[163] Recall that, amidst an array of fears, Bilbo's desire had disintegrated. Nevertheless, the Arkenstone revitalizes it, not primarily because he finds it attractive, but because he discovers it by means of "Thorin's description," for:

> there could not be two such gems, even in so marvellous a hoard, even in all the world . . . At last he looked down upon it and he caught his breath. The great jewel shone before he feet of its own inner light, and yet, cut and fashioned by the dwarves, who had dug it from the heart of the mountain long ago, it took all light that fell upon it and-changes it into ten thousand sparks of white radiance shot with glints of the rainbow. Suddenly Bilbo's arm went towards it drawn by its enchantment. His small hand would not close about it for it was a large and heavy gem; but he lifted it, shut his eyes, and put it in his deepest pocket.[164]

Thorin's ekphrastic ruminations on the stone become Bilbo's muse, and we see from the fact that his "arm went towards it drawn by enchantment" that this desire is not guided by rational aims. The depth of his desire is sealed by Tolkien's note that the hobbit "shut his eyes," almost as though he stood before something sacred, and "put it in his deepest pocket," as though to guard the singular treasure from Thorin's sight.

Bilbo immediately registers this act as theft: "Now I am a burglar indeed!" he thinks to himself.[165] Rationalizations follow in tow. At some point, he reflects, he will tell the dwarves about it, but for now he is content to remember that "they did say I could pick and choose my own share;

160. Tolkien, *The Hobbit*, 229.

161. Tolkien, *The Hobbit*, 229.

162. Milbank, *Chesterton and Tolkien as Theologians*, 130.

163. Tolkien, *The Hobbit*, 235.

164. Tolkien, *The Hobbit*, 235.

165. Tolkien, *The Hobbit*, 235.

and I think I would choose this, if they took all the rest!"[166] Even as his rationalizations emerge, however, he has an "uncomfortable feeling that the picking and choosing had not really been meant to include this marvelous gem, and that trouble would yet come of it."[167] He is right.

After pocketing the Arkenstone, Bilbo leads the dwarves to Smaug's lair. There they "caress and finger" the treasure.[168] Thorin searches single-mindedly for the Arkenstone, but tells no one he is doing so. As the rest of the company lose themselves in the hoard he "kept his head more clear of the bewitchment . . . Long before the dwarves were tired of examining the treasures, he became wary of it and sat down on the floor."[169] Here the dwarves' all-consuming desires seem to actually dwarf Bilbo's own, for he notes that he would give a good many precious goblets for some cheerful hospitality elsewhere, away from the Lonely Mountain. Does the sight of their excessive delight dull his own desire? Is his desire, again, simply sapped by fear? Or is his "success" in having pocketed the coveted Arkenstone a failure in that, in Dumouchel's words, "Only the Other's ability to be an obstacle can convince the subject that his or her fingers will close around something substantial"?[170]

As for Smaug's return, Bilbo has no reason to be concerned—at least for the moment. During the end of Bilbo's first interview with Smaug, the hobbit tells the dragon that "gold was only an afterthought" of the company's journey to his lair: "We came over hill and under hill, by wave and by win, for *Revenge*. Surely, O Smaug the unassessably wealthy, you must realize that your success has made you some bitter enemies."[171] The dragon scoffs at the possibility of any troupe taking "revenge" on a dragon so "old and strong, strong, strong."[172] Spurred in part by the fact that Bilbo stole a goblet, but likely also by the very possibility that someone would conceive of taking revenge against him, Smaug escalates revenge to the extreme. Unfortunately, the escalation is misplaced. Because Bilbo introduces himself to the dragon as "Ringwinner and Luckwearer . . . Barrel-rider," Smaug concludes that the hobbit is involved in "some nasty scheme of those miserable tub-trading Lake-men."[173] He has left his lair, then, in order to have his revenge on Lake-

166. Tolkien, *The Hobbit*, 235.

167. Tolkien, *The Hobbit*, 235–36.

168. Tolkien, *The Hobbit*, 239.

169. Tolkien, *The Hobbit*, 238.

170. Dumouchel, *The Ambivalence of Scarcity and Other Essays*, 26.

171. Tolkien, *The Hobbit*, 235.

172. Tolkien, *The Hobbit*, 224.

173. Tolkien, *The Hobbit*, 221.

town. Blind and mad with rage, he sets the town ablaze and knocks down the Great House with a swipe of his tail.[174] Bard the archer saves the town from total annihilation by shooting an arrow into a weak spot on the great beast's belly.

When Thorin and company learn from a thrush of Smaug's death they first "spr[ing] up and beg[in] to caper about for joy" but the messenger bird warns them that "legend of the wealth of Thror has not lost in the telling during many years; many are eager for a share of the spoil."[175] Further, the dragon's misplaced vengeance has incited another cycle of sought reciprocity, for "by the lake men murmur that their sorrows are due to the dwarves; for they are homeless and many have died, and Smaug has destroyed their town. They too think to find amends from your treasure."[176] The thrush expresses his desire for peace among dwarves and men and elves, but notes that such a peace "may cost you dear in gold."[177] At this Thorin bursts forth in rage: "None of our gold shall thieves take or the violent carry off while we are alive."[178] In resisting the possibility of reciprocity, Thorin knows he opens the gate of violence, and thus he and his fellow dwarves spend their time "fortifying the main entrance" and preparing for an ensuing attack—and rightfully so, as "the joined armies of the Lake-men and the Elves were hurrying towards the Mountain."[179]

Soon Bard approaches Thorin, asking "why do you fence yourself like a robber his hold? We are not yet foes, and we rejoice that you are alive beyond our hope."[180] He tells Thorin that it is by his own defeat of the dragon that the treasure has been delivered. Moreover, "I am by right descent the heir of Girion of Dale, and in your hoard is mingled much of the wealth of his halls and town, which of old Smaug stole."[181] In addition, Smaug destroyed the dwellings of Esgaroth, whose people aided the dwarves in their distress so many years earlier, when the dragon sent them into exile; in exchange for this aid the dwarves have "thus far brought ruin only, though doubtless undesired."[182] Although Bilbo hears these words as fair and true, Thorin does not admit that justice is in them. Instead, while he agrees to

---

174. Tolkien, *The Hobbit*, 247.
175. Tolkien, *The Hobbit*, 257.
176. Tolkien, *The Hobbit*, 257.
177. Tolkien, *The Hobbit*, 258.
178. Tolkien, *The Hobbit*, 258.
179. Tolkien, *The Hobbit*, 259.
180. Tolkien, *The Hobbit*, 262.
181. Tolkien, *The Hobbit*, 263.
182. Tolkien, *The Hobbit*, 263.

fairly pay the Lake-men for assistance previously received, "*nothing* will [he] give, not even a loaf's worth, under threat of force. While an armed host lies before [their] doors, [he] look[s] on [them] as foes and thieves."[183] In rejecting Bard's appeal, Thorin appeals to the presence of force, which, so his logic goes, invalidates any justice within them. He does not, however, reject the just components of their claims, but rather confirms the fact that "exchange in traditional societies is not a way of making profit but a means through which the social bond is continuously created and relations of solidarity enacted."[184] Both Bard and Thorin operate within such an economy.

In his slender volume *The Gift (Essai dur le don)*, Marcel Mauss contends that "gift-giving in a number of pre-capitalist cultures in the past," far from being a "spontaneous archaic generosity," was rather "an alternative social and economic system" comprised of "giving, receiving, and reciprocating, so that an obligation to give back was conferred on the receiver."[185] Alison Milbank demonstrates that, like Tolkien, Mauss was influenced by Nordic culture; *The Gift* finds evidence in the *Edda,* a collection of ancient Nordic literature, and its opening epigraph is the *Eddic* "a gift always looks for recompense."[186]

From the very beginning of *The Hobbit,* Bilbo's fidelity to a gift-exchange logic is tenuous. The morning after the dwarves' initial visit Bilbo wakes to find something quite different, something which we are all familiar: the contract, which I have analyzed at length earlier. Perhaps as he moves from his relatively modern bourgeois existence at Bag End through the pre-modern world of elves, goblins, dwarves and more, Bilbo begins to feel the thinness of a modern contract. From this vantage, we may wonder whether Bilbo is responding to the inadequacy of a mere modern contract when he takes the Arkenstone as a sort of pledge. Mauss notes that all sorts of Nordic contracts required a "pledge," *wadium,* (the English *wage*), which in the premodern contract served as the binding tie, allowing the contracting parties to "react with one another, since each possesses something of the other."[187] The *wadium* or "pledge" was "very much infused with the individuality of the donor," a description that most accurately denotes the Arkenstone, which is of course intimately tied to Thorin, and to the dwarves at large, as they carved and chiseled and polished it into its present state. Another important aspect of the pledge is its capacity to stimulate

183. Tolkien, *The Hobbit,* 263.

184. Dumouchel, *The Ambivalence of Scarcity and Other Essays,* 100.

185. Quoted in Milbank, *Chesterton and Tolkien as Theologians,* 118.

186. Milbank, *Chesterton and Tolkien as Theologians,* 119.

187. Marcel Mauss, *The Gift,* 79.

the recipient party into carrying out the contract. In Germanic culture the pledge-holder remained in an inferior state until he was freed of the pledge-wager. Bilbo seems to recognize this sense of obligation, the sense of danger that is part and parcel of receiving—in this case thieving—a pledge. Perhaps we can read Bilbo's relationship to the Arkenstone as a modern modification of the pledge. Perhaps it is his individualism that allows him to take the Arkenstone as his share of the contractual dividends without consulting Thorin and Company.

Bilbo's relationship to the Arkenstone only grows more complicated as the events unfold. As the Elves and Men remain camped outside of the Lonely Mountain, Thorin commands his fellow dwarves to look for the Arkenstone in every corner. He announces that he "will be avenged on anyone who finds it and withholds it."[188] Bilbo says nothing, as "the beginnings of a plan had come into his little head."[189] During his turn to take watch in the night, Bilbo steals away into the enemy camp.

Soon he is sitting beside a warm fire in a large tent, Elvenking and Bard gazing curiously upon him. "Really you know," Bilbo says, "things are impossible. Personally I am tired of the whole affair . . . But I have an interest in this matter—one fourteenth share, to be precise, according to a letter, which fortunately I believe I have kept."[190] His language is typically modern, appealing to both his own "interest" in this matter and the precious contract. Bilbo goes on to reveal secret information: Thorin's kin Dain is less than two day's march from the Lonely Mountain, five hundred dwarves with him, dwarves who have experience fighting the dreadful goblins. Bard openly wonders why Bilbo is betraying his friends, at which point Bilbo tells them that, in order "to avoid trouble for all concerned," he "will make . . . an offer."[191] He draws forth the Arkenstone and throws away the wrapping. Even the Elvenking, whose eyes are well acclimated to beautiful things, stands up in amazement, while Bard marvels at the stone in silence.

Bilbo goes on to tell them that the Arkenstone is the "Heart of the Mountain; and it is also the heart of Thorin. He values it above a river of gold. I give it to you. It will aid you in your bargaining."[192] Bard asks the hobbit how it is his to give, to which Bilbo replies "it isn't exactly; but, well, I am willing to let it stand against all my claim, don't you know. I may be a burglar

---

188. Tolkien, *The Hobbit*, 266.

189. Tolkien, *The Hobbit*, 266.

190. Tolkien, *The Hobbit*, 269.

191. Tolkien, *The Hobbit*, 270.

192. Tolkien, *The Hobbit*, 271.

... but I am an honest one."[193] The Elvenking, knowing in advance Thorin's coming ire, welcomes the hobbit to stay with them, but Bilbo insists that he is bound to his friends, especially after all that they have endured together. On his way back to the camp, the hobbit encounters Gandalf, who gives him a "Well done!" as he claps him on the back.[194] For Alison Milbank, Bilbo "learns the value of gift-exchange through his (albeit dubious) bestowal of the Arkenstone on the lakemen. He was attracted by its glitter and sought to hide his possession of it from the dwarves, but he freely gives it to the lakemen as a means of cementing peace."[195] Still, if the Arkenstone is Bilbo's (problematic) pledge, in giving it to Bard and the Elvenking, we can almost say that he collapses the gift-economy and contract upon themselves.

Mauss notes that in Nordic gift economies there is a danger represented in the thing given. "The gift" obtains a double meaning of the word. Like Plato's *pharmakon,* which alternately means both sophist and true philosopher, *gift* comes to obtain both positive and negative meanings at once: "on the one hand, a gift, on the other, poison."[196] We therefore witness the theme of a fatal gift in Germanic folklore. Rhine gold is deadly to those who conquer it, and there are "a thousand stories and romances of this kind."[197]

The end of *The Hobbit* gives ample evidence of the gift's ambiguity. First, Bard and the Elvenking again enter into diplomatic conversation with Thorin, asking whether "there then [is] nothing for which you would yield any of your gold?" When the King under the Mountain says no, Bard opens a casket and holds the jewel aloft. Thorin goes mute. "That stone is my father's," he says at last, "and it is mine . . . Why should I purchase my own?"[198] Then, accusing them of being thieves, he asks how they came upon this heirloom. Bard insists that he is not by any means a thief: "Your own we will give back in return for our own," he says.[199] When Thorin presses them as to their mode of acquisition, Bilbo comes forward and squeaks "I gave it to them."[200] Thorin, unsurprisingly furious, curses Gandalf for his choice of the hobbit, and threatens to throw the halfling to the rocks. Gandalf intervenes to stay Thorin's hand, and prompts Bilbo to explain himself. Bilbo in turn appeals to Thorin's promise that he "might choose [his] own fourteenth

193. Tolkien, *The Hobbit,* 271.

194. Tolkien, *The Hobbit,* 271–72.

195. Milbank, *Chesterton and Tolkien as Theologians,* 131.

196. Mauss, *The Gift,* 81.

197. Mauss, *The Gift,* 81.

198. Tolkien, *The Hobbit,* 274.

199. Tolkien, *The Hobbit,* 274.

200. Tolkien, *The Hobbit,* 274.

share," even as he acknowledges that he perhaps "took it too literally."[201] In a last appeal he asks Thorin to "take it that I have disposed of my share as I wished, and let it go at that!"[202] Instead, Thorin agrees to portion out one fourteenth share of the treasure for the "traitor," but he demands the Arkenstone. At last, he exiles Bilbo, and declares that "no friendship of mine goes with him," only to find Bilbo pressing back about the gold.[203] Thorin promises that it will follow after, but Bard steps forward and says that until it does, they will keep the Arkenstone. Relentless, Thorin again exiles Bilbo, and his declaration is nearly enacted when Bard steps forward and cautions against such haste, telling the dwarf king that he has until tomorrow to "see if you have brought from your hoard the portion that is to be set against the stone. If that is done without deceit, then we will depart, and the elf-host will go back to the Forest. In the meanwhile farewell."[204] The gift of the Arkenstone *has* shifted the stakes, even if it has not moved the hardened mind of Thorin. Perhaps Bilbo's deed makes such an impression upon Bard that the latter became willing to give up his claims upon Thorin's treasure if only Bilbo gains his own. At the same time, the gift of the Arkenstone is "poisonous" insofar as it has made Bilbo a near-scapegoat. From *Violence and the Sacred* onward, Girard has argued that people who begin as mimetic rivals unite their efforts against someone chosen as a scapegoat. In his *Leviathan*, Hobbes argues that it is "*precisely at the moment when the conflict is at its most intense*" that conflicting parties "cease hostilities and recognize that they need to work out a social contract."[205] As Michael Kirwan notes, Girard is scornful of this idea; he "jests here about Hobbes' Englishness, and imagines the 'war of all against all' concluding with people sitting down and sorting out their differences over a nice cup of tea."[206] Although Bilbo himself goes beyond mere contract though in risking the controversial gift of the Arkenstone, we may jest here too, musing whether he also becomes awfully English.

For Girard, mimetic desire more often becomes contagious, and violence spreads beyond its purported, original aims, so that any attempt to contain it or regain an equilibrium fails. As Kirwan explains, "in place of this original object of contention we now have the direct conflict of the

201. Tolkien, *The Hobbit*, 275.
202. Tolkien, *The Hobbit*, 275.
203. Tolkien, *The Hobbit*, 275.
204. Tolkien, *The Hobbit*, 276.
205. Michael Kirwan, *Discovering Girard*, 45.
206. Kirwan, *Discovering Girard*, 45–46.

opponents . . . the object is no longer central."[207] But at this crucial moment, the war of all-against-all becomes a war of all against one. According to Girard, the scapegoat is almost always innocent but the warring factions find in him the incarnation of guilt, and in exiling him or concentrating all of their violence upon him, they restore peace.

If *The Hobbit* contains a markedly different constitution of crisis and its resolution, we may first wonder whether such a difference would be of any consequence, being as it is a mere work of fantasy, a children's story, the first published part of a twentieth-century myth. In his short work *Sacrifice*, Girard, argues that myth is something "neither entirely fictive nor entirely real" but a transfiguration of something the author may not have completely understood."[208] We are thereby freed to avoid the modern delusion that reads myth as "projected into the realm of the imagination [for] this is how moderns are rid of their own violence."[209] Whereas for Girard the warring parties lose sight of the object of contention, in *The Hobbit* both Thorin and Bard remain acutely cognizant of the specific contents of their conflict, and their decisions are always informed by this knowledge. Although the Elves and men hold out for a change in Thorin that will bring reconciliation, their hopes are thwarted because the "knowledge that the Arkenstone was in the hands of the beseigers burn[s] in [the dwarves] thoughts" and makes them unwilling to participate in any art of compromise.[210] The scapegoat mechanism does appear, but in morphed form. First, as noted, Thorin tries to turn Bilbo into a scapegoat. The gift of the Arkenstone is riddled with ambiguity, and if the hobbit is guilty it is, in a sense, similar to the guilt of Oedipus. As Girard argues in *Oedipus Unbound,* the man who slept with his mother and killed his father is exiled in a manner that brings peace to the plague-ridden Athens. In *The Hobbit* we have neither an absolutely guilty nor an absolutely innocent scapegoat candidate.

But in the end this guilt or innocence does not need to be teased out with care, for instead of uniting with Thorin over the exile of Bilbo, Bard prevents such an exile and fixes more firmly his original terms: he rejects the scapegoat mechanism as a means of quelling the conflict, and thus rejects the possibility that former enemies might become friends. But he goes further. We might say that in demanding that Thorin give Bilbo his contracted share of the hoard, Bard insists upon justice at the very moment when the dwarf most desires vengeance. As Dumouchel outlines in

---

207. Kirwan, *Discovering Girard,* 48.

208. René Girard, *Sacrifice,* 49.

209. René Girard, *Sacrifice,* 49.

210. Tolkien, *The Hobbit,* 278.

"Revenge or Justice? Obama Gets Osama," the Greeks used two words for justice. *Dike* signifies the justice of relations between households, while *themis* refers to the justice of a given household.[211] Dumouchel goes on to note, however, that the distinction between two aspects of justice is not unique to the Greeks. Although one may be sympathetic to Thorin's rejection of any terms secured by force, he resists participation in *dike* in that he refuses to justly abide by the gift-economy, wherein "giving, receiving, and reciprocating" obligates the receiver to "give back."[212] When Thorin tries to forcefully exile Bilbo, on the other hand, Bard insists upon the just exchange of goods which would have secured peace; as he says, if Thorin would have given Bilbo his fourteenth share, elves and men would have left the King under the Mountain alone.

Bard's insistence on justice embodies the economy of gift; Bilbo alone would have received his just due, and thus the exchange of his fourteenth share for the Arkenstone would not have been a means of making a profit, but a way by which the social bond could have been renewed, and tensions ceased. Though Bilbo's gift may have inspired Bard's new terms, then, it certainly does not allow the bargain for peace which he had envisioned. Still, in a turn of events, we see the crisis of rivals turn into an "all-against-one," or rather "three-against-two"; amazement and confusion fall upon all as the goblins and the elves arrive and turn the men, elves, and dwarves from enemies into an alliance unified against a common threat. Men, elves, and dwarves win, even as Bilbo finds that "[v]ictory . . . seems a very gloomy business."[213] At the war's end Bilbo meets with Thorin for the last time, for the latter wishes to "part in friendship . . . and [he] would take back [his] words and deeds at the Gate."[214] His attempt to banish Bilbo, though it failed in action, still maintained the resonance that words are capable of holding, and thus this negation of scapegoating marks a significant turn. Also, though, his last words express a wish that the dwarves would imitate hobbits, rather than vice versa, for "[i]f more of us valued food and cheer and song above hoarded gold, it would be a merrier world. But sad or merry, I must leave it now."[215]

Thorin's successor Dain tells Bilbo that though the latter is willing to lay aside his claim of the hoard, he wishes to reward him "most richly of

---

211. Paul Dumouchel, "Revenge or Justice?: Obama Gets Osama," 10.

212. Milbank, *Chesterton and Tolkien as Theologians*, 118.

213. Tolkien, *The Hobbit*, 286.

214. Tolkien, *The Hobbit*, 288.

215. Tolkien, *The Hobbit*, 288

all."[216] Bilbo, in turn, insists that the absence of treasure is a relief, for he cannot imagine how he would have gotten all of the treasure back home without murder and war along the way: "In the end he would take only two small chests, one filled with silver, and the other with gold, such as one strong pony could carry."[217]

In the last pages of *The Hobbit,* gifts abound, making moot the now-crumpled contract with which Bilbo began his expedition, cooling mimetic desire and strengthening the social bond with so much exchange. At their parting, Bilbo gives the Elven king a necklace that Dain had given to him, and in turn the king names Bilbo "elf-friend and blessed."[218] As Alison Milbank observes, "Bilbo ends the novel bonded to the dwarves by heirloom gifts of their making which, as we learn in *The Lord of the Rings,* exceed all the wealth of the Shire and thus resist any calculation of market value."[219] Bilbo's "gold and silver [is] largely spent in presents, both useful and extravagant—which to a certain extent accounts for the affection of his nephews and nieces."[220]

If Marxist critic Ishay Landa is wrong to claim that the paradoxical thematic core underlying Tolkien's fiction is "the crisis of capitalist property relations at the beginning of the twentieth century culminating in the First World War and the Bolshevik revolution," he is right to alert us to the economic realities which Tolkien weaves thickly throughout *The Hobbit.*[221] Renounce riches he may, but Bilbo is unwilling to abandon all private property. With the finesse of classical circularity, the novel ends as it began: with a satirical portrait of modern legal claims. For as he returns to Bag End Bilbo is startled to find people of all sorts going in and out of his home, not even wiping their feet on the mat:

He had arrived back in the middle of an auction! "There was a large notice in black and red hung on the gate, stating that on June the Twenty-second Messrs. Grubb, Grubb, and Burrowes would sell by auction the effects of the late Bilbo Baggins, Esquire, of Bag-End, Underhill, Hobbiton Sale to commence at ten o'clock sharp."[222] Most all of his belongings had been commodified and sold. In part because their desires for the property are so strong, "it was quite a long time before Mr. Baggins was in fact admitted to

216. Tolkien, *The Hobbit,* 291.

217. Tolkien, *The Hobbit,* 291–92.

218. Tolkien, *The Hobbit,* 293.

219. Milbank, *Chesterton and Tolkien as Theologians,* 131.

220. Tolkien, *The Hobbit,* 302.

221. Landa, "Slaves of the Ring," 127.

222. Tolkien, *The Hobbit,* 301.

be alive again. The people who had got especially good bargains at the Sale took a deal of convincing."[223] The Sackville-Bagginses, in particular, who had bought the house itself, "never admitted that the returned Baggins was genuine, and they were not on friendly terms with Bilbo ever after. They had really wanted to live in his nice hobbit-hole so very much."[224] For Girard, the subject of mimetic desire is more fully convinced of the object's value insofar as the Other is an obstacle, and if the rivalry remains, the subject will only be satisfied when the Other is destroyed and slaughtered.[225] The Sackville-Bagginses' desire to acquire Bag End is so vicious, and Bilbo's reappearance as a living hobbit is such an obstacle, that they invent a fiction—the returned Baggins is not genuine—in which they, in a sense, slaughter and destroy the real Bilbo Baggins. In part because this does not work, because the real Bilbo does in fact inhabit his hole in the ground, we might not be amiss in suspecting that, via rumors, they turn their thwarted desire into a veritable contagion. For here at the novel's finale, if he maintains bonds with the elves, dwarves, and others who operate along the lines of the "gift-exchange," and if he maintains the house within which he can host them, Bilbo loses one of those necessary virtues of the modern world: respectability. "He was no longer quite respectable," we read, "He was in fact held by all the hobbits of the neighborhood to be queer."[226] The narrator tells us "he is sorry to say that [Bilbo] does not mind."[227] For all of the infamous importance of eucatastrophe, of happy endings in Tolkien's fiction, then, we can share this sorrow. For if Bilbo has escaped the worst constraints and detrimental desires of modern economy and acquisitive mimesis, the Shire remains ridden with it. Bilbo spends most of his days safe behind that penultimate symbol of bourgeois order which we meet on *The Hobbit's* first page: the "perfectly round door like a porthole, painted green, with a shiny yellow brass knob in the exact middle."[228]

On the last page of *The Gift*, Marcel Mauss gives us another circular symbol better able to mediate from the exact middle. He notes that in *Chronicles of Arthur* we read of how king Arthur, helped by a Cornish carpenter, invented the miraculous Round Table. While formerly the knights fought "'out of sordid envy,' in stupid struggle, duels and murders stained with blood the finest banquets," now, seated round the table, and

223. Tolkien, *The Hobbit*, 301.

224. Tolkien, *The Hobbit*, 301.

225. Dumouchel, *The Ambivalence of Scarcity and Other Essays*, 26.

226. Tolkien, *The Hobbit*, 302.

227. Tolkien, *The Hobbit*, 302

228. Tolkien, *The Hobbit*, 1.

everywhere Arthur took his table, "his noble company remained happy and unconquerable."[229] *The Lord of the Rings,* the circle around which the Fellowship must remain is the Ring of Power. So long as the members remain around it, around its bearer, they remain happy and unconquerable, but they do not, and just as Camelot collapses the Fellowship breaks. In *The Lord of the Rings* this is due as much to the corrupted desires of the characters as it is to the Ring's origins. Sauron, in naming himself "Lord of Gifts" used the rings he gave away as means of control and domination.[230] Alison Milbank argues that in *The Lord of the Rings* in particular Tolkien narrates both the good and the bad gift, whereas Mauss, "in his anxiety to prove the ubiquity and inescapability of the gift's reciprocation . . . only touches upon" this double business of gifts."[231] In *The Culture of the Teutons,* Vilhelm Grönbech, another scholar with whom Tolkien was likely familiar, "emphasizes both the importance of knowing the one from whom one is receiving and the fateful nature of the gift," even as he fails to identify the nature of this difference.[232] If Tolkien works out this difference in *The Lord of the Rings,* we must for now remain with Bilbo in his quiet hole in the ground, reaching out our hands alongside Gandalf to receive the gift as Bilbo, "laughing, hand[s] him the tobacco-jar."[233]

229. Mauss, *The Gift,* 106.

230. Milbank, *Chesterton and Tolkien as Theologians,* 129.

231. Milbank, *Chesterton and Tolkien as Theologians,* 139.

232. Milbank, *Chesterton and Tolkien as Theologians,* 139.

233. Tolkien, *The Hobbit,* 303.

Hobbes, Hobbits,
and the Modern State of Mordor

Myths of Power and Desire in *Leviathan*
and Tolkien's *Legendarium*

*L*ibido dominandi, the lust for power that holds such a central place in St. Augustine's *City of God,* is a point of focus that unites Tolkien,[1] René Girard, and Hobbes. Often this lust manifests as an overreach that leads to violent conflict. In his "Hobbes: The Sovereignty Race," Paul Dumouchel positions Thomas Hobbes as "certainly the social contract thinker closest to Girard" in that the former "is one of the rare philosophers who does not underestimate the role of violence in human affairs."[2] Hobbes, Girard, and Tolkien are also united in their insistence that desire is the primary "engine" of human nature. Finally, Hobbes and Tolkien are both mythmakers, Tolkien in the obvious sense, but, as we shall see, Hobbes' "Enlightenment" political philosophy is permeated by fictions and myths of his own making. These figures' overlapping and yet sometimes contradictory interpretations and mythologizations prompt us to consider what is most true in their respective responses to power and desire, especially as modern states and their discontents continue to play out their lusts for power in a war on and by terror coupled by a war on and by individuals' desired rights that escalates to extremes.

1. Surely Hobbes read a bootleg version of Bilbo's tales while he awaited the author copy of his *Leviathan,* which was printed "for Andrew Crooke, at the Green Dragon . . . ."

2. Dumouchel, *The Ambivalence of Scarcity and Other Essays,* 227.

In *Leviathan,* we read that there exists "for a generall inclination of all mankind, a perpetuall and restlesse desire of Power after power, that ceaseth onely in Death."[3] For Hobbes, man cannot live "whose Desires are at an end . . . Felicity is a continuall progresse of the desire from one object to another; the attaining of the former, being still but the way to the later."[4] Hobbes and Girard come close on yet another dimension of desire, even as we see important shades of difference. As I related elsewhere, for Girard, we borrow our desires from those whose very being we wish to possess. In Dumouchel's rendering, when we encounter an obstacle to our desires, only then do we begin to believe we are about to grasp something substantial. In *Leviathan,* Hobbes asserts the equality of all men, an equality that results in an equal hope that each individual's goals may be attained: "And therefore if any two men desire the same thing, which nevertheless they cannot both enjoy, they become enemies; and in the way to their End (which is principally their owne conservation, and sometimes their delectation only) endeavor to destroy, or to subdue one another."[5]

As Dumouchel clarifies, "Unlike Girard, Hobbes does not have an operator that necessarily makes desires converge on a single object."[6] Dumouchel sees this distinction as articulated in Hobbes's indication that such a conflict need not happen but might. The word *if* is key: "And from hence it comes to passe, that where an Invader hath no more to feare, than another mans single power; if one plant, sow, build, or possesse a convenient Seat, others may probably be expected to come prepared with forces united, to dispossesse, and deprive him."[7] Still, the desire for a single object which cannot be "enjoyed" by both leads, for Hobbes as for Girard, to an *escalated rivalry* in which each tries to subdue or destroy the other. If for Girard the escalation comes from mimetic contagion, the largely irrational desire for the being of the other, for Hobbes the escalation, which becomes what he calls the "war of all against all," comes from an entirely rational line of thought. Because it is possible that another individual may desire the same object that I either desire or possess, and because in spite of variations of strength we are each equally capable of destroying the other, we choose to engage in war. Probable invasion by the other rationally motivates invasion of the other.

3. Thomas Hobbes, *Leviathan,* 75.

4. Hobbes, *Leviathan,* 75.

5. Hobbes, *Leviathan,* 95.

6. Dumouchel, *The Ambivalence of Scarcity and Other Essays,* 235.

7. Hobbes, *Leviathan,* 95.

Interestingly for our purposes, Dumouchel describes this Hobbesian state of nature as a "stable chaos, a well-structured disorder, with mechanisms that maintain its stability."[8] Such "discord" never evolves into anything other than the war of all against all. In Tolkien's creation myth *Ainulindalë*, Melkor,[9] the Ainur[10] whose name means "mighty rising" or "uprising of power,"[11] manifests such a "stable chaos" in a mythical mode when weaving his individualized, deviated thoughts into music. In Melkor, a kind of individualism is born at the same time as the disposition that leads to a war of all against all. Although the creator God Ilúvatar wills that the Ainur "make in harmony together a Great Music,"[12] Melkor rejects this will, so that "straightway discord arose about him, and many that sang nigh him grew despondent, and their thought was disturbed and their music faltered; but some began to attune their music to his rather than to the thought which they had at first."[13] Therefore Melkor's discord advances to the point that, to the listening Ilúvatar, it is as though "about his throne there was a raging storm, as of dark waters that made war one upon another in an endless wrath that would not be assuaged."[14] Melkor's Music is an apt mythical metaphor for Hobbesian "well-structured disorder" in that even discordant music contains a kind of mathematical structure.

And yet, Tolkien departs from Hobbes and Girard: though he grants dramatic instantiations of the *libdo dominandi* and mimetic desire, he does not posit these as universally constitutive, does not deem them as psychologically key, except in those who depart from the will of Ilúvatar.[15] Such a rebellion is not the only rational line of pursuit, even if we reduce what is "rational" to the limited Hobbesian "good" of mere self-interest and survival;

8. Dumouchel, *The Ambivalence of Scarcity and Other Essays*, 238.

9. After Melkor thieves the Silmarils, Fëanor names him Morgoth.

10. An angel figure in Tolkien's mythology.

11. Tolkien, *Morgoth's Ring*, 350.

12. Tolkien, *The Silmarillion*, 3.

13. Tolkien, *The Silmarillion*, 4–5.

14. Tolkien, *The Silmarillion*, 5.

15. I should also note, however, that among the Ainur who have *not* rebelled, desire is not always driven by contaminated mimesis, a fact proven by this most central moment: Then there was unrest among the Ainur; but Ilúvatar called to them, and said: 'I know the desire of your minds that what ye have seen should verily be, not only in your thought, but even as ye yourselves are, and yet other. Therefore I say: *Eä!* Let these things Be! And I will send forth into the Void the Flame Imperishable, and it shall be at the heart of the World, and the World shall Be; and those of you that will may go down into it. And suddenly the Ainur saw afar off a light, as it were a cloud with a living heart of flame; and they knew that this was no vision only, but that Ilúvatar had made a new thing: Eä, the World (*Silmarillion* 9).

remaining in harmony with the Great Music of God would achieve this end. Adherence to the Creator's will is apprehended as a definitive danger for Melkor, however, in that he seems to assess himself as at least prospectively equal to Ilúvatar, and thus somehow, in a Hobbesian sense, is threatened by any manifestation of superiority and authority on the part of God. Hobbes gives us further insight into the psychology of Melkor in his assessment of the high value individuals attribute to honor: "For every man looketh that his companion should value him at the same rate he sets upon himself, and upon all signs of contempt or undervaluing naturally endeavors, as far as he dares . . . to extort a greater value from his contemners, from damage: and, from others, by the example."[16] Hobbes posits an "equivalence between vain and rational people"[17]; joy itself comes from contemplating one's own power in an act of conquest, remembering that life is a race which has "no other goal, no other garland, but being foremost."[18] In *Ainulindalë*, Melkor's music, like a rationalized grasping after primacy, "had achieved a unity of its own"; it is "loud, and vain, and endlessly repeated" in a "clamorous unison" that seems like the score of a Hobbesian state of nature. However, Ilúvatar disrupts Melkor's self-interested song of supremacy, raising up "both his hands, and in one chord, deeper than the Abyss, higher than the Firmament, piercing as the light of the eye of Ilúvatar, the Music ceased."[19]

If Ilúvatar thwarts Melkor's strides toward being foremost, we can easily see how the latter might nevertheless retain his sense of supremacy in a manner analogous to an ambitious bureaucrat who, though recognizing his inferiority beside, say, the president of an institution, nevertheless cultivates a set of imitators who provide a constant reminder that his superiority is an elevated and honored attribute. He becomes an example, and thus we can assume that according to his own rationale his honor increases both by his initial damage of Ilúvatar's theme, and by his accrual of followers. Among those who rebel, and whose ways of being are habituated to rebellion against Ilúvatar, we witness the primacy of lust for power and mimetic desire. Again, near the very beginning of *The Silmarillion*,[20] we read that the

---

16. Hobbes, *Leviathan*, 95–96.

17. Paul Dumouchel, *The Ambivalence of Scarcity and Other Essays*, 239.

18. Eric Voegelin, et al., *Collected Works of Eric Voegelin*, 63.

19. Tolkien, *The Silmarillion*, 5.

20. As *The Silmarillion* unfolds, we find that Melkor is often driven by such desire:

> But when the Ainur had beheld this habitation in a vision and had seen the Children of Ilúvatar arise therein, then many of the most mighty among them bent all their thought and their desire towards that place. And of these Melkor was the chief, even as he was in the beginning the

rebel Ainur is driven by what Girard might call metaphysical desire—desire for the being of the other—at its most metaphysical:

> To Melkor among the Ainur had been given the greatest gifts of power and knowledge, and he had a share in all the gifts of his brethren. He had gone often alone into the void places seeking the Imperishable Flame; for desire grew hot within him to bring into Being things of his own, and it seemed to him that Ilúvatar took no thought for the Void, and he was impatient of its emptiness.[21]

Melkor does not pine for an object that Ilúvatar possesses, as in conventional mimetic desire. What he most desires is the capacity to bring things into Being.

In Tolkien's *The Lord of the Rings*, desire remains central to the Enemy's nature; it is integral to his manner of ruling. When in "The Shadow of the Past" Gandalf first tries to explain the unfolding crisis of Middle-earth to Frodo, he says "in a deep voice: 'This is the Master-ring, the One Ring to rule them all. This is the One Ring that he lost many ages ago, to the great weakening of his power. He greatly *desires* it—but he must *not* get it.'"[22] In "Flight to the Ford," after Frodo puts on the Ring for the first time in an attempt to hide from the Black Riders' terroristic tactics, we read that, "He bitterly regretted his foolishness, and reproached himself for weakness of will; for he now perceived that in putting on the Ring he obeyed not his own desire but the commanding wish of his enemies."[23]

---

greatest of the Ainur who took part in the Music. And he feigned, even to himself at first, that he desired to go thither and order all things for the good of the Children of Ilúvatar, controlling the turmoils of the heat and the cold that had come to pass through him. But he desired rather to subdue to his will both Elves and Men, envying the gifts with which Ilúvatar promised to endow them; and he wished himself to have subject and servants, and to be called Lord, and to be a master over other wills.

Also, in the *Valaquenta*, we read of Melkor:

From splendour he fell through arrogance to contempt for all things save himself, a spirit wasteful and pitiless. Understanding he turned to subtlety in perverting to his own will all that he would use, until he became a liar without shame. He began with the desire of Light, but when he could not possess it for himself alone, he descended through fire and wrath into a great burning, down into Darkness. And darkness he used most in his evil works upon Arda, and filled it with fear for all living things.

21. Tolkien, *The Silmarillion*, 4.
22. Tolkien, *The Lord of the Rings*, 50–51.
23. Tolkien, *The Lord of the Rings*, 199.

Sauron, The Dark Lord, is fundamentally driven by desire, which dramatically limits his capacity to comprehend the motives and movements of others. The Fellowship—excepting Boromir—is only able to avoid despair in the face of his power insofar as they do *not* imitate his desire. Toward the end of the Council of Elrond, Gandalf notes that "the only measure that he knows is desire, desire for power; and so he judges all hearts. Into his heart the thought will not enter that any will refuse it, that having the Ring we may seek to destroy it."[24] Here we have Tolkien's counter to the totalization of desire posited by Girard and Hobbes: it is possible for persons to govern their own lusting desire. It is possible for the circle of violent reciprocity contained within the ring to melt in the heat from whence it came.

To complete the Hobbesian movement from subjects orchestrated by desire to the political forms that most perfectly corresponds to such persons, we must move beyond Tolkien's poetic psychology of desire and investigate the political structures that correspond to Sauron's lust for dominion. The question guiding the second part of our investigation will then be whether, and in what senses, Sauron's rule corresponds to Leviathan, who masters others largely by striking fear into their hearts. Hobbes writes of Leviathan as:

> (to speak more reverently) of that Mortall God . . . For by this Authoritie, given him by every particular man in the Common-Wealth, he hath the use of so much Power and Strength conferred on him, that by terror thereof, he is inabled to forme the wils of them all . . . And he that carryeth this Person, is called Soveraigne, and said to have the Soveraigne Power; and every one besides, his Subject."[25]

This passage provokes us to ponder the sort of sovereignty that Sauron maintains, especially in that nothing immediately suggests that it was established via contract.

Sauron was originally a Maia, sent into Middle-earth to help the Ainur order the world. He did not always carry connotations that beg comparison with the Hobbesian Leviathan. As Hayden Head notes, in Tolkien's *Akallabêth*, Sauron "provokes the Númenóreans' envy of the immortal Elves and the Valar to the point that they sail against Aman, the Undying Lands. The Valar had attempted to inhibit the Númenóreans' envy by imposing a ban against sailing toward the West."[26] The proud Númenóreans are particularly piqued by his use of the title "Lord of the Earth," an attribution that car-

---

24. Tolkien, *The Lord of the Rings*, 269.

25. Hobbes, *Leviathan*, 132.

26. Hayden Head, "Imitative Desire in Tolkien's Mythology: A Girardian Perspective," *Mythlore* 26, no. 1/2 (2007), 142.

ries notes of Hobbes' depiction of Leviathan as "Lord of the proud." In this instance, as I have elsewhere observed, Sauron operates not by assuming direct rule, but by convincing king Ar-Pharazôn to war against the Valar. Here we have a Sauron whose primary weapon is guileful persuasion. He assures Ar-Pharazôn that though the gift of eternal life is not destined for all, surely it is reserved for "Ar-Pharazôn, mightiest of the sons of Earth, to whom Manwë alone can be compared, if even he. But great kings do not brook denials, and take what is their due."[27] The Valar punish both Ar-Pharazôn and Sauron, but, consequences of their haughty raid on the angelic realm aside, it is worth noting that Sauron *is* persuasive: he elicits obedience.

His masterful guile reaches its climax in the gift of the rings. On the threshold of the Third Age, he assumes the name of Annatar, the Lord of Gifts, and ingratiates himself among Men, whom "he found the easiest to sway of all the people of the Earth."[28] At last, however, Sauron achieves his higher aim of captivating the Elves, appealing to their desire "ever to increase the skill and subtlety of their works."[29] While the Elves use the skills Sauron teaches them to make many rings, the "Lord of Gifts" forges the powerful "One Ring to rule all the others, and their power was bound up with it"; upon gathering all the Rings of Power, "he dealt them out to the other people of Middle-earth, hoping thus to bring under his sway all those that desired secret power."[30]

By the time of the Third Age, Sauron, "Having failed to enhance his 'being' by deceiving the Númenóreans, attempts to do so by establishing a tyranny over Middle-earth—that is, by crushing every rival, real or imagined."[31] Tolkien himself traces the transmogrification of Sauron as follows: "He had gone the way of all tyrants: beginning well, at least on the level that while desiring to order all things according to his own wisdom he still at first considered the (economic) well-being of other inhabitants of the Earth. But he went further than human tyrants in pride and the lust for domination," an excess that the author attributes to Sauron's immortal spirit.[32] Tolkien goes on to note that Sauron "desired to be a God-King, and was held to be this by his servants, by a triple treachery."[33] First, Sauron followed Morgoth because he adored the latter's strength, and thus fell with

27. Tolkien, *The Silmarillion*, 282.

28. Tolkien, *The Silmarillion*, 343.

29. Tolkien, *The Silmarillion*, 344.

30. Tolkien, *The Silmarillion*, 344–45.

31. Head, "Imitative Desire in Tolkien's Mythology," 143.

32. Tolkien et al., *Letters*, 243.

33. Tolkien et al., *Letters*, 243.

the object of his imitation into the heart of evil, rising to the rank of Morgoth's lieutenant in Middle-earth. Second, after the Valar defeated Morgoth, Sauron betrayed his alliance, motivated merely by fear, and did not present himself before the judgment of the Valar, as would be expected, to ask for pardon. Finally, "When he found how greatly his knowledge was admired by all other rational creatures and how easy it was to influence them, his pride became boundless."[34]

In his being driven primarily by desire, and in his demand that all rivals be crushed by his sole dominion, Sauron emerges as a Hobbesian individual. He emerges as a Hobbesian sovereign insofar as many pledge him obedience, and insofar as he strives after an artificial but orderly political realm built upon the state of nature, in which it is "rational to submit to the judgment of the sovereign, whatever the content of that judgment."[35] Whereas in Hobbes the Soveraigne is the image *of the people,* in *The Lord of the Rings* Sauron's character demands that individuals be made in his image. However, while Hobbes intimately identifies each subject with the Soveraigne, he limits the extent of their identification to one willed thing: "What is *desired (willed)* by 'each subject' is the existence of absolute sovereignty, or, more precisely, it is the peace for which the absolute sovereignty is the necessary instrument."[36] Note the claim that Leviathan embodies what is *desired* by the subjects. The question of *why* they desire such a sovereign is crucial. For Hobbes, submission to a Leviathan is largely a matter of self-preservation:

> The final Cause, End, or Designe of men (who naturally love Liberty, and Dominion over others,) in the introduction of that restraint upon themselves . . . is the foresight of their own preservation, and of a more contented life thereby; that is to say, of getting themselves out from that miserable condition of Warre, which is necessarily consequent . . . to the naturall Passions of men, when there is no visible Power to keep them in awe."[37]

What is the relation of Orcs to that "miserable condition of Warre"? Do we have any evidence that they submit themselves to Sauron in order to secure self-preservation? In his "Political Institutions in Tolkien's Middleearth," Dominic J. Nardi, Jr., argues that Orcs serving Sauron receive not

34. Tolkien et al., *Letters,* 243
35. David Dyzenhaus, "Introduction," 6.
36. Hobbes, *Leviathan,* 143.
37. Hobbes, *Leviathan,* 128.

only "collective defense" but also "war booty."[38] While collective defense would seem to be a guarantee of life, the reference to "war booty" reminds us of an important difference between Hobbes' imagined subjects and sovereign, and Sauron and his underlings. In *Leviathan*, Hobbes is principally concerned with constructing a social order that will definitively prevent *civil* discord. In *The Lord of the Rings*, any assurance of protection that Sauron grants his Orcs is principally driven by the preservation of that "structured disorder," an aim he inherits from Morgoth, whose music "had achieved a unity of its own," it was "loud, and vain, and endlessly repeated" in a "clamorous unison."

Part of what gives *Leviathan* its force is Hobbes's capacity to evoke intense psychological experiences that support his argument concerning human nature. *The Lord of the Rings* has been faulted for granting us very limited direct contact with the Orcs, very little that gives us that intensity of psychological content. Hal Colebatch has noted that a "book about Orcs from the inside would have been a different kind of book, perhaps something like *The Lord of the Flies* . . . "[39] Reference to *Lord of the Flies* is interesting here in that Michael Kirwan establishes a connection between Rene Girard and Hobbes via William Golding's novel in which a group of island-stranded schoolboys "revert to a state of murderous nature until order is restored at the end by the arrival of a naval ship [Hobbesian sovereign.]"[40] Colebatch, too, then, intuits the interconnection between Hobbes and Orcs. Although Tolkien doesn't give us a story told from such a vantage, we do gain at least a glimpse into the ways of Orcs, a glimpse that is all the more accurate in that they are acting as they would without the strictures that might come from countenancing others.

In "The Choices of Master Samwise," just after the monstrous spider Shelob, Sauron's "pet," has paralyzed Frodo, we gain a limited but elucidating glimpse into the subjects of Mordor. Gorbag and Shagrat, two Orcs, greet one another cynically, in an exchange that bleeds with a barely cloaked "warre of all against all."[41] At first glance, it would seem that Sauron nurtures an internal hostility among his subjects. After the Orcs claim Frodo's spider-spun body, Sam notices that "the captains of the two parties seemed

38. Nardi, "Political Institutions in J.R.R. Tolkien's Middle-earth," 116.

39. Colebatch, *Return of the Heroes*, 143. Additionally, Robert Tally Jr. notes that "the story of such creatures—rational though simple, seduced and tortured by dark forces, yet with the possibility of redemption—might make for a cracking good tale in its own right" ("Let Us Now Praise Famous Orcs," 26).

40. Kirwan, Michael. *Discovering Girard*, 45.

41. Tolkien, *The Lord of the Rings*, 735.

to be bringing up the rear, debating as they went."[42] Once in earshot, their debate emerges as childish, a contention over whose rabble is "making such a racket," but soon we find that they are concerned about noise levels because they "don't want Shelob on us."[43] Next we find that Lugbúrz, the name the Orcs give to Mordor's seat of power, Barad-dûr, wants Frodo's body, but both Shagrat and Gorbag are visibly bothered that the reasons such a body may be desirable are withheld from them. Gorbag complains that "[t]hey don't tell us all they know, do they? Not by half. But they can make mistakes, even the Top Ones can."[44] Shagrat interrupts him with a shush, worried that they might be overheard, as "they've got eyes and ears everywhere." One could argue that Hobbes would favor this sort of surveillance in that individuals, bent on seeking self-interest, would nonetheless be more likely to be chastened into doing their respective duties if they knew they were being watched—watched, importantly, by those with power. On the other hand, surveillance, or the attempt at omniscience, may signal an impotency: when one cannot rule by the fear instilled by force, one tries to rule by the fear felt when a Great Eye is ever watching.

In "Theoscopy: Transparency, Omnipotence, and Modernity," Stefanos Geroulanos writes of a condition called "theoscopy," which he describes as follows:

> To be forever seen without seeing back is to succumb to a mercy and grace carved in religious force, to walk in fear and faith of a tremendous power one cannot face. It is to live a paranoid existence of nakedness before a God who is all-seeing, hence omniscient and omnipotent, and who accordingly metes out a social experience and a knowledge of oneself and one's history that is based on this awareness of being seen.[45]

In Middle-earth, surveillance begins not with Sauron, but with Fëanor, who makes the *palantíri* both a means of communication and a way by which to see things across a vast spanse of space. Of the *palantíri* in Saruman's tower, Gandalf notes that, "alone it could do nothing but see small images of things far off and days remote. Very useful, no doubt, that was to Saruman; yet it seems that he was not content. Further and further abroad he gazed, until he cast his gaze upon Barad-dûr. Then he was caught!"[46] Here we see the way by which voluntary surveillance blends with the theoscopy

42. Tolkien, *The Lord of the Rings*, 736.
43. Tolkien, *The Lord of the Rings*, 736.
44. Tolkien, *The Lord of the Rings*, 737.
45. De Vries and Sullivan, *Political Theologies*, 633.
46. Tolkien, *The Lord of the Rings*, 598.

of which Geroulanos writes. However, in place of an all-seeing, all-knowing God, we encounter Sauron, whose Orcs have the impression that he is all seeing, even as he us painfully unable to hone his sight on more than one locale at once. The nature of his surveillance find fullest expression in the Eye of Sauron.

In Foucault's work *Discipline and Punish*, which examines, among other things, power and surveillance, he writes, "there is no . . . knowledge that does not presuppose and constitute . . . power relations."[47] In this rendering, as Cherylynn Silva notes, "while Sauron does have actual power, the characters' knowledge of that power enhances and extends it so much so that even when he is disembodied, their fear of Sauron remains."[48] This is illustrated in a somewhat banal way by the Orcs' sense that they are being overheard, but it connects more directly with an instrument of surveillance when Saruman allies himself with Sauron because, in using the *palantiri*, he comes to believe the information Saruman feeds him, to the point that it seems "over the power of Mordor there can be no victory." Silva shows us that Saruman articulates Foucault's sense that "power produces truth through knowledge."[49] However, the supposedly secret surveillance "knowledge" which the *palantir* provides Saruman is only in part true. The illusion of increased omniscience, though, makes it difficult to treat this "knowledge" as fiction, a phenomenon that both Saruman and Denethor demonstrate in the turns that they take after they use the *palantiri*. In *Unfinished Tales*, Tolkien writes:

> The *palantíri* were no doubt never matters of common use or common knowledge, even in Númenor. In Middle-earth they were kept in guarded rooms, high in strong towers, only kings and rulers, and their appointed wardens, had access to them, and they were never consulted, nor exhibited, publicly. But until the passing of the Kings they were not sinister secrets. Their use involved no peril, and no king or other person authorized to survey them would have hesitated to reveal the source of his knowledge of the deeds or opinions of distant rulers, if obtained through the Stones.[50][51]

47. Foucault, *Discipline and Punish*, 27.
48. Silva, "One Ring to Rule Them All," 15.
49. Silva, "One Ring to Rule Them All," 15.
50. Tolkien, *Unfinished Tales*, 119.
51. Tolkien explicates the nature of the Stones in *Unfinished Tales*:

> A viewer could by his will cause the vision of the Stone to concentrate on some point, on or near its direct line. 19 The uncontrolled "visions" were

When Saruman obtains the keys of Orthanc, this guileless surveillance disappears and the Stones show what comes of their ill use: having "gained a special knowledge of the Stone," he strove to possess it, and Beren the Steward was likely sure that the Stone would find no safer supervisor than the "head of the Council opposed to Sauron."[52]

It is ultimately Sauron, not Saruman, who fully shifts the Stones into purveyors of power. On first glance their mode of operation seems to protect against a Panoptic surveillance. Tolkien notes that "The *palantíri* could not themselves survey men's minds, at unawares or unwilling; for the transference of thought depended on the wills of the user on either side, and thought (received as speech) was only transmittable by one Stone to another in accord."[53] Panopticism, on the other hand, takes the form not of the *palantíri*, but of the Ring of Power. If Frodo wears the Ring he is, being invisible, able to evade observation. However, in so doing, he becomes subject to Sauron's all-seeing eye. As his use of the Ring grows, he more keenly feels the weight of the Sauron's vision, interiorizing it "to the point that he

---

small, especially in the minor Stones, though they were much larger to the eye of a beholder who placed himself at some distance from the surface of the palantír (about three feet at best). But controlled by the will of a skilled and strong surveyor, remoter things could be enlarged, brought as it were nearer and clearer, while their background was almost suppressed. Thus a man at a considerable distance might be seen as a tiny figure, half an inch high, difficult to pick oat against a landscape or a concourse of other men; but concentration could enlarge and clarify the vision till he was seen in clear if reduced detail like a picture apparently a foot or more in height, and recognized if he was known to the surveyor. Great concentration might even enlarge some detail that interested the surveyor, so that it could be seen (for instance) if he had a ring on his hand.

But this "concentration" was very tiring and might become exhausting. Consequently it was only undertaken when information was urgently desired, and chance (aided by other information maybe) enabled the surveyor to pick out items (significant for him and his immediate concern) from the welter of the Stone's visions. For example, Denethor sitting before the Anor-stone anxious about Rohan, and deciding whether or not at once to order the kindling of the beacons and the sending out of the "arrow," might place himself in a direct line looking north-west by west through Rohan, passing close to Edoras and on towards the Fords of Isen. At that time there might be visible movements of men in that line. If so, he could concentrate on (say) a group, see them as Riders, and finally discover some figure known to him: Gandalf, for instance, riding with the reinforcements to Helm's Deep, and suddenly breaking away and racing northwards.

52. Tolkien, *Unfinished Tales of Númenor and Middle Earth*, 422.
53. Tolkien, *Unfinished Tales of Númenor and Middle Earth*, 429.

is his own overseer."[54] Those who wear the Ring with enough frequency become constantly fearful, sure that they will be seen. Thus he is in constant fear of being watched, whether he is physically visible or not, and the Ring fulfills the Panoptic dynamic: "it is the fact of being constantly seen, of being able always to be seen that maintains the disciplined individual in his subjection."[55] As Silva argues, "When wearing the Ring, Frodo's situation parallels that of the prisoners under the surveillance of the Panopticon: the prisoners are kept under endless surveillance, and yet they are invisible to each other."[56] While Frodo wears the Ring, he is seen by Sauron's Eye even as he cannot, with any clarity, see the world around him.

Still, Sauron lacks the "perfect disciplinary gaze" which would "make it possible for a single gaze to see everything constantly."[57] Sauron himself depends on both the Ringwraiths and the *palantíri*. Moreover, he depends on the weak wills of individuals who must freely employ the *palantíri*. Silva argues that his "reliance on the Ringwraiths also demonstrates his imperfect gaze. They demonstrate his affinity with the Hobbesian sovereign, who relies more on force than surveillance."[58] Sauron requires the Ringwraiths if he is to seize Frodo and the Ring, and yet they are, for all of their capacity to inspire awe—to terrorize—surprisingly feeble. Further, in *The Return of the King*, we see that, as Sam and Frodo cross Mordor, Sauron's inability to assume the Panopticon's power to see everywhere simultaneously is fatal. Focused on the final battle, Sauron fails to see the Ringbearer until it is too late. Too late, "the Dark Lord was suddenly aware of him, and his Eye piercing all shadows looked across the plain to the door that he had made; and the magnitude of his own folly was revealed to him in a blinding flash, and all the devices of his enemies were at last laid bare."[59] Perhaps under the sovereignty of Sauron the Foucaultian economy that knowledge always constitutes power relations is true. However, Frodo completes his quest to Mount Doom in part because Sauron's incapacity for total omniscience equals an incapacity for total omnipotence. This phenomenon is revealed most strikingly when:

> From all his policies and webs of fear and treachery, from all his stratagems and wars his mind shook free; and throughout his realm a tremor ran, his slaves quailed, and his armies halted,

54. Foucault, *Power/Knowledge*, 155.

55. Foucault, *Power/Knowledge*, 187.

56. Silva, "One Ring to Rule Them All," 16.

57. Foucault, *Power/Knowledge*, 173.

58. Silva, "One Ring to Rule Them All," 17.

59. Tolkien, *The Lord of the Rings*, 946.

and his captains suddenly steerless, bereft of will, wavered and despaired. For they were forgotten. The whole mind and purpose of the Power that wielded them was now bent with overwhelming force upon the Mountain.[60]

If Geroulanos is right that panopticism embodies a form of societal policing wherein those in power seek to inhabit a mode reserved for God alone, Sam and Frodo reveal to Sauron that no matter his policies and reincarnations, no matter his powers and machinations, the Dark Lord will lack not only the omniscience and omnipotence of Ilúvatar, but also the grace and mercy of that Creator God who has carved these things into even the seeming doom of Frodo's quest to interrupt the Eye before it can even approximate the near-total surveillance of the Panopticon.

Returning, then, to another episode upon that Mountain, to Shagrat's claim that "they've got eyes and ears everywhere," although we can somewhat securely suppose that surveillance is consonant with Hobbesian Sovereignty, we can also read an implicit pronouncement of Sauron's disqualification as Hobbesian Sovereign; his strategic manipulation of and proliferation of surveillance makes him more akin to a Benthamite prison warden who has not yet mastered the Panoptic system. It would seem that the Orcs inhabit a mode of life that is nearer a Hobbesian "state of nature" than a social order transformed by Leviathan, and the individuals that inhabit a Benthamite Panopticon are Hobbesian indeed. For the Orcs, more than for any others in Middle-earth, there is "no knowledge of the face of the earth, no account of time, no arts, no letters; no society; and which is worst of all, continuall feare, and danger of violent death; and the life of man, solitary, poore, nasty, brutish, and short."[61] If Sauron is obeyed at all, it is mostly because his subjects know fear for their own lives.

The Orcs go on to dream of better days, when the war's over, and to Shagrat's insistence that "they say" the war is going well, Gorbag first allows only a skeptical "[t]hey would . . ." but then goes on to say that if Mordor does win the war, "there should be a lot more room," and that, if the pair get the chance, "you and me'll slip off and set up somewhere on our own with a few trusty lads, somewhere where there's good loot nice and handy, and no big bosses."[62] Finally, he again reiterates his prior suspicion that "even the Biggest [Bosses] can make mistakes," and that "[a]lways the poor Uruks [a type of Orcs] to put slips right, and small thanks."[63] What we have, then,

60. Tolkien, The Lord of the Rings, 946.
61. Hobbes, Leviathan, 97.
62. Tolkien, The Lord of the Rings, 738.
63. Tolkien, The Lord of the Rings, 738.

is two Orcs who want to get themselves *out* of the condition of war that the sovereignty of Sauron facilitates, both externally and internally. We can read their desire to relocate with "trusty lads" as evidence of the natural love of dominion over others which Hobbes posits, but the main current that carries throughout their conversation is a deep anti-authoritarianism; their experience under the dominion of a despot seems to spur a penchant for anarchy ("somewhere where there's . . . no big bosses") even as it seems to have left in them an internalized desire to be rulers rather than ruled. Hobbes speaks of a "terror thereof" whereby Leviathan "is inabled to forme the wils of them all," but here, at least upon first glance, the wills of the underlings appear to be in disagreement with their Master.

The Orcs' overheard conversation merely *confirms* the core Hobbesian claims that we have thus far considered: a) men are driven by a restless desire to acquire one thing after another, and b) men are naturally in a state of war. Although their fantasies of anarchic relocation are real, the psychological dissonance between the Orcs and their Big Bosses (and the Biggest Boss, Sauron) is not inconsequential from a Hobbesian vantage point, even if Sauron, as Sovereign, is still obeyed, if begrudgingly. In Chapter 29 of *Leviathan,* Hobbes insists that his Sovereign can only achieve his ends if the subjects rationally understand the need for such an overlord. Likewise, Dumouchel writes, "If the people are not convinced of the well-foundedness of the Sovereign's essential rights, then the Sovereign has no sword."[64] The anarchic aspirations of Shagrat and Gorbag, then, would suggest that the Sovereign "has no sword." Before we arrive at such a conclusion, however, we need to gain a better grasp both of the sort of creature Hobbes was after, and of Tolkien's own ideas concerning the genesis and nature of Orcs.

In his *Leviathan in the State Theory of Thomas Hobbes,* Carl Schmitt suggests that Hobbes's state as *homo artificialis* comprises both body and soul and is in the end a machine.[65] Descartes established the necessary metaphysical reconfiguration of the modern state when he conceived the human body as a machine. From here Hobbes consummated this new anthropology of man in that he posited his *huge man,* the state, as a machine, and therefore the "mechanization of the concept of the state thus completed the mechanization of the anthropological image of man."[66] For Hobbes, machines are products of high human creativity, and thus contain greater

---

64. Dumouchel, *The Ambivalence of Scarcity and Other Essays,* 232.
65. Schmitt, *Leviathan in the State Theory of Thomas Hobbes,* 234.
66. Schmitt, *Leviathan in the State Theory of Thomas Hobbes,* 37.

mythical than mechanical meanings. In *Leviathan* we have man, "a *mecha-nism with a soul*," turned into a huge man—the state.[67]

Hobbes's mythic conception of the modern state can illuminate the political meaning of Mordor. His mechanical vision of the person finds corollaries in Tolkien's note on the nature of Orcs, who, as *made/corrupted* not *created ex nihilo*, are "more like puppets filled (only at a distance) with their maker's mind and will, or ant-like operating under direction of a queen-centre."[68]

We find evidence of this in the chapter "Mount Doom," where we read that, "From all his policies and webs of fear and treachery, from all his strata-gems and wars his mind shook free; and throughout his realm a tremor ran, his slaves quailed, and his armies halted, and his captains suddenly steerless, bereft of will, wavered and despaired. For they were forgotten." Christopher Tolkien contends that his father had this passage in mind when he mused that the subjects of Sauron "had little or no *will* when not actually 'attended to' by the mind of Sauron."[69] Remember that Leviathan "is inabled to forme the wils of them all."

Tolkien spends a good many jottings trying to probe the nature of Orcs, the heart of his ruminations being that only Ilúvatar can create creatures with independent reasoning powers and wills. Like Hobbes, he sees the need for consistency between Orcs' character traits and their social and political proclivities. Tolkien goes beyond psychology and begins with metaphysics: "Any creature that took him [Sauron] for Lord[70] . . . became soon corrupted in all parts of its being."[71] From metaphysics Tolkien moves to language. Puzzling over Orcs' capacity for speech, he insists that talking does not nec-essarily signify possession of a rational soul. In a fascinating conclusion, Tolkien notes that Orc-talk is "really reeling off 'records' set in them by Melkor. Even their rebellious critical words—he knew about them."[72] In this sense our earlier concern that Shagrat and Gorbag's anarchistic dreams sug-gest a threat to Sauron's sovereignty may be somewhat assuaged. Hobbes too hones in on the interconnection between language and power. In Chapter 18 of *Leviathan* he contends that the subjects' opinions must be controlled because their actions proceed from opinions: government of the subjects'

---

67. Schmitt, *Leviathan in the State Theory of Thomas Hobbes*, 93–94.

68. Tolkien, *Morgoth's Ring*, 412.

69. Tolkien, *Morgoth's Ring*, 413.

70. Notice the emphasis on *willed* subjection in *took him for Lord*, as here we have an emphasis on decision that is reminiscent of Hobbes.

71. Tolkien, *Morgoth's Ring*, 412.

72. Tolkien, *Morgoth's Ring*, 410.

actions, therefore, begins with government of the subjects' opinions, their words—their speech. It would seem that Sauron takes this farther than Hobbes in that he "devised a language" for the Orcs.[73] Hobbes's Sovereign does not devise a language, but does something analogous in that he decides which doctrines will procure peace and which will be silenced by censure, who may speak in public, on what, etc. As Voegelin observes, "the passage could be written by a modern minister of propaganda."[74] Or, we might add, the lieutenant of Morgoth.

There is one last loophole in Hobbes's *Leviathan* that may open grounds for correlation between the Sovereign and Sauron. Hobbes's reputation hinges on his being positioned among the social contract theorists. One of the clearest articulations that the social contract authorizing the Sovereign needs to be agreed upon by the subjects comes in Chapter 17, where we read that each man says to each man, *"I authorize and give up my right of governing myself, to this man, or to this assembly of men, on this condition: that thou give up thy right to him, and authorise all his actions in like manner."*[75] However, although Hobbes explains that in order to live contentedly men must, "conferre all their power and strength upon one Man, or upon one Assembly of men, that may reduce all their Wills, by plurality of voices, into one Will,"[76] in a remarkable passage that is pertinent for our purposes, he mutes any difference between Sovereignty by Institution and Sovereignty Despoticall; the manner by which a Leviathan acquires his authority is of little concern: "That men who choose their Soveraign, do it for fear of one another, and not of him whom they Institute; but in this case they subject themselves to him they are afraid of. In both cases they do it for fear."[77] Beside the social contract, then, is a kind of "natural contract" that comes about when the Sovereign acquires his authority by force, as when a parent induces his or her child to obey by means of threats of violence. The subject can signify, "either in expresse words, or by other sufficient signes of the Will, that so long as his life, and the liberty of his body is allowed him, the Victor shall have the use thereof, at his pleasure."[78] This natural acquisition of sovereignty is somewhat inconsistent with Hobbes' premise that in nature all are equal enough that the state of nature is stabilized by its relative instability. However, again, Hobbes blurs the distinctions by insisting that

73. Tolkien, *Morgoth's Ring*, 411.
74. Voegelin, Gebhardt, and Hollweck, *Collected Works of Eric Voegelin*, 70.
75. Hobbes, *Leviathan*, 132.
76. Hobbes, *Leviathan*, 152–53.
77. Hobbes, *Leviathan*, 153.
78. Hobbes, *Leviathan*, 155.

in any case men submit to a Sovereign out of fear. Who is this Hobbesian subject, so driven by fear that he cares not whether his Sovereign has assumed authority by force or collective consent?

Perhaps we can see in Hobbes' *Leviathan* the *invention* of a certain type of individual, of a certain human being, a parallel to Melkor's "making" of a certain species of individual subjects. In this sense, Hobbes is not the revered realist of legend, but a myth-maker, whose *individual* is a work of phantasy. Machiavelli, writes Pierre Manent, "wants to force us to fix our attention exclusively, or almost exclusively, on pathologies. He wants to force us to lose what, after having read him, we shall be tempted to call our 'innocence.'"[79] Hobbes does something similar by creating before our eyes a universally-valid portrait of human nature as necessarily engaged in a competitive struggle driven by ever-increasing desire for power and fear of death. One wonders whether he "discovered" the true nature of human beings and then theorized his Sovereign or whether he created a human individual which would necessarily justify the Sovereign. In the case of the Orcs, Sauron himself did not *make* them, but his Master did, and the tale of their genesis is terrible. Morgoth (then called Melkor) imprisoned Elves, which "by slow arts of cruelty were corrupted and enslaved; and thus did Melkor breed the hideous race of the Orcs in envy and mockery of the Elves, of whom they were afterwards the bitterest foes . . ."[80] We further learn that in their innermost recesses the Orcs, "loathed the Master whom they served in fear, the maker only of their misery. This it may be was the vilest deed of Melkor, and the most hateful to Ilúvatar."[81]

Niels Werber helps us to consider the idea that Orcs are invented to serve a political purpose when he argues that:

> Orcs are the outcome of engineered processes of deprivation and, typical for a modern discourse of genetics, of improvement. What they lack in comparison to their genetic ancestors is humanity and individuality (from the narrator's perspective) or weakness, hesitation, and disloyalty (from the perspective of the Dark Lord). Their deprivation is, from another standpoint, their improvement in strength and obedience.[82]

The same could be said of the Hobbesian human, for whom "[t]here is no such *Finis ultimus,* (utmost ayme,) [and] *Summum Bonum* (greatest

79. Manent, *An Intellectual History of Liberalism*, 13.

80. Tolkien, *Silmarillion*, 47.

81. Tolkien, *Silmarillion*, 47.

82. Werber, "Geo- and Biopolitics of Middle-Earth," 235.

Good,) as spoken of in the Books of the old Morall Philosophers."[83] Depraved, fearful, lustfully competitive, the Hobbesian human being is, from the standpoint of the Sovereign, an "improvement" in that he can more justifiably induce terror in his subjects. If men may imagine that unlimited sovereignty may bring forth "many evil consequences, yet the consequences of the want of it, which is perpetuall warre of every man against his neighbour, are much worse."[84]

It is Tolkien, however, who is the realist when it comes to power dynamics resultant from sovereignty achieved despotically. He writes that the Orcs, who, like Hobbes's subjects, serve the Master in fear, *loathe* him. Shagrat and Gorbag give abundant evidence of this. Hobbes, on the other hand, gives us the story of a depraved being who, in gratitude for the protection given by the sovereign, grants Leviathan the use of his body "for his pleasure" without any apparent dissonance or dissent.

The terror that Sauron strikes, his immense power put on public display in the towering Barad-dûr, does not put an end to Warre. The existence of a figure aspiring to absolute sovereignty hastens and escalates conflicts that would otherwise be extant but either more latent or more mild. If Leviathan, a Mortall God, strikes a peace-inducing terror into the populace internal to his realm, Sauron, the Imortall[85] Lieutenant of the angelic Melkor, strikes a war-inducing terror into even the most sluggish and apolitical members of the populace—the Shirefolk.

We can of course wonder whether either of these artistic creations—Sauron and his Mordor, the Sovereign and his Leviathan, can make an impression on the minds of those living under the reign of technocracy. Tolkien's vision would seem to be of interest as an act of nostalgia for an unrecoverable isle of the past. And can we not simply pinch ourselves to remember that Mordor is a mere fantasy, no matter how many times Tolkien mapped it, and that Sauron is in the end lieutenant over a body of subjects equally fantastical? Has not history demonstrated that Hobbes's theory of the state did not materialize in England, for "the English people decided against such a state" on the grounds that "the content of Hobbes' concept was regarded as despotism"?[86] And yet the cold hard facts indicate that *The Lord of the Rings* remains unchained from pre-mechanical England, the despotism Hobbes defended and the totalitarianism he intimated remain, if not uni-

83. Hobbes, *Leviathan*, 75.

84. Hobbes, *Leviathan*, 160.

85. Nardi notes that "Sauron is . . . immortal [which] gives Sauron an even greater bargaining position because he can outwait any Orc demands for greater rights or resources" (119).

86. Schmitt, *Leviathan in the State Theory of Thomas Hobbes*, 79–80.

versal, recurrently visible on the world stage. If we understand the passions as operating not always and everywhere but sometimes and somewhere as Hobbes describes them, and if we grasp the historical-political echoes of Tolkien's Secondary World rendering of a *libido dominandi* that regathers and explodes, recedes and, after days or decades or centuries resurfaces with sheer force, then we suddenly behold the illuminating shadows that both Hobbes and Tolkien cast on our times. This illumination increases when we witness "the possibility of disruption permanently present in the national state," wherein "at any moment the passions may break loose again; inspired leaders may arise, find their sectarian followers, and blow up the common-wealth in a new civil war," or, say a war on or by means of terror.[87] Perhaps Schmitt is not entirely wrong to suggest that in such a rationalistic world as ours, which has culminated in technocracy, "on the thought processes of total technology Leviathan can no longer make a sinister impression. It trusts itself to be able to place him, like other saurian and mastadons, under protection in a preserve and display him as a museum curiosity in a zoo."[88] And yet, Schmitt admits, "no clear chain of thought can stand up against the force of genuine, mythical images."[89] Voegelin assures us that Hobbes's "failed symbol" of total control is bona fide in that "this technique of control by the mortal God is probably the inevitable instrument of peaceful order among men who have lost their immortal God."[90] Whoever uses such im-ages, however, "easily glides into the role of a magician who summons forces that cannot be matched by his arm, his eye, or any other measure of his human ability."[91]

Yet here Tolkien's metaphysical realism is once again cast into relief, for if on the one hand we live under the ever-present threat of bourgeois hobbits habituated to boredom, paranoid Morgoths advancing or inspiring acts of terror, militant Mordors barely restrained by borders increasingly difficult to mark, we also have a grace that builds upon nature. Wolfgang Palaver notes that, whereas "Hobbes expressly rules out any possible way of escaping man's violent nature . . . Girard's theory argues expressly for openness to transcendence and . . . sees in God the only way to overcome the violence of an intrinsically competitive mimesis."[92] Tolkien's world is ultimately more realistic than Hobbes's in that within it, as within our own

87. Voegelin, Jurgen, and Hollweck, *Collected Works of Eric Voegelin*, 71.

88. Schmitt, *Leviathan in the State Theory of Thomas Hobbes*, 82.

89. Schmitt, *Leviathan in the State Theory of Thomas Hobbes*, 81.

90. Voegelin, Jurgen, and Hollweck, *Collected Works of Eric Voegelin*, 71.

91. Schmitt, *Leviathan in the State Theory of Thomas Hobbes*, 82.

92. Palaver, "René Girard's Mimetic Theory," 99.

world, "There is [] such [a thing as] *Finis ultimus*, (utmost ayme,) [and] *Summum Bonum* (greatest Good,) as spoken of in the Books of the old Mor-all Philosophers," which allows the heroes of *The Lord of the Rings* to desire and be towards a common good, to establish a political order in spite of the supposed superiority and centrality of the desire for power manifested by the Modern State of Mordor.[93] But first, we slaves of technocracy must be freed from the magic of the Machines, who persistently proclaim that the *Summum Bonum* is efficiency or expediency rather than a form of happiness which the old Morall Philosophers used to call *beatitude*.

Tolkien and the Technocratic Paradigm

Of the regimes Plato catalogues in *The Republic*, we do not read of technocracy, and yet increasingly the political form of liberal democracy under late capitalism seems to be most rightly characterized as *techno-cracy*, which we can understand as both "rule by those who possess technology," and the "rule of technology over humankind." Just as Tolkien, like Hobbes, mythologized elements of the Modern State in Mordor, he also countenances technocratic logic in a narrative mode. His manner of doing so finds consonance in the philosopher Gabriel Marcel's contention that "unless we make a truly ascetic effort to master techniques and put them in their proper subordinate place, they tend to assemble themselves, to organize themselves, around the man who rejects. It is a mysterious and significant fact about our contemporary world that nihilism is tending to take on a technocratic character, while technocracy is inevitably nihilist."[94] In his 2015 Encyclical *Laudato Si'*, Jorge Bergolio critiques the notion that technology is a mere "neutral instrument."[95] Modern man has "taken up technology and its development according to an undifferentiated and one-dimensional paradigm."[96] This "technocratic paradigm" lauds the concept of a subject who acquires control over all of the objects it encounters using rational and logical methods. With the scientific method as its primary if not exclusive modus operandi, the subject inhabiting the technocratic paradigm seeks to master, possess, and manipulate reality: "It is as if the subject were to find itself in the presence of something formless, completely open to manipulation. Men and women have constantly intervened in nature, but for a long time this meant being in tune with and respecting the possibilities offered by the things

93. Hobbes, *Leviathan*, 75.
94. Marcel, *Man Against Mass Society*, 195.
95. Bergolio, *Laudato Si'*.
96. Bergolio, *Laudato Si'*.

themselves."[97] In the pre-technocratic period, man approached nature as a receiver, gaining from her what she allowed. Now, however, man disregards all dimensions of an object that falls outside of the technocratic paradigm's criteria, all the while working to maximize that which can be extracted from that which he masters. Jorge Bergolio's diagnosis of the problem of technology, which he calls the "technocratic paradigm," is not novel. Rather, his is a continuation of a line of questioning put to technology by a number of early twentieth-century thinkers: Christian theologian Romano Guardini, whom Jorge Bergolio quotes throughout the encyclical; German philosopher Martin Heidegger, to whom *Laudato Si'* is, as we shall see, indebted; and the Christian author J.RR. Tolkien. If we find a diagnosis of the technocratic paradigm, which he refers to as "the Machine," in Tolkien's letters, we find an unexpected anodyne in the poetic paradigm inculcated in his fantasy fiction.

In a letter to Milton Waldman, Tolkien writes of his *legendarium*, "Anyway, all this stuff is mainly concerned with the Fall, Mortality, and the Machine . . . "[98] When the desire to be "Lord and God" of one's own private creation combines with rebellion against the "laws of the Creator," we become driven by a desire for Power, and "for making the will more quickly effective"; thus, "the Machine" gains importance. Tolkien goes on to explicate what he means by "the Machine":

> By the last I intend all use of external plans or devices (apparatus) instead of development of the inherent inner properties or talents—or even the use of these talents with the corrupted motive of dominating: bulldozing the real world, or coercing other wills. The Machine is our more obvious modern form though more closely related to Magic than is usually recognized . . . The Enemy in successive forms is always 'naturally' concerned with sheer Domination, and so the Lord of magic and machines; but the problem: that this frightful evil can and does arise from an apparently good root, the desire to benefit the world and others—speedily and according to the benefactors own plans—is a recurrent motif.[99]

As Romano Guardini outlines in *The End of the Modern World*, the modern era justified technology as essential to the promotion of man's well-being. However, "in so doing, it masked the destructive effects of a ruthless

97. Bergolio, *Laudato Si'*.

98. Tolkien et al., *Letters*, 145.

99. Tolkien et al., *Letters*, 146.

system."[100] If technology were nothing more than that which makes "the will more quickly effective," corrupted human will, and not technology, would be responsible for misuse; the machine would be mere *instrument*. However, as Heidegger contends in "The Question Concerning Technology," we will remain chained slavishly to technology, whether we reject it or passionately affirm its goodness, insofar as we "regard it as something neutral."[101] According to the instrumentalist understanding of technology as a mere tool, "everything depends on our manipulating technology in the proper manner as a means."[102] Heidegger finds impoverished all attempts to define technology *technologically*, because such approaches fail to locate the true essence of technology, which is nothing technological.

In spite of the vast valley that stands between their philosophical and theological foundations,[103] Tolkien and Heidegger stand on common ground when they assess modern man's claims concerning the nature of technology, and the reductionist definitions that we so inadequately wield as we try to comprehend and use it. At first glance, however, it may seem as though Tolkien's initial argument that technology makes "the will more quickly effective" partakes of the instrumentalist's presuppositions. However, he goes on to note that "[t]he Machine is our more obvious modern form, though it is more closely related to Magic than usually recognized."[104] In calling attention to the correlation between Machine and Magic, Tolkien echoes Heidegger's claim that technology's essence is non-technological when he argues that there is something more than mechanical in the essence of the Machine. Far from being a mere means, technology is a "way of revealing."[105] Tracing the etymology of "technology," we find that it stems from the Greek word *Technikon*, which signifies that which belongs to *techne*. For the Greeks, *techne* signifies not merely the activities of the

100. Guardini, *The End of the Modern World*, 56.

101. Heidegger, "The Question Concerning Technology," 4.

102. Heidegger, "The Question Concerning Technology," 5.

103. Martin Heidegger stands at the center of that influential circle of persons who malign much of the philosophical theology of the West by considering it idolatrous syncretism of metaphysics and theology in which God's being and the impenetrable mysteries of his existence have been subjected to the philosophical-scientific modes of analysis, and there by de-mystified and, ultimately, dangerously reduced. Tolkien's work is marked by lucid imprints of this very tradition of philosophical theology—be it the work of Plato, St. Augustine, or St. Thomas Aquinas.

104. Tolkien et al., *Letters*, 146.

105. Heidegger, "The Question Concerning Technology," 12.

craftsman, but the "arts of the mind and the fine arts. *Techne* belongs to bringing-forth, to *poiesis*; it is something poietic."[106]

Can we find consonance between Heidegger's claim that technology is fundamentally a kind of *poiesis* or "revealing" and Tolkien's contention that there is an affinity between the Machine and Magic? For Heidegger, "the revealing that rules in modern technology is a challenging" which puts to nature the unreasonable demand that it supply energy that can be extracted and stored as such."[107] Modern technology's challenging—a violent confrontational engagement with the natural world—forever expedites in that it exposes and unlocks, and is always directed toward advancing something else, for instance, "driving on to the maximum yield at minimum expense."[108] Coal is extracted not merely so that it can be used in various homes, or in a power plant, but so that it can be "on call," ever available to deliver' the sun's warmth. The sun is seen not as, say, the god Helios, as in Greek mythology, or a symbol of either the Good, as in Plato's *Republic*, or of the "Sun of Justice," but as "warmth that is challenged forth for heat," which powers steam, allowing a factory's gears to continue turning. Unlike the modern mechanized food industry, the work of the pre-modern farmer did not "challenge" the soil of the field.[109] This line bears striking resemblance to *Laudato Si*'s assessment of the "receptive" nature of pre-modern technology. Heidegger exemplifies this modern "challenging" most memorably in an extended consideration of "two Rhines." On the one hand, we have "The Rhine" as revealed by the German poet Holderline's *poiesis*, and, on the other hand, "The Rhine" as "water power supplier," as "river . . . damned up into the power plant."[110] We may object that the Rhine is still a river in the landscape, but, Heidegger insists, "[H]ow? In no other way than as an object on call for inspection by a tour group ordered there by the vacation industry."[111] As we can see, the core problem resultant from modern technology is that it comes to *exclude other modes of revealing*. Under the technological gaze, all objects "disappear[] into the objectlessness of standing-reserve," a stock of various energies that can be called upon.[112] Eventually, however, the technological gaze fixes itself upon man *per se*, and

---

106. Heidegger, "The Question Concerning Technology," 13.
107. Heidegger, "The Question Concerning Technology," 14.
108. Heidegger, "The Question Concerning Technology," 15.
109. Heidegger, "The Question Concerning Technology," 15.
110. Heidegger, "The Question Concerning Technology," 16.
111. Heidegger, "The Question Concerning Technology," 16.
112. Heidegger, "The Question Concerning Technology," 19.

"he comes to the point where he himself will have to be taken as standing-reserve."[113] Instead of recognizing his perilous state, at this very moment man so threatened "exalts himself to the posture of the lord of the earth . . . This illusion gives rise in turn to one final delusion: It seems as though man everywhere and always encounters only himself."[114]

Strikingly, Tolkien also incorporates the modern mill as an exemplification of the Machine. On the first page of the "Prologue," we learn that hobbits "do not and did not understand or like machines more complicated than a forge-bellows, a water-mill, or a hand-loom, though they were skillful with tools," indicating the creature's decisive adherence to premodern technology.[115] We gain an even sharper sense of the water-mill's import when Sam Gamgee gazes into the Mirror of Galadriel, only to find there a nightmare scenario: "Sam noticed that the Old Mill had vanished, and a large red-brick building was being put up where it had stood. Lots of folk were busily at work. There was a tall red chimney nearby. Black smoke seemed to cloud the surface of the Mirror. / 'There's some devilry at work in the Shire,' he said."[116] The scene leaves little need for interpretation, as it resounds with a Dickensian, *Hard Times*-critique of industrialization via the Modern Machine. Finally, after Sam and Frodo have destroyed the Ring in Mount Doom, and they have returned to a markedly impoverished Shire, Farmer Cotton narrates the disturbing changes brought to the mill[117]:

> Take Sandyman's mill now. Pimple knocked it down almost as soon as he came to Bag End. Then he brought in a lot o' dirty-looking Men to build a bigger one and fill it full o' wheels and outlandish contraptions. Only that fool Ted was pleased by that, and he works there cleaning wheels for the Men, where his dad was the Miller and his own master. Pimple's idea was to grind more and faster, or so he said. He's got other mills like it. But you've got to have grist before you can grind; and there was no more for the new mill to do than for the old. But since Sharkey came they don't grind no more corn at all. They're always a-hammering and a-letting out a smoke and a stench, and there

---

113. Heidegger, "The Question Concerning Technology," 27.

114. Heidegger, "The Question Concerning Technology."

115. Tolkien, *The Lord of the Rings*, 1.

116. Tolkien, *The Lord of the Rings*, 362–63.

117. In his Preface to *The Lord of the Rings*, Tolkien addresses the decline of the old mill: "Recently I saw in a paper a picture of the last decrepitude of the once thriving corn-mill beside its pool that long ago seemed to me so important. I never liked the looks of the Young miller, but his father, the Old miller, had a black beard, and he was not named Sandyman" (*LOTR* xxi).

isn't no peace even at night in Hobbiton. And they pour out filth
a purpose; they've fouled all the lower Water, and it's getting
down into Brandywine. If they want to make the Shire into
a desert, they're going the right way about it.[118]

Pimple's[119] openly-stated intention is to "grind more and faster," a veritable paraphrase of Tolkien's contention that the machine is meant, at least
in part, to make the will more quickly effective. The actual application of
Pimple' intent, however, captures Tolkien's further definition of the Machine
as "all use of external plans or devices (apparatus) instead of development
of the inherent inner properties or talents—or even the use of these talents
with the corrupted motive of dominating: bulldozing the real world, or coercing other wills."[120] Through Farmer Cotton's account we see that Pimple's
is a technological gaze, under which all objects, in the words of Heidegger,
"disappear[] into the objectlessness of standing-reserve."[121] *Laudato Si'* continues the implications of this objectlessness in is contention that, under
the technocratic paradigm, man perpetually finds himself in "the presence
of something formless, completely open to manipulation."[122] He lusts for a
machine that will grind faster and more, but ignores the inherent properties
of nature and so fails to see that "you've got to have grist before you can
grind; and there was no more for the new mill to do than for the old."[123] He
"bulldozes" the real world and, eventually, hammering away and building
a greater Machine seems to become an end in and of itself, as indicated by
Cotton's complaint that "they don't grind no more corn at all"; the most
prolific product seems to be "filth" which fouls the waters. As the Machine
grinds on, the Shire itself, which is objectless under Pimple's gaze, is soon
to become a "desert": a geographic metaphor for objectlessness. Hauntingly, Heidegger notes that when the technological gaze has looked long
enough, man himself will become "standing-reserve." We see this again in
Pimple, who brings in "a lot o' dirty-looking Men," outside "resources" that
are noteworthy only insofar as their energy and labor is on call for Pimple's
demands. In addition to "bulldozing the real world," Tolkien continues, the
Machine is concerned with "coercing other wills," which ultimately shows-
forth in sheer domination.

118. Tolkien, *The Lord of the Rings*, 1013.
119. Remember that Pimple is the alias of Lotho Sackville-Baggins.
120. Tolkien et al., *Letters*, 156.
121. Heidegger, "The Question Concerning Technology," 19.
122. Jorge Bergolio, *Laudato Si'*.
123. Tolkien, *The Lord of the Rings*, 1013.

Importantly, Tolkien describes the Ring as a symbol of "the will to mere power, seeking to make itself objective by physical force and mechanism, and so inevitably by lies."[124] Here in the Ring-maker's emphasis on "mechanism" and "physical force," as well as purported or attempted "objectivity," we hear echoes of a Heideggerian analysis of modern technology. Although a "mechanism," it ultimately only challenges-forth when its user imposes physical force over others and other things, and in so doing aspires to a sort of mastery over reality that "discovers" all things as primarily "standing reserve." In a letter to Rhona Beare, Tolkien explains the Ring in a manner that reveals further Heideggerian affinities:

> The Ring of Sauron is only one of the various mythical treatments of the placing of one's life, or power, in some external object, which is thus exposed to capture or destruction with disastrous results to oneself. If I were to—philosophize this myth, or at least the Ring of Sauron, I should say it was a mythical way of representing the truth that potency (or perhaps rather potentiality) if it is to be exercised, and produce results, has to be externalized and so as it were passes, to a greater or less degree, out of one's direct control. A man who wishes to exert—power must have subjects, who are not himself. But he then depends on them.[125]

Understood as an exemplar of modern technology, the Ring of Sauron demonstrates the fact that insofar as we insert our power and life into the machine, that life and power pass "out of [our] control." In other words, it is not merely that we, as modern wimps, are more dependent on machines. The danger is greater: our *wills* themselves become "standing-reserve" for the Ring.[126]

---

124. Tolkien et al., *Letters*, 160. It is worth noting an intriguing connection between the Ring, the Machine, and Hegel's master-slave dialectic. As Peter Kreeft polemicizes, modern man pines not for human slaves, because we have substitutes for them: machines. The Industrial Revolution made slavery inefficient and unnecessary. But our addiction is the same whether the slaves are made of flesh, metal, or plastic. We have done exactly what Sauron did in forging the Ring. We have put our power into things in order to increase our power. And the result is, as everyone knows but no one admits, that we are now weak little wimps, Shelob's slaves, unable to survive a blow to the great spider of our technological network. We tremble before a nationwide electrical blackout or a global computer virus. . . In our drive for power we have deceived ourselves into thinking that we have become more powerful when all the time we have been becoming less. We are miserable little Nietzsches dreaming we are supermen. For in gaining the world we have lost our selves (187–88).

125. Tolkien et al., *Letters*, 279.

126. Tolkien et al., *Letters*, 279.

In *Laudato Si'*, Jorge Bergolio continues Heidegger's work of unravelling the "neutrality" argument: "Science and technology are not neutral; from the beginning to the end of a process, various intentions and possibilities are in play and can take on distinct shapes."[127] In Tolkien's *The Lord of the Rings*, the character Boromir, more than any other, approaches the Ring as a neutral instrument. During the Council of Elrond, when Elves, Men, Dwarf, Hobbits, and Wizard gather to decide what should be done with the One Ring of the Dark Lord, Boromir asks:

> Why do you speak ever of hiding and destroying? Why should we not think that the Great Ring has come into our hands to serve us in the very hour of need? Wielding it the Free Lords of the Free may surely defeat the Enemy. That is what he most fears, I deem. 'The Men of Gondor are valiant, and they will never submit; but they may be beaten down. Valour needs first strength, and then a weapon. Let the Ring be your weapon, if it has such power as you say. Take it and go forth to victory!'[128]

In arguing that "Valour needs first strength, and then a weapon," Boromir is one more voice enunciating the idea that the Ring is, as at least part of Tolkien's analysis of the Machine suggests, merely an instrument to sharpen and quicken the will. In Heidegger's articulation of this disposition, "Everything depends on our manipulating technology in the proper manner as means."[129]

> Elrond, however, opposes Boromir's naïve diagnosis and proposition: We cannot use the Ruling Ring. That we now know too well. It belongs to Sauron and was made by him alone, and is altogether evil. Its strength, Boromir, is too great for anyone to wield at will, save only those who have already a great power of their own. But for them it holds an even deadlier peril.[130]

Sauron's *intentions* have been so infused into the "instrument" that all of its prospective wearers will, in the words of *Laudato Si'*, "take on distinct shape."[131]

The solution to this solipsistic-humanistic technological challenging is, for Heidegger, to be found in what the Greeks called *poiesis, techne,* or art, through which they "brought the presence of the gods, brought the dialogue

---

127. Bergolio, *Laudato Si'*.
128. Tolkien, *The Lord of the Rings*, 267.
129. Heidegger, "The Question Concerning Technology," 5.
130. Tolkien, *The Lord of the Rings*, 267–68.
131. Bergolio, *Laudato Si'*.

of divine and human destinings, to radiance."[132] Jorge Bergolio acknowl-edges the same—sans romantic valorization of the Greeks—when he notes that it "cannot be maintained that empirical science provides a complete explanation of life, the interplay of all creatures and the whole of reality. If we reason only within the confines of the latter, little room would be left for aesthetic sensibility, poetry, or even reason's ability to grasp the ultimate meaning and purpose of things."[133] However, for the purposes of our present investigation, in order to delve further into the difference between poetic and modern-technological modes of revealing-concealing, we must, with Tolkien, determine that which both binds and separates the Machine and Magic. Further, with Tolkien, we must further make distinctions between types of magic.

Tolkien uses the word "magic" to mean manifold things. Indeed, in another letter, he admits to being "afraid that I have been far too casual about 'magic' and especially the use of the word."[134] He goes on to offer an explanation of magic that is remarkably similar to the instrumentalist argument concerning technology. Tolkien admits to a latent distinction, in *The Lord of the Rings,* between *goeteia,* or "bad magic," on the one hand, and *magia,* or "good magic," on the other. In his tale, Tolkien contends, "nei-ther is . . . good or bad (per se), but only by motive or purpose or use."[135] However, he does point to a "supremely bad motive" which is "domination of other 'free' wills."[136] Here, then, we come to a crucial passage that links magic to Machine:

> The Enemy's operations are by no means all *goetic* deceits, but 'magic' that produces real effects in the physical world. But his *magia* he uses to bulldoze both people and things, and his *goete-ia* to terrify and subjugate. Their *magia* the Elves and Gandalf use (sparingly): a *magia,* producing real results (like fire in a wet faggot) for specific beneficent purposes. Their *goetic* effects are entirely artistic and not intended to deceive: they never deceive Elves (but may deceive or bewilder unaware Men) since the dif-ference is to them as clear as the difference to us between fiction, painting, and sculpture, and 'life.'[137]

132. Heidegger, "The Question Concerning Technology," 34.

133. Jorge Bergolio, *Laudato Si'.*

134. Tolkien et al., *Letters,* 199.

135. Tolkien et al., *Letters,* 199.

136. Tolkien et al., *Letters,* 199.

137. Tolkien et al., *Letters,* 199.

First, we note that although some opponents of the Enemy do use *goeteia,* they use it for "entirely artistic" purposes, never intending to deceive in a moral sense, but only in the sense of creating supreme fictions as distinct from life. Whereas the technological gaze "enframes" in that it excludes all but its narrow challenging, disguising the nearness of the world, and "even this, its disguising," the *goetic* effects of Gandalf and the Elves are *evident,* are undisguised: being altogether artistic, they allow others to better know Beauty.[138] In his assessment of the Enemy's operations, Tolkien returns again to the image of bulldozing, this time both people and things, but adds the aim to "terrify" which is part of his will to subjugate. At last, then, the link between Magic and the Machine becomes utterly lucid:

> The Enemy, or those who have become like him, go in for 'machinery' — with destructive and evil effects — because 'magicians,' who have become chiefly concerned to use *magia* for their own power, would do so (do do so). The basic motive for *magia* — quite apart from any philosophic consideration of how it would work—is immediacy: speed, reduction of labour, and reduction also to a minimum (or vanishing point) of the gap between the idea or desire and the result or effect.[139]

Neither Gandalf nor the Elves "go in for machinery," no matter their use of the *goetic.* The motives of machine and magic meet insofar as their aims are "reduction to a minimum (or vanishing point) of the gap between the idea or desire and the result or effect." In his famous lecture "On Fairy-Stories," Tolkien makes yet another clarifying distinction, even if it at first adds yet another meaning to his use of "magic," and thus demonstrates that he was rightly concerned with prospective ambiguity in this regard. Magic, he notes, "is *power* in this world, domination of things or wills," while enchantment "does not seek delusion, nor bewitchment and domination; it seeks enrichment, partners in making and delight, not slaves."[140] It would seem, then, that *enchantment* serves as a kind of corollary force that stands as more good, true, and beautiful than magic and the technocratic spell. The technocratic paradigm emerges in part as a result of and in part as a harbinger of disenchantment. As Charles Taylor relates, disenchantment "designat[es] one of the main features of the process we know as secularization" [287]. The German word for "disenchantment" is "Entzauberung," which contains the word "Zauber," or *magic*: it literally translates as *de-magicification.*[141]

138. Heidegger, "The Question Concerning Technology," 46.

139. Tolkien et al., *Letters,* 199.

140. Tolkien, "On Fairy Stories," 369.

141. Charles Taylor, quoted in Gregory Stackpole, "Charles Taylor On Disenchantment."

Taylor traces "two main" features of the enchanted world that "disenchantment did away with." The first was that the world "was once filled with spirits [God, angels, Satan, demons, spirits of the wood] that were "almost indistinguishable from the loci they inhabit," etc.] and moral forces [that] impinged on human beings" (the boundary between humans and these were "porous"). The second was that "meaning [was] within the cosmos" because it was a "Great Chain of Being"—being was understood to have levels, and to be hierarchical, so that some things would share meaning and even power."[142]

For Tolkien, this enchantment comes about through "fairy-stories" such as, we can add, his own *legendarium,* from *The Silmarillion* to *The Return of the King.* How, though, would something like Tolkien's *legendarium* grant us recovery of that which has been lost from our sight by looking at things too long now with technological gazes? In "On Fairy-Stories" Tolkien argues that Fairy is deeply concerned with:

> Recovery (which includes return and renewal of health) is a regaining—regaining of a clear view. I do not say "seeing things as they are" and involve myself with the philosophers, though I might venture to say "seeing things as we are (or were) meant to see them"—as things apart from ourselves. We need, in any case, to clean our windows; so that the things seen clearly may be freed from the drab blur of triteness or familiarity—from possessiveness.[143]

But this still seems too abstract. Tolkien insists that fairy-stories are concerned largely with fundamental, simple things, "but these simplicities are made all the more luminous by their setting . . . It was in fairy-stories that I first divined the potency of the words, and the wonder of the things, such as stone and wood, and iron; tree and grass; house and fire; bread and wine."[144] The importance of this passage cannot be overstated. Part of the problem with the technocratic paradigm is its submersion of its subjects into a characteristically modern prejudice: meaning is in the mind, not in *things. The Lord of the Rings* may help us to "see things as we were meant to see them," but this doesn't simply mean that it cleanses our perception; it shows us the *being* of things, things freed from the technocratic paradigm and gaze. Consider Sam's return home after he has laid down his life to help Frodo destroy the Ring of Power. Tolkien takes Sam home, even as we too come to grasp our place amidst these enchanted, ordinary things:

142. Stackpole, "Charles Taylor On Disenchantment."

143 Tolkien, "On Fairy Stories," 373.

144. Tolkien, "On Fairy Stories," 375.

And he went on, and there was yellow light, and fire within; and the evening meal was ready, and he was expected. And Rose drew him in, and set him in his chair, and put little Elanor upon his lap.

He drew a deep breath. "Well, I'm back," he said.[145]

A cynical reading of this passage might resist it as sentimental, or even clichéd. But in her article "'My Precious': Tolkien's Fetishized Ring," Alison Milbank offers a far more enchanting interpretation: "The objects of fire, food, light, and shelter unite here to signify human warmth and community. By making Sam function as a chair for his little daughter in a family trinity, the text affirms the familial relation of objects to persons. Chairs are only chairs; they have no magical qualities, but they allow human connection."[146] Freed from the objectlessness of standing reserve, objects can signify themselves—parts of a whole which is beyond our possession.

And yet we cannot end with the Shire; rather, it is necessary to develop a political map that does justice to the overarching political organization with which the novel ends: monarchy. For just as Tolkien helps us to recover the sense that technology is not merely neutral, he helps us to recover the grandeur of kingship, and, more so, the primacy of the common good.

145. Tolkien, *The Lord of the Rings*, 1031.

146. Milbank, "'My Precious': Tolkien's Fetishized Ring," 43.

Middle-earth and the Return of the Common Good

The tyrant, more than the good king, reigns in the contemporary political imagination, even as in recent times the most tyrannical have eschewed the title. As political philosopher Pierre Manent observes in *Seeing Things Politically*, "If a man like Stalin was able to present himself simply as the 'General Secretary,' and if, at the same time, it was possible for him to be considered a paragon of humanity and the father of the arts and sciences, this is to some degree because . . . we had become incapable of using a single word: the word 'tyrant.'"[1]

In the society of late democratic capitalism we, too, have become incapable of giving the proper name to the phenomenon of misguided personalism, the undue exaltation of each individual as an end in and of herself. "A society constituted by persons who love their private good above the common good, or who identify the common good with the private good, is a society not of free men, but of tyrants, 'and thus the entire people becomes like one tyrant,'" who lead each other by force, the head of all being simply the strongest, cleverest tyrant, and the subjects being only lesser, frustrated tyrants."[2] Thankfully, this mass tyranny, wherein a common conception of justice is jettisoned, insofar as it emerges in a democracy, may not end in as cataclysmic a manner as a one-man tyranny. As Aquinas argues, "If the government should fall away into injustice, it is more fitting that it should belong to many so that it may be weaker, and so that they may hinder one another. Among the forms of unjust rule, therefore, democracy is the most

1. Manent, *Seeing Things Politically*, 5.
2. De Koninck, "On the Primacy of the Common Good."

tolerable and tyranny is the worst."[3] Such a society of tyrants is especially likely when the common good has been banished from public life, or when the common good has been replaced with a generic utilitarian greatest happiness for the greatest number.[4] And yet such a society is not by any means unlikely when, in the wake of totalitarian, communist abuses of the "collective" or common good, many remain suspicious of any organizing force beyond private interests. As De Koninck writes in his preface, "Totalitarian regimes recognize the common good as a pretext for subjugating persons in the most ignoble way."[5] Still, he asks, "Shall we be so lax as to allow totalitarianism this perversion of the common good and of its primacy?"[6]

Exaltation of the personal good, after all, can lead to a society of tyrants that is little less troubling—and in some ways more so—than a single tyrant who has corroded the common good rightly understood. But the memories of this corrosion and corruption haunt the imagination like that specter of communism which once haunted Europe, and in fiction, in *The Lord of the Rings* itself, such figures move us because, if grotesque, they seem applicable. Consider Saruman, the only one to explicitly use the phrase "common good" in the entire novel. During Gandalf's second visit to Isengard, Saruman, in a last effort to persuade his fellow wizard, suggests that the "lesser folk" should "wait on our decisions! For the common good I am willing to redress the past, and to receive you."[7]

And yet, Tolkien's *The Lord of the Rings* helps us to recover reverence for a rightly-ordered common good, and it is one of the great ironies of the novel that this education into the common good comes about in part through the interdependence of Sam, Frodo, and Sméagol.

Whose Compassion, Which *Misericordia?*: Taming Pity and the Problem of Sméagol

In *A World Beyond Politics?* Manent takes up the task of distinguishing the different versions of humanism and humanitarianism, in large part to demonstrate their indebtedness to—and incompatibility with—Christian love of neighbor. Manent's aim is to unveil the paucity and fragility of modern humanism's moral foundations. For Jean-Jacques Rousseau, one of the fathers of this humanism, pity is a moral sentiment that is able to

3. Aquinas, *De Regno*, 18-19.

4. De Koninck, "On the Primacy of the Common Good."

5. De Koninck, "On the Primacy of the Common Good."

6. De Koninck, "On the Primacy of the Common Good."

7. Tolkien, *The Lord of the Rings*, 581.

unify human beings in a world witnessing the death of the common good. Christian love is never aimed at the neighbor in-and-of-herself, but at the *Imago Dei* that is found in every human being. Even "Nietzsche, though furiously anti-Christian, nonetheless says that to love the neighbor for the love of God is the most refined moral sentiment attained by human beings."[8] Manent helps us distinguish humanitarianism from Christian love in part through a linguistic analysis, for the foundation of humanitarianism is not *agape* (sacrificial love) or *caritas* (charity) as much as it is compassion, or pity, in the sense that Rousseau uses the word. For Rousseau, capacity for pity is universal because all human beings have a body that is subject to the strong possibility of suffering; human beings are inevitably objects of suffering. Further, because of the universality of suffering, human beings will undoubtedly be subjects of suffering: "Physical suffering is immediately grasped or imagined," Manent writes. "One sympathizes with a toothache, a nervous colic, and two days without eating or drinking more easily than with a moral humiliation, an intellectual preoccupation, or a spiritual anguish."[9] In sum, the physicality of pity, rooted as it is in the senses, allows us to "communicate immediately with the other, without the mediation of complex ideas. Pity can be relied on to bind people because it is a sentiment, an affect, or a disposition that does not demand any moral transformation or transcendence of self."[10]

For instance, the visible suffering of an Other says to me, "You too could undergo this," and therefore I make an effort to assuage his suffering. But, in fact, I do not in truth experience this suffering that I perceive so vividly: "I know well that I do not effectively experience it and so I rejoice that I am exempt from it. I experience the pleasure of not suffering. Therefore, there is nothing idealistic or utopian in pity as the foundation of social morality."[11] As Manent maintains, altruistic pity is morally economical, demanding very little from mankind: "there is nothing in pity that is heroic, since its wellspring is the selfishness of each person. Rousseau was giving us the blueprint that has effectively prevailed in liberal democratic society."[12]

In "The Taming of Sméagol," Frodo recollects an earlier conversation with Gandalf in which he considered it "a pity [that] Bilbo did not stab the vile creature, when he had the chance."[13] Gandalf replies that it was "Pity

---

8. Manent, *A World Beyond Politics?, 188.*

9. Manent, *A World Beyond Politics?, 189.*

10. Manent, *A World Beyond Politics?, 189.*

11. Manent, *A World Beyond Politics?, 190.*

12. Manent, *A World Beyond Politics?, 190.*

13. Tolkien, *The Lord of the Rings,* 615.

that stayed his hand. Pity, and Mercy: do not strike without need."[14] Just after he draws out Sting, at the moment when Sam insists they should kill the creature, Frodo notes that though he is afraid of Gollum, he "will not touch the creature. For now that I see him, I do pity him."[15]

To what "species" of pity are Frodo and Sam appealing? Are they, in appealing to pity, advocating a baseline morality that fosters ethical acts even to such despicable creatures as Sméagol? It is imperative that we grasp the meaning of pity in *The Lord of the Rings* because suffering and pain permeate the narrative, and thus the common good will involve, in part, a right response to that suffering.

In his work *Dependent Rational Animals,* Alasdair MacIntyre argues that most philosophers' quests for an understanding of human nature and the good life are deeply inadequate. Why? Because human beings are profoundly vulnerable to various sorts of affliction—injury, illness, disablement, etc.—and this disability makes dependence upon others central to our exploration of human nature, the common good, and moral commitment. MacIntyre notes that feminist philosophers have done much to remedy previous philosophers' blindness to dependence, especially by making the mother/child relationship—in which the child is utterly vulnerable and dependent—the paradigm for moral relationships. MacIntyre asks "what difference to moral philosophy would it make, if we were to treat the facts of vulnerability and affliction and the related facts of dependence as central to the human condition?"[16] To pursue this question, we would do well to consider the kind of disablement that consists in gross disfigurement, "where the horrifying and disgusting appearance of the sufferer becomes an obstacle to addressing her or him as a human being."[17] Now, Gollum is no human being, but it is well known that Tolkien sewed a strong thread between human beings and hobbits, and between hobbits and Gollum, for though Frodo squirms at the thought that he might be related to the creature, Gandalf clearly states that Gollum came from a "clever-handed and quiet-footed little people . . . of hobbit kind."[18] Gollum, more than any other character in *The Lord of the Rings,* presents the problem of disfigurement and related questions of the nature and implications of MacIntyre's dependence. What may we learn about ourselves from grappling with such difficulties? It is necessary, first, to avoid the dual mistakes of either pretend-

14. Tolkien, *The Lord of the Rings,* 615.

15. Tolkien, *The Lord of the Rings,* 615.

16. MacIntyre, *Dependent Rational Animals,* 4.

17. MacIntyre, *Dependent Rational Animals,* 136.

18. Tolkien, *The Lord of the Rings,* 52.

ing that the sufferer—Gollum, in this case—"does not in fact present an horrifying appearance . . . [and] being too distracted by that appearance to be able to deal rationally with the sufferer."[19] A 1946 psychological study found that seventy-seven percent of the subjects inferred from a description of someone as intelligent, skillful, industrious, warm, determined, that the person would be good-looking. A 1998 study found that one in three people believe that people in wheelchairs are less intelligent.

At the outset, we can learn from contact with Gollum that we have been influenced irrelevantly by feelings of dislike, disgust, and even horror, and have made purportedly rational judgments based on our responses to disfigurement.

MacIntyre asks that we sustain our consideration of dependence by unflinchingly grappling with more extreme cases, in which the physically and mentally incapacitated are bereft of all but the most minimal responses to others. It is worth noting that according to John Locke, who argued that "personhood" is contingent on active rationality and affective responses, such *persons* would not actually qualify as "persons." MacIntyre of course rejects this Lockean reductionism, and presses on to the problems that this Lockean logic imply: Can such persons be any more than passive objects of benevolence? Is it possible for disfigured, vulnerable, "dependent rational animals" to partake of the common good? What virtues, what qualities of character would we need if we were to receive from others what we need them to give us and give to others what they need to receive from us?

It is only through the practice of reasoning through the needs of others who are dependent on us—we must keep in mind that we also are dependent on others—that we can begin to identify their individual goods in the course of identifying our common goods. We can only identify both individual goods and common goods through shared deliberation, and through this process we learn to reason practically about the common good; we learn to, in effect, "reason politically."[20] Thus, when we engage in relationships that necessitate a consideration of ourselves as both depended-upon and dependent, we find that many of our goods are shared goods: what is good for Gollum is in fact good for Sam and Frodo. What is good for Frodo is good for Sam. What is good for Sam is good for Frodo. Consideration of what part certain goods are to play in my life are inseparable from the part that such goods are to play in the life of our community.

Here, however, is the catch that casts us back to the problem of Rousseau and the nature of pity: none of the aforementioned virtues can come to be

19. MacIntyre, *Dependent Rational Animals*, 136.
20. MacIntyre, *Dependent Rational Animals*, 140.

without pity, for we cannot recognize dependence and respond rightly to disfigurement without pity—at the bare minimum—or something which is both similar to it and yet surpasses it. Aquinas raises this objection in his *Summa Theologiae,* asking how taking pity could be a defect in the person who pities, given that God himself pities. This "something," which is both similar to pity and yet surpasses it, is *misericordia.* Thomas Aquinas probes the problem of *misericordia,* which can be translated as "pity" but which we ought to leave in Latin to avoid the connotative meaning of pity as pure sentiment, unguided by reason—sentimentality, a sign of moral failure. Most literally, *misericordia* means "miserum cor" or pitying heart. *Misericordia,* Aquinas teaches (citing St. Augustine), is a heartfelt grief or sorrow over another's distress, "impelling us to succor him if we can."[21] In order to establish the *motives* of pity, Aquinas turns to Aristotle, who in his *Rhetoric* defines pity as "sorrow for a visible evil, whether corruptive or distressing."[22] Such evils, he writes, provoke pity even more if they are contrary to deliberate choice, "when it is the result of an accident, as when something turns out ill, whereas we hoped well of it."[23] Finally, Aristotle argues, "we pity most the distress of one who suffers undeservedly."[24] Pity rightly practiced hinges on this word: *undeservedly.* Aquinas explains that it is of the nature of a fault to be voluntary, and as it is voluntary, it "deserves punishment rather than mercy."[25] However, because a fault "may be, in a way, a punishment, through having something connected with it that is against the sinner's will," it may call for *misericordia,* for pity.[26]

Although pity can be felt or demonstrated wrongly, then, it would be wrong and even dangerous for us to banish it from our hearts and minds. Both Aquinas and Aristotle note that a virtuous person looks upon his friend as another self, and so he counts his friend's grief as his own. But Aquinas, agreeing here with Rousseau, notes that a person can also feel pity with those who are not his friends, especially when he realizes that what has happened to another may happen to himself. The old and the wise, he says, know well that they may fall upon evil times, "as also feeble and timorous

21. Aquinas, *Summa Theologiae,* II-II, Q.30.

22. Aquinas, *Summa Theologiae,* II-II, Q.30.

23. Aquinas, *Summa Theologiae,* II-II, Q.30.

24. Aquinas, *Summa Theologiae,* II-II, Q.30.

25. Aquinas, *Summa Theologiae,* II-II, Q.30.

26. Aquinas, *Summa Theologiae,* II-II, Q.30.

persons, are more inclined to pity."[27] Others are naturally unlikely to know pity, especially "those who deem themselves happy, and so far powerful as to think themselves in no danger of suffering any hurt."[28] The proud are inclined to think that those who suffer have merited it; thinking the suffering wicked, they refrain from pity. The angry also are bereft of pity, for, as we read in Proverbs 27:4: "Anger hath no mercy, nor fury when it breaketh forth."

How, then, can we learn to pity rightly? First, we must learn the parameters of pity rightly understood. In the *Summa*, Aquinas considers the objection that pity cannot be a virtue. As Aristotle teaches, virtue is above all else a choice, "the desire of what has been already counselled."[29] But pity seems to hinder counsel. In addition, mercy seems to belong to the appetitive power; as a feeling, it cannot be an intellectual virtue, and because God is not its object, it cannot be a theological virtue. Finally, because it does not belong to justice, and is not about passions, pity cannot be a moral virtue. Aquinas admits that distress over another's distress may be a mere movement of the sensitive appetite. But we must not on these grounds discard it, as "in another way, it may denote a movement of the intellective appetite, in as much as one person's evil is displeasing to another. This movement may be ruled in accordance with reason, and in accordance with this movement regulated by reason, the movement of the lower appetite may be regulated."[30] Augustine, too, knew that this was true, for in *The City of God* he argues that "this movement of the mind obeys the reason, when mercy is vouchsafed in such a way that justice is safeguarded," for instance when we give to the needy or forgive the repentant.[31] Pity, then, *misericordia*, is a virtue, insofar as it is practiced justly, which is to say according to reason.

Tolkien's text contains a remarkable reference to this virtue, which is evident through Gandalf's response to Frodo. When at first Frodo admits that he does "not feel any pity for Gollum," and contends that "he deserves death," that he wishes Bilbo would have stabbed "the vile creature, when he had the chance!" Gandalf insists that, on the contrary, Bilbo embodied "Pity, and Mercy: not to strike without need."[32] Does the text suggest that Frodo does in fact possess *misericordia*, or is his response limited to the shallow pool of pity? Doesn't his pity only expose him to Sméagol's secret

27. Aquinas, *Summa Theologiae*, II-II, Q.30.

28. Aquinas, *Summa Theologiae*, II-II, Q.30.

29. Aquinas, *Summa Theologiae*, II-II, Q.30.

30. Aquinas, *Summa Theologiae*, II-II, Q.30.

31. Aquinas, *Summa Theologiae*, II-II, Q.30.

32. Tolkien, *The Lord of the Rings*, 615.

designs, and doesn't any sense that Sméagol, Frodo, and Sam all share some common project that promises a common good merely set the hobbits up for Sméagol's deception? After all, though they depend upon the creature to show them the way to Mount Doom, he leads them instead to Shelob, circumventing his fealty with a labyrinthine logic worthy of only the most cynical law clerk. Shelob herself is naturally incapable of the common good, insofar as she is not a rational creature; as De Koninck notes, knowledge of irrational animals is bound and restricted to the sensible and singular. Explicit action toward a common good presupposes knowledge which is universal, and this knowledge presupposes a rationality which Shelob lacks. We learn that "her lust was not [Gollum's] lust. Little she knew of or cared for towers, or rings, or anything devised by mind or hand, who only desired death for all others, mind and body, and for herself a glut of life, alone, swollen till the mountains could no longer hold her up and the darkness could not contain her."[33] In an "inner chamber of his cunning, which he still hopes to hide from her," and which he certainly hides from Sam and Frodo, Gollum plots the Ringbearer's death, hoping that he and Shelob can partake of a common evil insofar as what will satisfy her craving for sweet meat will bring about a scenario wherein, once she "throws away the bones and the empty garments, we shall find it, we shall get it, the Precious, a reward for poor Sméagol who brings nice food."[34]

Gollum perfectly incarnates De Koninck's contention that "[e]ven the secrets of the heart must be conformed and ordered to the common; they are purely means; they must always be conformed to the order established by God."[35] Although we may be inclined to think otherwise, even in our most interior, secret thoughts, "we are not ourselves the supreme rule, otherwise those secret thoughts," if they are good, "would be good simply because they are our singular possession, and because they concern only us."[36]

Although Gollum is not, like Shelob, capable only of operating on the level of senses—that is, though he does have a rational capacity, Gollum's long possession of the Ring has left him with a mind preoccupied almost exclusively with his own private good. And so he loses his dignity, as to achieve it, he would, De Koninck demonstrates, need to "submit[] his private good to the common good."[37] Sméagol is not alone in this regard. We must not, like Sam and Frodo, try to dig an intellectual or imaginative trench between

33. Tolkien, *The Lord of the Rings*, 723–24.
34. Tolkien, *The Lord of the Rings*, 724.
35. De Koninck, "On the Primacy of the Common Good."
36. De Koninck, "On the Primacy of the Common Good."
37. De Koninck, "On the Primacy of the Common Good."

him and ourselves. Our good, the good of the intellect, is not assured by our own nature. As the sensitive life is first in us, we are unable to achieve acts of reason except by passing first through the senses, and, "as long as man is not rectified by the cardinal virtues which must be acquired, he is drawn principally towards the private good against the good of the intellect."[38]

We can justly argue that Frodo demonstrates genuine *misericordia* towards Sméagol. Sméagol, on the other hand, absorbs the goods of this public virtue into the hell of his own private good. In Sméagol we witness a profound loss of dignity, as he has habitually withered away his own rationality. As Aquinas hauntingly argues, "By sinning, man sets himself outside the order of reason, and consequently, he loses human dignity, as namely man is naturally free and existing for himself, and he places himself in some way in the servitude of animals . . . for the bad man is worse than an animal."[39] In placing themselves under the guide of a more-than-animalistic creature, Frodo and Sam ultimately subject themselves to his worse-than-animal aims.

After Sméagol nearly succeeds in actualizing his web of deceit, the problem of pity emerges again at the very Crack of Doom. As Gollum struggles to throttle his master, Sam sees "these two rivals with other vision. A crouching shape, scarcely more than the shadow of a living thing, a creature now wholly ruined and defeated, yet filled with a hideous lust and rage; and before it stood stern, untouchable now by pity, a figure robed in white, but at its breast it held a wheel of fire."[40] From out of this struggle the figure robed in white, the figure "untouchable now by pity" tells the creature wholly defeated, "If you touch me ever again, you shall be cast yourself into the Fire of Doom."[41] No longer does Frodo pause before the possibility of death as fitting punishment for Sméagol.

And yet the only one capable of killing the creature himself stalls at the threshold of death. First he leaps forward, blade drawn, but when Sméagol pathetically imagines a future wherein he "dies into the dust," Sam's hand wavers:

> His mind was hot with wrath and the memory of evil. It would be just to slay this treacherous, murderous creature, just and many times deserved; and also it seemed the only safe thing to do. But deep in his heart there was something that restrained him: he could not strike this thing lying in the dust, forlorn,

38. De Koninck, "On the Primacy of the Common Good."
39. Aquinas, *De Regno*, 6.
40. Tolkien, *The Lord of the Rings*, 944.
41. Tolkien, *The Lord of the Rings*, 944.

ruinous, utterly wretched. He himself, though only for a little while, had borne the Ring, and now dimly he guessed the agony of Gollum's shrivelled mind and body, enslaved to that Ring, unable to find peace or relief ever in life again. But Sam had no words to express what he felt.[42]

Now Sam, not Frodo, chooses the virtue of *misericordia* over the virtue of *justice*. "It would be just to slay this treacherous, murderous creature," he says, repeating the word "just" as though to incite himself into being the instrument of that justice.[43]

At the precipice of the Cracks of Mount Doom, Tolkien takes us beyond the politics of Middle-earth and into divine *misericordia*. After all of the narrow escapes, all of the certain dooms, Frodo fails. "'I have come,' he said. 'But I do not choose now to do what I came to do. I will not do this deed. The Ring is mine!'"[44] At first it seems as though this passage situates Frodo as incapable of ethical action. He *cannot* choose to do what he came to do. As Aristotle argues in *Nicomachean Ethics,* and as Aquinas affirms, an action is ethical only insofar as it is freely chosen. Actions that are truly forced are not to be judged according to ethical categories. But Frodo is not actually *beyond* choice, or incapable of choice. He makes his choice, and he chooses his private—not, by the way, his proper personal—good over the common good of the common project around which so much of Middle-earth has rallied. Frodo has committed a personalist error insofar as he is acting as though "individual persons are themselves goods willed first of all for themselves, and in themselves superior to the good of the accidental whole whose constitution out of them is a kind of consequence and complement of their own existence."[45] Only one who has lost sight of the consonance of personal good and common good, who has eclipsed the common good with an exaggerated elevation of the private good, could so fail.

Of this moment at the Crack of Doom Tolkien writes in his letters:

> Frodo had done what he could and spent himself completely (as an instrument of divine Providence) and had produced a situation in which the object of his quest could be achieved. His humility (with which he began) and his sufferings were justly rewarded by the highest honour; and his exercise of patience

---

42. Tolkien, *The Lord of the Rings,* 944–45.

43. Tolkien, *The Lord of the Rings,* 945.

44. Tolkien, *The Lord of the Rings,* 945.

45. De Koninck, "On the Primacy of the Common Good."

and mercy toward Gollum gained him Mercy; his failure was redressed."[46]

This "redress" comes in grotesque form, as "Gollum's long hands draw up-wards to his mouth; his white fangs gleamed, and then snapped as they bit. Frodo gave a cry, and there he was, fallen upon his knees at the chasm's edge."[47] Notice that Tolkien does not give us a scene wherein Frodo, first failing, recovers and collects himself in time to shove Sméagol off the cliff. Instead, "even as his eyes were lifted up to gloat on his prize," Sméagol steps too far, quavers at the edge for just a moment, and falls. "Out of the depths came his last wail *Precious*, and he was gone."[48] In Tolkien's interpretation of his own work, he gives us a hobbit who gains *misericordia* from God for showing *misericordia* toward Gollum. However, we must add to Tolkien's interpretation two things. First, if Gollum's biting of the finger is the form of this *mercy*, then *misericordia* can also take the form of a kind of punish-ment. That is, if grace, in this moment, finishes what Frodo alone fails to accomplish, it does so in a manner that permanently mars Frodo's body. Grace does not merely perfect nature, it also punishes it even as it achieves a good common to all of Middle-earth. Perhaps this punishment is part of the perfection. Whatever the case, this *misericordia-iustitia* has more than Frodo as its end. For, if Frodo's quest was all along one wherein his proper personal good would come as a consequence of the common good, and if his failure had been final, would have had consequences that would have covered Middle-earth, so the justice-mercy of God, proper to his particular person, is also superabundant:

> Let us recall once more that the common good is said to be com-mon in its superabundance and in its incommensurability with the singular good. The properly Divine good is so great that it cannot be the proper good even of the whole of creation; the latter will always have in some way the character of a part.[49]

The Return of *De Regno*: Aragorn and Aquinas on Kingship and the Common Good

At least one critic, Colleen Donnelly, has rightly read in Tolkien the eleva-tion of a society "where the needs of the 'common good' of the whole society

46. Tolkien et al., *Letters*, 326.
47. Tolkien, *The Lord of the Rings*, 946.
48. Tolkien, *The Lord of the Rings*, 946.
49. De Koninck, "On the Primacy of the Common Good."

and one's contribution to it far exceed the significance of an individual's needs and accomplishments."[50] We see this in that Middle-earth is saved not merely through the lone quest of Frodo, or by Aragorn descending in some single-handed *deus ex machina,* but through the commitment of innumerable characters—kings and seemingly insignificant hobbits, among others—to the common good. Fealty to political protagonists is part of the education into the common good. As Tolkien noted in a radio interview with Denys Gueroult of the BBC, "I'm rather wedded to those kinds of loyalties, because I think (contrary to most people) that touching your cap to the squire may be bad for the squire but damn good for you."[51] Without the loyalty of followers—if all, for instance, strive to hold the position of leader—the common good will not return.

In hailing the return of the common good to Middle-earth in the form of a king, Tolkien decidedly departs from modern suspicions that one ruler is synonymous with, or inevitably turns into, tyranny. Here he finds good company with Thomas Aquinas, who, in his treatise on kingship, contends that a single ruler is best able to "procure the unity of peace." Aquinas himself, living long before the terrible tyrannies of the twentieth century, grasps that many hesitate to choose kingship as the best regime because they are fearful that it will degenerate: "Because both the best and worse can occur in a monarchy—that is, under government by one—the evil of tyranny has rendered the dignity of kingship odious to many."[52] Those who have experienced—or imagined—life under the rule of one who syphons that which should be designated for the common good for his own personal stores, and who "oppresses his subjects in a variety of ways, according to the different passions to which he is subject as he tries to secure whatever goods he desires," are rightfully terrified of tyranny. Those who strive after virtue, and who are capable of excellence may be especially wary, in that tyrants "who rule their subjects rather than benefit them put every obstacle in the way of their progress, being suspicious of any excellence in their subjects that might threaten their own wicked rule."[53]

Saruman comes to mind as one who, despite claiming to desire partnership with Gandalf as he strives after dominion, may well be trying to configure a way by which he can stifle the excellence of his fellow wizard, for tyrants "endeavor to prevent their subjects from becoming virtuous and increasing in nobility of spirit, lest they refuse to bear their unjust

50. Donelly, "Feudal Values, Vassalage, and Fealty in *The Lord of the Rings*," 17.

51. Donelly, "Feudal Values, Vassalage, and Fealty in *The Lord of the Rings*," 17.

52. Aquinas, *De Regno*, 15.

53. Aquinas, *De Regno*, 13.

dominion."[54] We have a further picture of this in Saruman's manifestation as Sharkey in the Shire. When the Fellowship arrives home, the thick hospitality so characteristic of their home has been replaced by an austerity coupled with paranoia in the inn.[55] As we noted earlier, Gandalf observes of that metaphysical tyrant Sauron that "the only measure that he knows is desire, desire for power; and so he judges all hearts. Into his heart the thought will not enter that any will refuse it, that having the Ring we may seek to destroy it."[56] Likewise, Aquinas gives us a portrait of the tyrant as one who "endeavor[s] to prevent anyone from becoming powerful or rich, because, suspecting their subjects according to their own evil conscience, they fear that, just as they themselves use power and riches to do harm, so the power and wealth of their subjects will be used to do harm to them in return."[57] Aquinas does not, then, gloss over or unduly dismiss the perils of one-man rule, but argues that "the rule of many turns into tyranny more rather than less frequently than that of one."[58] If several rule, and dissension divides them, often one who is superior will appropriate dominion over the community.

In *De regimine principum*, Aquinas notes that individuals differ in terms of their private interests, but with regard to the common good they are united: "It is fitting, therefore, that . . . there should be something which promotes the common good of the many," and that when things are organized into a unity "something is found that rules them all."[59] This something is the king, the ruler who in his oneness accords with the principle that "those things are best which are most natural": as the body is ruled by one part (the heart), and the soul is ruled by reason, and, "in the whole universe one God is the Maker and Ruler of all."[60]

54. Aquinas, *De Regno*, 14.

55. Tolkien, *The Lord of the Rings*, 999.

56. Tolkien, *The Lord of the Rings*, 269.

57. Aquinas, *De Regno*, 14.

58. Aquinas, *De Regno*, 17.

59. Aquinas, *De Regno*, 7.

60. Aquinas, *De Regno*, 11.

Monotheism and Political Theology in Middle-earth: Erik Peterson's "Monotheism as a Political Problem" and Tolkien's Divine Court in *The Silmarillion*

Aquinas's affiliation, by analogy, of one God and one Ruler, is not without problems. In "Monotheism as a Political Problem," Erik Peterson calls our attention to an antiquity wherein a deep-seated political theology authorized earthly monarchical rule by means of the heavenly rule of one God. When the Trinitiarian theology established at the Council of Nicaea prevailed over Arianism—which, in subjugating the Son to the Father, opened the possibility of such a political theology within Christianity—the "supranational kingship of Christ" was revealed to admit no imperial or national rivals.

Tolkien may not overtly posit Aragorn as analogous to Ilúvatar, but the fact that Ilúvatar, the one Creator God of Middle-earth, is depicted with language fit for a king, makes the link between the two more than implicit. Before we proceed with a direct analysis of Aragorn's kingship, then, we must consider to what extent the earthly king is God's viceregent on Middle-earth, and what dangers emerge when we consider the political problems inherent in such divine authorizations as articulated by Erik Peterson.

In *The Silmarillion,* after the Ainur, or angels, make a map, in music, of the World, "Ilúvatar gave to their vision Being, and set it amid the Void, and the Secret Fire was sent to burn at the heart of the World; and it was called Eä."[61] Tolkien told Clyde Kilby that "the Secret Fire sent to burn at the heart of the World in the beginning was the Holy Spirit."[62] Christopher Scarf contends that we see "implicitly at least, two persons of the Holy Trinity mirrored in Ilúvatar (the Allfather) and in the 'Secret Fire.'"[63] Tolkien explicitly strives to make his myth consonant with a cosmos created and loved by a Trinitarian God. In his letter to Milton Waldman, Tolkien's participation in political theology is profoundly apparent. Here he analyzes the Ainur as "angelic powers, whose function is to exercise delegated authority in their spheres (of rule and government, *not* creation, making or remaking) . . . Their powerful wisdom is derived from their knowledge of the cosmogonical drama, which they perceived as a drama . . . and later as a 'reality.'"[64] Here, Tolkien appears to echo Plato in that power is directly connected to knowledge. Further, the political dimension of angelic existence is made

---

61. Tolkien, *Silmarillion*, 15.

62. Quoted in Scarf, *The Ideal of Kingship in Lewis, Tolkien, Williams*, 128.

63. Scarf, *The Ideal of Kingship in Lewis, Tolkien, Williams*, 128.

64. Tolkien et al., *Letters*, 146.

clear in that they exercise "delegated authority . . . of rule and government."[65] These Ainur, which "certain angelic Beings (created but at least as powerful as the gods of human mythologies)," were the "agents and viceregents of Eru (God)."[66] Tolkien contends that they "can be accepted—well, shall we say badly, by a mind that believes in the Blessed Trinity."[67] Tolkien directly affiliated viceregents with those who act in the name of the king, a fact that Christopher Scarf corroborates: "The Anglo-Saxon king was also, as 'king by the grace of God, *dei vicarious,* vicar of God, thus his viceregent."[68] It is entirely within reason, then, to read Tolkien's Eru as a monarch.

Still, in the early drafts of *The Silmarillion,* such as those found in *The Lost Road,* Tolkien first uses the word king in a negative sense, when "Morgoth forged for himself a great crown of iron, and he called himself the King of the World."[69] Of course, Morgoth gives *himself* this title, just as Stalin granted to himself the title of "General Secretary"; these rulers' self-given titles bring to mind Aristotle's understanding of tyranny as a perversion of kingship.[70] In other words, Tolkien's elevation of the rule of one, and of kingship, is not so sanguine that it leaves out the total domination that tempts the ambitious to one-man rule.

In *The Silmarillion,* the larger narrative clearly shows that not all who assume the title king embody its dignity. Morgoth wants "to be called Lord, and to be a master over other wills," and he claims the earth as "his own kingdom," but Manwë, the goodly angelic being who is described as "king" of the Valar, reproves him: he says, "This kingdom thou shalt not take for thine own, wrongfully, for many others have labored here no less than though."[71] Christopher Scarf clarifies that Manwë intervenes "using his authority as Ilúvatar's viceregent."[72] Tolkien incorporates the language of "kingdom" yet again when he writes, in "Valaquenta," that the Ainur who entered the world have the task of laboring "in the regions of Ea [until] the Kingdom of Earth" is made."[73]

Manwë 's criticism of Melkor's (Morgoth's) lust for singular rule is clearly not a wholesale condemnation of kingship as a political form. In *The*

65. Scarf, *The Ideal of Kingship in Lewis, Tolkien, Williams,* 132–33.

66. Scarf, *The Ideal of Kingship in Lewis, Tolkien, Williams,* 128.

67. Tolkien et al., *Letters,* 146.

68. Scarf, *The Ideal of Kingship in Lewis, Tolkien, Williams,* 118.

69. Tolkien, *Silmarillion,* 87.

70. Scarf, *The Ideal of Kingship in Lewis, Tolkien, Williams,* 130.

71. Tolkien, *Silmarillion,* 8.

72. Scarf, *The Ideal of Kingship in Lewis, Tolkien, Williams,* 132.

73. Tolkien, *Silmarillion,* 15.

Silmarillion Manwë himself receives the title "King of the World of Valar and Elves and Men."[74] Still further, we can find more direct links between Ilúvatar and kingship by turning to the Hebrew Bible, the presence of divine kingship of which, Christopher Scarf claims, must surely have exercised an at least subconscious influence on Tolkien's myth.

"Though God in Ancient Hebrew does not have a crown," Alison Salvesen notes, "he does have a throne, symbolizing his kingship."[75] Here we can make a connection with Ilúvatar, as in *The Book of Lost Tales* we find that the Ainur sing before "the seat of Ilúvatar . . . after the Great End," the word *seat* signifying, like Yahweh's, "divine throne."[76] Ilúvatar ruled his heavenly host as a theocracy under his kingship, and Like Yahweh, Ilúvatar is the sole Creator of Tolkien's mythology. This similarity does not override the important fact that while Yahweh creates through Wisdom, though, Ilúvatar does so through thought.

Ilúvatar's delegation is pronounced through the Valar's acting as sub-creators, to the point that, for Tolkien scholar Verlyn Flieger, these angels are "more comparable" to *Elohîm,* the Hebrew word for God "as multiplicity," by which she means not multiple gods but rather "God in all his aspects."[77] And yet, Tolkien's 1951 letter to Waldman clearly delineates Manwë as a secondary figure, not an *aspect* of God. Tolkien hedges the theological place of the Ainur carefully, explaining that the Valar "take the imaginative but not the theological place of 'gods.'"[78] Christopher Scarf well-establishes the correlation between Tolkien's angels and Hebrew angelology, in which angels "who were elemental spirits connected sometimes with natural phenomenon like the wind, clouds, fire, etc." even as the Valar are "spirits" of Water (Ulmo), Winds (Manwë), Fire (Melkor). We see that Ilúvatar "is depicted as being *with* the Valar, *his* 'choir of angels,' like Yahweh with 'the whole host of heaven standing around him,'" and, as such, is revealed as "the One"; the God of Tolkien's mythology thus appears to be as monotheistic as Yahweh in the Hebrew Bible.[79]

But if in his *legendarium* Tolkien takes great pains to create a mythology as though written both before and yet entirely consistent with the revelation of Christ "in parallel with the Israelites' Hope, in *Morgoth's Ring* Tolkien expects that one day Ilúvatar would need to 'intervene in person'

74. Scarf, *The Ideal of Kingship in Lewis, Tolkien, Williams,* 133.

75. Quoted in Scarf, *The Ideal of Kingship in Lewis, Tolkien, Williams,* 137.

76. Scarf, *The Ideal of Kingship in Lewis, Tolkien, Williams,* 139.

77. Flieger, *Splintered Light,* 54.

78. Tolkien et al., *Letters,* 284.

79. Tolkien, *Morgoth's Ring,* 141.

because of what was, in Christian terms, the Fall, here the Fall of the angels through Melkor."[80]

Tolkien takes a decidedly Thomistic stance concerning kingship, even as he articulates an affinity with anarchy. He admits that his "political opinions lean more and more to Anarchy (philosophically understood, meaning abolition of control not whiskered men with bombs) or to 'unconstitutional' Monarchy."[81] How can Tolkien embrace unconstitutional Monarchy when the implications of such sovereignty in modernity veritably guarantee the secularization of originally theological concepts, a phenomenon articulated by Peterson's interlocutor Carl Schmitt in his work *Political Theology*?

It seems that, just as Thomas Aquinas is unwilling to surrender the goods of kingship because the existence of tyrants has demeaned its dignity, Tolkien is unwilling to surrender even those things that Hitler has coopted and corrupted. If one of these, as we saw earlier, is the Nazi degradation of the true and good nobility of the northern myths, which Tolkien wishes to restore to their proper goodness, another is the Holy Roman Empire. The official title of the German kingdom, which existed as empire from 911 through 1806, was the Holy Roman Empire. For Nazi leader Alfred Rosenberg, Emperor Otto, who reigned from 936–973 A.D., "had been the founder of a 'German national church,' and had brought the papacy in subjection to himself."[82] Rosenberg further read the Saxon lords as forerunners of the German colonization of eastern territories. Himmler, the same man who instituted an archaeological expedition to tie Nazi Germany with Atlantis, under the influence of astrologists and fantasists close to the SS, saw himself as the "reincarnation" of Holy Roman Emperor Henry I, and believed that he would "complete his work of the subjection of the East."[83] Himmler went so far as to celebrate the 1,000th anniversary of Henry's death, in 1936, by praising him as a powerful ruler who did not tolerate the Church getting involved in political events. Hitler himself praised Charlemagne's cultural creativity, his capacity to organize, and his renunciation of individual freedom, but he again saw himself as completing on a more global scale what Charlemagne only achieved toward the south.

Tolkien, too, mythologized the Holy Roman Empire, but whereas Hitler strove to do so in a fashion that would, like Hegel and Saruman, allow his Second Reality to eclipse the First, Tolkien's is explicitly a *legend*, a Secondary World, even if, as Bradley Birzer notes, "it . . . became a myth

80. Tolkien, *Morgoth's Ring*, 142.

81. Tolkien et al., *Letters*, 63.

82. Blamires, *World Fascism*, 321.

83. Blamires, *World Fascism*, 321.

for the restoration of Christendom itself."[84] For Tolkien, the Holy Roman Empire connotes not political mastery of the Church, but Anglo-Saxon missionaries such as St. Boniface of Crediton, who carried classical and Christian traditions to barbarian Europe, thereby initiating the synthesis of medieval world. St. Boniface would come to crown Pepin, Charles Martel's son, opening the gates for papal recognition of Charlemagne's "revived Holy Roman Empire in 800 A.D.," this initiating not political mastery of the Church, but a unification of the natural political order and the supernatural Church.[85] Tolkien himself saw in Aragorn's return to his rightful throne that "the progress of the tale ends in what is far more like the re-establishment of an effective Holy Roman Empire with its seat in Rome."[86] As Birzer unveils, in Tolkien's own private writings he "equated numerous parts of Italy with various geographical aspects of Gondor . . . In his diary, for example, Tolkien recorded that with his trip to Italy, he had 'come to the head of Christendom: an exile from the borders and far provinces returning home, or at least to the home of the fathers.'"[87] Still more, Tolkien wrote to a friend that he had holidayed "in Gondor, or in modern parlance, Venice."[88] Not only kingship, but kingship in the vein of the Holy Roman Empire, then, sits and reigns from the center of Tolkien's *legendarium*.

Of course, the Holy Roman Empire has provoked innumerable discontents. Erik Peterson argues that when the God of the Jews was fused with the monarchical principle of the Greek philosophers, divine monarchy becomes primarily a means of political-theological propaganda used by the Jews. "This political-theological propaganda," he continues, "was taken over by the Church in its expansion into the Roman Empire."[89] At this point the Church was brought into conflict with pagan political theology, which posited both a reigning divine Monarch and reigning national gods. Christian critics contended that national gods could not rule because the Roman Empire should logically signal the end of national pluralism. Finally, "the divine Monarchy was bound to flounder on the Trinitarian dogma, and the interpretation of the Pax Augusta on Christian eschatology. In this way not only was monotheism as a political problem resolved and the Christian faith liberated from bondage to the Roman Empire," but we witnessed a "fundamental break" with every political theology that appropriates "the Christian

84. Birzer, *Tolkien's Sanctifying Myth*, 42.

85. Birzer, *Tolkien's Sanctifying Myth*, 43.

86. Quoted in Birzer, *Tolkien's Sanctifying Myth*, 43.

87. Birzer, *Tolkien's Sanctifying Myth*, 43.

88. Birzer, *Tolkien's Sanctifying Myth*, 43.

89. Peterson, "Monotheism as a Political Problem," 104.

proclamation for the justification of a political situation."[90] Christianity, Peterson claims, signals the end of political theology, which could only exist within paganism and Judaism. Peterson ends his essay with a bold proclamation: just as the mystery of the Trinity exists not in Creation but only in the Godhead, so "the peace that the Christian seeks is won by no emperor, but is solely a gift of him who 'is higher than all understanding.'" An Augustinian through-and-through (his marvelous essay begins with a prayer to St. Augustine), Peterson goes beyond Augustine in his absolute rejection of the peace which can be brought by an emperor.[91] It is possible to reject the equation of "One God = One King" without capitulating the goods of either political peace or a Christian Emperor.[92]

In his *City of God* Augustine considers what we might mean when we say that a Christian emperor is "blessed."[93] We certainly do not mean that they are happy through an extended reign, or because, dying in peace, they bequeathed their kingdoms to their heirs. Nor do we mean that they are "blessed" because they "conquered the enemies of the republic, or because they were warned in time to put down the rebellions of the seditious citizens."[94] Augustine does not denounce these things as evil; he merely rejects them as carrying the particular weight of the word *blessed*, a distinction he is eager to make because those emperors who have worshipped pagan gods, who did not belong to the City of God, have likewise experienced such things. Rather,

> We call those Christian emperors happy who govern with justice, who are not puffed up by the tongues of flatterers or the services of sycophants [Wormtongues], but remember they are men. We call them happy when they think of sovereignty as a ministry of God and use it for the spread of true religion, when they fear and love and worship God . . . when they are slow to punish, quick to forgive; when they punish, not out of private revenge, but only when forced by the order and security of the

90. Peterson, "Monotheism as a Political Problem," 104.

91. Peterson also, by the way, shows his selectivity when he excludes the evidence of the word "monarch" in the psalms from informing the outcome of his argument. "It is inappropriate," he writes, "to take the word 'monarchy' so seriously in a hymn. The language of prayer and hymnody has its own laws (72).

92. I should note, in this context, that I find problematic Augustine's praise of those emperors—Christian or otherwise—who, for instance, coerce Donatists to return to the Catholic fold, his claim that they serve "Him by enforcing with suitable rigor such laws as ordain what is righteous, and punish what is reverse" (Augustine, *Letters*, 428).

93. Augustine, *City of God*, 117.

94. Augustine, *City of God*, 117.

republic, and when they pardon, not to encourage impunity, but with the hope of reform; when they temper with mercy and generosity the inevitable hardness of their decrees.[95]

Augustine's words, if they rightly posit the goods of heaven as supreme, do not call for a chasm between the peace and justice of this world and the hereafter. Aragorn might almost wear these words as his royal garments, but for the fact that he reigns long before the birth of Christ. Certainly, though, Augustine's characterization of the Christian Emperor paves the way for Tolkien's embrace of the Holy Roman Empire—though not the Roman Empire itself, and not in a falsely triumphalist, propagandizing way.

In a 1944 letter to his son Christopher, Tolkien muses on a future ruled by Communism and Americanism. He trembles before the prospect of a world defined by the Americans' "great standardized amalgamations with their mass-produced notions and emotions," and wonders "what kind of mass manias the Soviets can produce."[96] Christopher and himself, Tolkien proposes, "belong to the ever-defeated never altogether subdued side," a third contingent that resists both Americanism and Communism, hoping that "propaganda defeats itself, and even produces its opposite effect."[97] What they are seeing with the ascendancy of Nazi Germany, with the battle between Nazism, Americanism, and Communism, he contends, has "always been going on in different terms . . . [and] I should have hated the Roman Empire in its day (as I do), and remained a patriotic Roman citizen while preferring a free Gaul and seeing good in Carthaginians."[98] Such a blending of the Roman and barbarian ethos did indeed come—in the form of the Holy Roman Empire.

However, Tolkien's "application" of Middle-earth to the Holy Roman Empire further problematizes any efforts to relegate his understanding of the relationship between Ilúvatar, Aragorn, and kingship to a world before the full revelation of the Trinitarian God. His indication that Aragorn incarnates a reestablishment of the Holy Roman Empire in the sense of a redeemed relationship between the Church and the Emperor situates Tolkien among a long line of Catholics given to anticipating the Return of a King. In his peculiar book *Catholic Prophecy,* Yves Du Pont collects hundreds of prophecies that span more than a millennium, and, sifting through them, he constructs a narrative wherein, after the Church is disorganized, leaderless, and split, Europe is invaded by agents of atrocity. Into this doom enters a

95. Augustine, *City of God*, 118.
96. Tolkien et al., *Letters*, 89.
97. Tolkien et al., *Letters*, 89.
98. Tolkien et al., *Letters*, 89.

soldier around whom Christians rally, even as their chances are overwhelmingly slim. After a series of cataclysms, a new Roman Empire emerges, and its Emperor, a Christian King, works hand-in-hand with the Pope.

I cannot here cite, in a comprehensive manner, the varied prophecies which Du Pont assembles as the basis of his narrative, but will excerpt just a few, so as to give a sense of the parts:

> *Monk Adso* (10th century): Some of our teachers say that a King of the Franks will possess the entire Roman Empire. He will be the greatest and last of all the Monarchs.[99]

> *Melanie Calbat* (The Seeress of La Salette, 19th Century): After a frightful war a Great King will arise and his reign will be marked by a wonderful peace and a great religious revival.[100]

> *St. Cataldus* (5th Century): The Great king will wage war until the age of forty. He will assemble great armies, and hurl back the tyrants out of his empire.[101]

As Dupont, whose first book on prophecy was published in Paris in 1959, remarks in his commentary to the prophecies:

> All this talk about Kings, Thrones, and Kingdoms may well seem so hopelessly out-of-date that the reader may be tempted to dismiss all these prophecies as rank nonsense. I am well aware of this; we have all been brought up in the belief that popular forms of government mean progress, and that democracy and progress are inseparable. Under these premises, a return to non-popular forms of government, it is thought, must needs mean a return to the Dark ages.[102]

With his detachment from popular forms of government, and his language of "return," this may well be Tolkien writing. Du Pont goes on to caution rosy-colored assessments of the modern world. He contends that "history of past civilization[s] shows that governments have been in the main non-popular, and no one will deny that some of the extinct civilizations reached very high standards indeed."[103] Further, wars under these non-popular forms of government, unlike they do now—and, we might add, unlike Sauron's war—"did not involve the *whole* nation and the *whole* people . . . but only the regular armies of professional soldiers . . . the myth

---

99. Du Pont, *Catholic Prophecy*, 18.

100. Du Pont, *Catholic Prophecy*, 13.

101. Du Pont, *Catholic Prophecy*, 13.

102. Du Pont, *Catholic Prophecy*, 27.

103. Du Pont, *Catholic Prophecy*, 27.

of 'popular sovereignty' soon gave rise to the very real curse of popular involvement in war," a curse which Tolkien, who fought in World War I under this regime of large-scale conscription, knew too well.[104]

Tolkien, as a Catholic whose sympathies lay with monarchy, and deeply familiar with the medieval world, and privy to prophecy at least in that it prophecies of the legends come true in both *The Hobbit* and *The Lord of the Rings,* may have been doing more, with his *legendarium,* than creating a mythology into which he absorbed and preserved the heritage of Christendom. He may have been imaginatively anticipating the fulfillment of so many Catholic prophecies in *The Return of the King.* It is in this sense that he also goes beyond a mere literary indebtedness to the Arthurian "Golden Age king," which Stratford Caldecott,[105] among others, establishes.[106] Tolkien infamously resisted the allegorical imagination, and found unsatisfying the Arthur story and any other "Christian myths" which "conform [themselves] to [their] own supreme archetype, the story of Christ, which is both myth and history. Just as Christ gathered his twelve disciples, so Arthur gathered his knights."[107] Jane Chance helps us further distinguish Aragorn from the "Germanic king Theoden," who "serves primarily heroically after his contest with Wormtongue, giving leadership in battle and loving and paternal treatment of his warriors outside it," riding at the head of his troop as they near the city.[108] As "Christian king," Chance contends, Aragorn is defined by "his moral heroism as a healer rather than his valor as a destroyer," characteristics that fulfill the words of Ioerth, Gondor's wise woman, who declares *"The hands of the king are the hands of a healer, and so shall the rightful king be known."*[109] Long before his ascendancy as King Elessar, Aragorn cares for Frodo after the horrors of Weathertop, as well as Frodo and Sam after Moria, and, after the battle of the Pelennor Fields,[110] he tends Merry, Eowyn, and Faramir. As Karen Simpson Nikakis notes, the imposition of order on the realm can only come after Minas Ithil is "utterly destroyed," so that the

104. Du Pont, *Catholic Prophecy*, 27.

105. Although Tolkien denied the influence of the Arthurian legends on his own, Caldecott makes a compelling case that this influence did in fact exist, not least because "King Elessar [Aragorn] is associated with a green stone (the Elfstone after which his house is named) . . . For in Wolfram von Eschenback's tale *Parzifal,* the Holy Grail is formed out of a green stone that fell from Lucifer's crown when he was struck down by St. Michael" (164).

106. Caldecott, *The Power of the Ring*, 164.

107. Caldecott, *The Power of the Ring*, 163.

108. Chance, *Tolkien's Art*, 176.

109. Chance, *Tolkien's Art*, 176.

110. Tolkien, *The Lord of the Rings*, 844–53.

land can begin to heal.[111] This healing of the land itself reaches its peak in the blossoming of the White Tree, the eldest of trees that eclipses the withered tree in the Court of the Fountain in Gondor.[112]

Aragorn's "Christian kingship" is further exemplified in his decision to die in a sacrificial manner. Nikakis turns beyond the last pages of the novel to the Appendices of *The Return of the King,* wherein Aragorn *decides* the time of his death. At the appointed time, he is "laid down on the long bed that had been prepared for him," and he declares, to Arwen, "Lo! We have gathered and we have spent, and now the time of payment draws near"—this after has been given to him "not only a span thrice that of Men of Middle-earth, but also the grace to go at my will, and *give back the gift.*"[113] Substitutionary sacrifice melds with gift in Aragorn's Christian death.

Aragorn is also "Christlike" in his humility, not least in his hesitation before assuming the throne. If the tyrant is in part defined in the aforementioned desire and even demand for "recognition," then Aragorn is remarkable in that, though rightful heir, he has spent countless years as an unrecognized Ranger, a suffering servant whose unremarkable appearance brings to bind the messianic prophecies of Isaiah. His apparent lack of pedigree moves the increasingly tyrannical Denethor to refuse "to be the dotard chamberlain of an upstart . . . I will not bow to such a one, last of a ragged house long bereft of lordship and dignity."[114] Having spent long years unrecognized, chastened to a sacrificial life without reward, even after the battle of the Pelennor Fields Aragorn resists Eomer's insistence that he make his claim upon the kingship of Gondor. "I deem the time unripe," Aragorn says, "and I have no mind for strife except with our Enemy and his servants."[115] Even at the brink of the Last Battle, Aragorn hopes in the fealty of the lords and leaders, rather than imposing his sovereignty like Leviathan:

> As I have begun, so I will go on. We come now to the very brink, where hope and despair are akin. To waver is to fall. Let none now reject the counsels of Gandalf, whose long labours against Sauron come at last to their test. But for him all would long ago have been lost. Nonetheless I do not yet claim to command any man. Let others choose as they will.[116]

111. Nikakis, "Sacral Kingship," 83.

112. Nikakis, "Sacral Kingship," 83.

113. Tolkien, *The Lord of the Rings*, 1037.

114. Tolkien, *The Lord of the Rings*, 854.

115. Tolkien, *The Lord of the Rings*, 861.

116. Tolkien, *The Lord of the Rings*, 880.

That Tolkien paints Aragorn as a counterpoint to the tyrant is clear in "The Black Gate Opens," where, as Chance notes, "only one view—that of the Dark Lord, voiced by his 'Mouth,' the Lieutenant—predominates."[117] Sauron demands servitude, does not defer to the wills of those who would voluntarily serve. The Lieutenant, Tolkien writes, "would be their tyrant and they his slaves."[118] Once more Aragorn is the subject of mockery, when the Lieutenant asks whether "any one in this rout" has the "authority to treat with me . . . Or indeed with wit to understand me."[119] Aragorn, the king whom the Lieutenant has described as "brigandlike," meets this mockery with silence. Perhaps, again in Christian fashion, he is only "recognized" in his death, when "a great beauty was revealed in him, so that all who after came there, looked on him in wonder; for they saw that the grace of his youth, and the valour of his manhood, and the wisdom and majesty of his age were blended together."[120]

Still further, we can grasp the sense in which Aragorn is a "Christian King" by turning to "Beowulf: The Monsters and the Critics," the lecture in which Tolkien praises the good pagan things found in *Beowulf*, that "heathen, noble, and hopeless" poem.[121] In the "history of kings and warriors" the *Beowulf* poet finds that "all glory . . . ends in night," in "the common tragedy of inevitable ruin."[122] Beowulf emerges as a king who has "the noble pagan's desire for the *merited praise* of the noble—the idea expressed in the Anglo-Saxon term *lof*." Beowulf expects the pagan's "just esteem" or *dom*, which are only merited insofar as the hero offers "absolute resistance, perfect because [they are] without hope." This northern "theory of courage" finds voice in Aragorn, when he exhorts Legolas and Gimli that "with hope or without hope we will follow the trail of our enemies."[123] Still more, like the just Anglo-Saxon king, the "just king Aragorn" will not "use his soldier's loyalty to enhance his own personal glory."[124] Aragorn's blood, then, seems to have (at least) three streams:

> As a sacral monarch, he was like the Anglo-Saxon Saint-Kings, Oswald and Edmund. Aragorn did not, of course, follow a Cross when he went into battle, but he *did* wear his Elfstone, the

117. Chance, *Tolkien's Art*, 178.

118. Tolkien, *The Lord of the Rings*, 890.

119. Tolkien, *The Lord of the Rings*, 887.

120. Tolkien, *The Lord of the Rings*, 1038.

121. Tolkien, *Monsters and the Critics and Other Essays*, 119.

122. Tolkien, *Monsters and the Critics and Other Essays*, 119.

123. Tolkien, *The Lord of the Rings*, 420.

124. Chance, *Tolkien's Art*, 119.

mythological equivalent. Tolkien's Ideal King, Aragorn, like the *Rex Pacificus* of the Anglo-Saxons, and the king of the ancient Hebrews, brought peace, prosperity, and justice to the lands.[125]

Distributive Justice, Thomistic Freedom

A king worthy of the title must foster the common good. Often "lay" readers and "scholars" alike do not adequately explore the importance of justice in Aragorn's reign. *The Lord of the Rings*, Colleen Donnelly writes, "ends with one overlord, one supreme ruler, uniting all people and creating an ordered society out of the chaos and ruin of war."[126] As Jane Chance notes, "the political and social healing that follows on the return of the King restores harmony and order to the ruled individually and to bodies of the ruled, to the communities that make up Middle-earth."[127] Aragorn honors all who served him, and, "As both Chance and McFadden have thoroughly demonstrated, the judgments the newly crowned Aragorn delivers upon his defeated enemies are equally impressive. Those Easterlings who surrender to him are pardoned and made free. 'The slaves of Mordor' are also freed and given their territory. Peace is made with the Men of Harad."[128] Although he reigns in majesty, he does not hesitate to give the Forest of Drúedain to Ghân-buri-Ghân and his folks, "to be their own for ever."[129] Of course, this gift of freedom is given to the Ghân-buri-Ghân, a primeval people, a tribal people whom the king also promises to help protect—a protection that requires considerable measure of the kingdom's ("government's") resources. Yes, the last third of *The Lord of the Rings* ends with the return of Aragorn who has "come into [his] inheritance . . . by the labour and valor of many," but his return signals not merely the preservation of peace and unity: with his assumption of the throne we witness a contagious commitment to *justice*. We see the culmination of a concern with the common good which permeates the lives of even the most unsuspected hobbits. If we have often missed the centrality of justice to the novel, if we have failed to see that *The Return of the King* is also, and perhaps even more so, *The Return of the Common Good* to Middle-earth, this is in part because we have failed to read the work of the Teutophile Tolkien through a Thomistic lens. It is

125. Chance, *Tolkien's Art*, 119.

126. Donnelly, "Feudal Values, Vassalage, Fealty," 25.

127. Chance, *Mythology of Power*, 104.

128. Sinex, "'Monsterized Saracens,'" 189.

129. Tolkien, *The Lord of the Rings*, 976.

only by bringing Catholic political ethics to bear upon the novel that we can see the marriage of *solidarity* and *subsidiarity,* Aragorn as the paradigmatic *just* king concerned with the common good, and the "small-scale," "somewhat 'anarchic' absence of law and policing, with the king a long way off," a distributist connection which both Alison Milbank and Stratford Caldecott have established.[130]

As Chesterton famously quipped, Distributism finds that the problem with Capitalism is not that there are too many capitalists, but too few. Upon the Fellowship's return to the Shire, Farmer Cotton notes that Lotho, whose commerce with Saruman marks the beginning of the Shire's dissolution, "wanted to own everything himself, and then order other folks about. It soon came about that he already did own a sight more than was good for him; and he was always grabbing more, though where he got the money was a mystery . . ."[131] Here we see echoes of Pope Pius XI's insistence, in *Quadregisimo anno,* that "if the social and public aspect of ownership be denied or minimized, the logical consequence is 'individualism.'"[132] Such passages, from both Tolkien and Pope Pius XI, chafe against Robert Sirico's "neo-conservative Catholic" claims that "low-paying factory jobs represent the best and brightest opportunity the poor may have" and that "[c]aps on income are counterproductive if what we want is more for the poor."[133] True, Lotho reaches the pinnacle of his corruption when he joins the Shire government as "Chief Shirriff," but Tolkien establishes a clear link between excesses of the private sphere and those of the government. This is not to say that Tolkien is against private property, or in favor of extensive government regulation of its use. Indeed, his treatment of Lotho is a penultimate example in that critics of the greedy hobbit's excessive ownership respects the principle of commutative justice, which—in the words of Pius XI—demands that we "faithfully . . . respect the principle of possession of others" even as, for instance, "a man's superfluous income is not left entirely to his own discretion," for he must submit to the obligations "of charity, beneficence, and liberality which rest upon the wealthy."[134] Lotho's wife Lobelia in a sense meets the demands of justice on behalf of her husband's avarice even as she abides by the aforementioned obligations. By the novel's end, the scrupulously bourgeois hobbit of the first chapter is so crushed by news of her husband's murder that she gives the coveted Bag End back to Frodo

---

130. Milbank, *Chesterton and Tolkien as Theologians,* 13.

131. Tolkien, *Lord of the Rings,* 1012.

132. Pius XI, *Quadragesimo Anno.*

133. Sirico, *Defending the Free Market,* 94–103.

134. Pius XI, *Quadragesimo Anno.*

and "[leaves] all that remained of her money and of Lotho's for [Frodo] to use in helping hobbits made homeless by the troubles,"[135] which ends the longstanding feud between Bilbo, his nephew, and the Sackville-Bagginses, and thereby helps to initiate an era *freed* from petty competitiveness and rivalry, and committed to a common good.

From the vantage point of Catholic distributivists, a major part of the problem with the regime of liberalism is its impoverished understanding of "freedom" or "liberty." Liberty has come to be synonymous with individuality. "Imitation is suicide," Ralph Waldo Emerson once wrote. According to the *zeitgeist* of modern liberalism, we betray the dignity of our individuality when we allow social norms to govern and shape our lives. "No law can be sacred to me but that of my own nature," Emerson insists. "Good and evil are but names readily transferable to that or this; the only right is what is after my constitution; the only wrong what is against it."[136] The great imperative of life is to be true to oneself, even at the cost of tossing over the baggage of inherited moral norms. In 1859, John Stuart Mill published *On Liberty*, in which he argues that authentic personal freedom requires more than protection from official government coercion. We are social animals, and we remain vulnerable to the unofficial but quite real coercions of communal expectation. In order to undertake what Mill famously called "experiments in living," we need to be able to escape from "the tyranny of the prevailing opinion and feeling." The best society, therefore, is one that sets aside, as far as possible, the question of good and evil, giving individuals the greatest psychological freedom to decide how to live their lives. To the extent that we seek to provide the opportunity for deep personal freedom to every person, we should use the power of the state to ensure an expansive view of liberty.

Tolkien was keenly sensitive to this impoverished understanding of freedom, of liberty. In a 1944 letter Tolkien sent to his son Christopher, he describes the "difficulties of discovering what common factors if any existed in the notions associated with freedom, as used at present."[137] He concludes that "I don't believe there are any [common factors], for the word has been so abused by propaganda that it has ceased to have any value for reason."[138] Regretfully, *The Hobbit Party* only furthers this abuse. Aragorn the king, however, does not.

In order to obtain Tolkien's vision of freedom we must return to Pope Leo XIII's *Aeterni Patris,* in which he beckons Catholics to learn again the

135. Tolkien, *Lord of the Rings*, 1021.

136. Emerson, *The Essay on Self-Reliance*, 15.

137. Quoted in Witt and Richards, *Hobbit Party*, 189.

138. Witt and Richards, *Hobbit Party*, 189.

meaning of liberty at the feet of the Thomas Aquinas, the Angelic Doctor of the Church:

> For the teachings of Thomas on the true meaning of liberty, which at this time is running into license on the divine origin of all authority, on laws and their force, on the paternal and just rule of princes, on obedience to the higher powers, on mutual charity one towards another—on all of these and kindred subjects have very great and invincible force to overturn those principles of the new order which are well known to be dangerous to the peaceful order of things and to public safety.[139]

Instead of turning to the Angelic Doctor, in *The Hobbit Party* Witt and Richards learn the meaning of "liberty" from Michael Novak, whose *The Spirit of Democratic Capitalism* is a panegyric for the rise of "property rights, rule of law, stable financial institutions, and economic freedom."[140] Indeed, Novak adopts and baptizes the Enlightenment understanding of freedom as "the formal ability to choose, not a freedom for any particular good."[141] Against this reductionist definition of freedom John Medaille asks whether it is "true freedom to be able to display pornographic images on billboards or the airwaves? Certainly there are commercial reasons for doing so, and one could argue, as Novak does, that commercial freedom must allow the flourishing of all vices."[142] Thomistic freedom is more demanding. As Medaille notes, freedom can only be adequately described if we consider not merely our *ability* to choose (its formal aspect), but the *object* of our choice (its material aspect). According to an Enlightenment understanding of freedom—the freedom we learn from the marketplace—Frodo makes an entirely legitimate choice when he says, on the brink of Mount Doom, that he does "not choose now to do what [he] came to do. [He] will not do this deed."[143] After all, the Ring *is* his, especially if we see it as a piece of property: by rights, he owns it. In the novel this choice is of course tragic, the incarnation of unhinged freedom, and it nearly prevents the reign of the Returned King.

---

139. Leo XIII, *Aeterni Patris*.
140. Witt and Richards, *Hobbit Party*, 55.
141. Medaille, *The Vocation of Business*, 208.
142. Medaille, *The Vocation of Business*, 209.
143. Tolkien, *The Lord of the Rings*, 945.

On the Primacy of the Common Good
against the Shirefolk

At first glance, the final ending of *The Lord of the Rings* ends with an archetypal domestic, private scene. Sitting in his chair, wife at his side and daughter on his lap, Samwise Gamgee draws a deep breath and says, "Well, I'm back." The epilogue, however, demonstrates Aristotle's claim, in the *Nicomachean Ethics,* that "though it is worthwhile to attain the end merely for one man, it is finer and more godlike to attain it for a nation and for city states."[144] In *Politics* we read that "when several families are united, and the association aims at something more than the supply of daily needs, the first society to be formed is the village."[145] Marking his full fruition as a political animal Sam's last recorded deeds include an extended term as Mayor of the Shire, from 1427 until he was re-elected in 1434, 1441, 1448, 1455, 1462 and 1469, serving until 1476.[146] This comes to nearly forty years in office. In Aristotle's formulation, "the state is by nature clearly prior to the family and to the individual, since the whole is of necessity prior to the part; for example, if the whole body be destroyed, there will be no foot or hand."[147] This is something that, before the War of the Ring, Shire-folk could not accept, and thus they were unprepared for the way in which larger political affairs would come to transform their families and their village.

We find numerous passages indicating that the hobbits' education into a common good that involves but surpasses their personal goods is an education that other characters require as well. A major reason why the common good, like the rightful king, has veritably disappeared from Middle-earth is that persons lack a common project. At the novel's start, "The hobbits did not pay much attention to . . . [that which] . . . did not at the moment seem to concern hobbits."[148]

Elrond's Council is, in large part, a forum wherein partakers can gain a sense of the common good through increased perception of the common evil of which Sauron is the host. Elrond's correction of the dwarves could well be applied to any species present: "But you do not stand alone. You will learn that your trouble is but a part of the trouble of all the western world. The Ring! What shall we do with the Ring, the least of the rings, the trifle that Sauron fancies? That is the doom that we must deem."[149] And thus they

144. Aristotle, *Nicomachean Ethics*, 4.
145. Aristotle, *Politics*.
146 Tolkien, "Appendix A" in *The Lord of the Rings*, 1033.
147. Aristotle, *Politics*.
148. Tolkien, *The Lord of the Rings*, 156.
149. Tolkien, *The Lord of the Rings*, 242.

have their common project, through which they will recover both the common good and their common king.

Aragorn, who as Ranger has long sought a good that stretches beyond his species, has habituated himself to goods of the genus. Aragorn has sacrificed common goods that are more familiar—such as goods to family, and to more proximate public office, in order to protect the wider world of Middle-earth. He would know well what De Koninck means when he writes:

> Further, if a rational creature cannot limit itself entirely to a subordinate common good, such as the good of the family or the good of public society, this is not because its singular good as such is greater; rather it is because of its order to a superior common good to which it is principally ordered. In this case the common good is not sacrificed for the good of the individual as individual, but rather for the good of the individual considered as ordered to a more universal common good. Singularity alone cannot be the reason per se. In every genus the common good is superior.[150]

Thus habituated to a more universal common good, Aragorn is able to correct Boromir's excessive sense that he and Gondor are the only ones protecting the freedom and peace of Middle-earth.[151]

De Koninck cautions us against the lie, perpetuated by collectivists and personalists alike, that the "common good" is ever at enmity with the "personal good." In such a formulation, the common good is "identified . . . as an alien good," a problem which breeds others: "All love would be confined to the particular."[152] If the common good is alien, "considering that one must love oneself more than one's neighbor, one would have to conclude it necessary to love one's own particular good more than any common good, and this latter would be worthy of love only insofar as it could be reduced to one's particular good."[153] In *The Lord of the Rings*, this false dichotomy is done away with in that the proper common good is also local good, as when Eomer fights for "the Mark," Aragorn for "Dunedain," and Frodo and Sam "for the Shire," each are also fighting for the wider world. They are not fighting wars that are more common merely out of love for their own particular goods; rather, they are here demonstrating a sense that "we are first of all and principally parts of the universe."[154] We, and our given nations, cities, and

150. De Koninck, "On the Primacy of the Common Good."
151. Tolkien, *The Lord of the Rings*, 245–48.
152. De Koninck, "On the Primacy of the Common Good."
153. De Koninck, "On the Primacy of the Common Good."
154. De Koninck, "On the Primacy of the Common Good."

families, are not "wholes, absolutes," so that "to be a part" is secondary. In such a case, "love of the singular good [would be] the measure of the common good."[155] We see Bilbo coming at last to know this when, in response to the old hobbit's claim that he "started" the whole affair of the Ring, Gandalf says, "If you had really started this affair, you might be expected to finish it. But you know well enough now that *starting* is too great a claim for any, and that only a small part is played in great deeds by any hero."[156]

Tolkien educates through irony. Bilbo is a bourgeois; thus Gandalf makes him a burglar. Frodo calls for Sméagol's death; thus Sméagol saves him from his own—and more. What Romano Guardini says of Socratic irony may well be said of Tolkienian:

> In the last resort its object is not to expose, to wound, to despatch, but to help. It has a positive aim: to stimulate movement and to liberate. It aims at serving truth. But would it not be better to teach directly, to refute, warn, challenge? Only when the truth in question can be communicated in this way. Socrates's concern is, above all things, for an inward mobility, a living relation to being and truth, which can only with difficulty be elicited by direct speech. So irony seeks to bring the centre of a man into a state of tension from which this mobility arises.[157]

The increasing immersion of the hobbits into the political life reaches its pinnacle, ironically, with what at first glance we might call anarchic rebellion. "The Scouring of the Shire" gives us a jubilant depiction of what a superficial gloss might consider sedition in the wake of the dramatically-altered Shire, one wherein "some new houses had been built: two-storeyed with narrow straight-sided windows, bare and dimly lit, all very gloomy and un-Shirelike."[158] Architectural decline, an absence of public or common beauty, is, however, only one arm of this alteration. Upon their arrival, the Fellowship learns from Hob that, "We grows a lot of food, but we don't rightly know what becomes of it. It's all these 'gatherers' and 'sharers,' I reckon, going round counting and measuring and taking off to storage. They do more gathering than sharing, and we never see most of the stuff again."[159] The text does not give us a numerical breakdown of the severe taxation that Hob relates, but we do see that among the "common folk" food

---

155. De Koninck, "On the Primacy of the Common Good."
156. Tolkien, *The Lord of the Rings*, 270.
157. Guardini, *The Death of Socrates*, 6.
158. Tolkien, *The Lord of the Rings*, 999.
159. Tolkien, *The Lord of the Rings*, 999.

is scarce enough that Pippin, Frodo, and company have to piece together their own foodstuffs in order to make a meal.

While food has been "shared" elsewhere, if one thing is in abundance, in the Shire, it is Rules. In naming them "rules" rather than "laws," Tolkien seems to intentionally avoid affiliating this arbitrary litany of dos and don'ts with a legitimate, authoritative law that merits obedience. Here he echoes Thomas Aquinas, who in his *Summa* argues that "[e]very law laid down by a human being has the nature of law only insofar as it is derived from the law of nature. But if in some respect it is in disagreement with the natural law, it will not be law, but a corruption of law."[160] We get a more concrete sense of the arbitrariness of the rules when the leader of the Shirriffs proclaims that the Fellowship is "arrested for Gate-breaking, and Tearing up of Rules, and Assaulting Gate-keepers, and Trespassing, and Sleeping in Shire-buildings without Leave, and Bribing Guards with Food."[161] *Bribing. Breaking. Tearing up. Assaulting.* The hyperbolic depictions of the Fellowship's arrival in the Shire reveal the loose connection between allegation and actuality.

On what grounds, though, can those opposed to the current regime both declare its injustice and disrupt the government? This arrest demonstrates the crushing stringency of the current regime, the disproportionality between crime and punishment; it suggests injustice. Why have those hobbits who have remained behind not worked, in any meaningful way, to overturn the reigning powers? Merry supposes that the Shire-folk have "been so comfortable so long they don't know what to do."[162] For this reason, he moves to "[r]aise the Shire!" to incite all hobbits to rebel. Farmer Cotton welcomes this returning wind: "I've been itching for trouble all this year," he says, "but folks wouldn't help."[163] Again, on the surface, though, the movement spurred by Cotton, Merry, and others has characteristics that mark it as seditious, in the sense that sedition is "a kind of discord." Cotton may be tongue-in-cheek when he calls his actions "trouble," but we see the possibility of divisiveness as an end in itself when, after Sam finds "the whole village roused," the village-folk light a large fire, in part to enliven things, "and also because the Chief forbids it."[164] Importantly, as the Shirriffs witness this fire, and the barriers that surround it, they are at first dumbfounded, but then take off their feathers and "join in the revolt."[165] One of the objections

160. Thomas Aquinas, *Summa Theologiae*, I-II, 95.
161. Tolkien, *The Lord of the Rings*, 1001.
162. Tolkien, *The Lord of the Rings*, 1007.
163. Tolkien, *The Lord of the Rings*, 1008.
164. Tolkien, *The Lord of the Rings*, 1009.
165. Tolkien, *The Lord of the Rings*, 1009.

that Thomas Aquinas grants concerning sedition is that, though delivering a multitude from tyrannical rule is praiseworthy, "this cannot easily be done without some dissension in the multitude, if one part of the multitude seeks to retain the tyrant, while the rest strive to dethrone him."[166] That *most* Shirriffs join the revolt suggests at first that the part which seeks to dethrone the Chief is considerably larger. However, once the division between the parts erupts into war, and once the war has claimed its carnage, we learn that while "nineteen hobbits were killed, and some thirty were wounded," almost "seventy of the ruffians lay dead on the field, and a dozen were prisoners."[167] Perhaps the hobbits are simply superior warriors, but this significant difference also suggests that those in the service of the Chief remain a large number until the end. This raises the problem of the nature of the hobbits' revolt: again, is it sedition?

Aquinas argues that discord against that which is evidently good is a sin, whereas discord against that which is not evidently good "may be without sin."[168] Does the fact that a large number of "ruffians" remained with the Chief's government until the end suggest that, if this government is unjust, this unjust character is "not evident"? Or, does the fact that so many Sherriffs rather quickly abandoned their loyalties to the Chief suggest the opposite? Aquinas notes that disturbance against a tyrannical government is not seditious, but also notes that this grows out of the fact that a tyrannical government is "directed, not to the common good, but to the private good of the ruler."[169] Whatever small benefits or privileges those loyal to the Chief may enjoy, it seems clear that they are problematic in that: a) we may not easily identify them as *goods,* only privileges or benefits; b) that insofar as they do receive benefits and privileges, these seem to grow out of a structure that only allows such things at the expense of others; c) and finally that the Chief himself claims a level of "private good" that far surpasses the goods obtainable by both those he unjustly rules and those in his service.

Aquinas goes on to contend that sedition does not come from disturbing a government "unless indeed the tyrant's rule be disturbed so inordinately, that his subjects suffer greater harm from the consequent disturbance than from the tyrant's government."[170] How we discern this question of "greater harm," then, seems to be of great importance. It would seem, on the one hand, that the revolt could be seen as causing "greater harm," in that it

166. Aquinas, *Summa Theologiae,* II-II, Q.42.

167. Tolkien, *The Lord of the Rings,* 1016.

168. Aquinas, *Summa Theologiae,* II-II, Q.42.

169. Aquinas, *Summa Theologiae,* II-II, Q.42.

170. Aquinas, *Summa Theologiae,* II-II, Q.42.

brought about more deaths. However, we see that under the Chief's reign his subjects are becoming Orc-like, an observation Sam makes to Hob when he says, "No welcome, no beer, no smoke, and a lot of rules and orc-talk instead."[171] By "orc-talk" he means the petty in-fighting and pusillanimous accusations the inhabitants of the altered Shire level at one another. Aquinas insists that the disturbance of an unjust government is not seditious in that "it is the tyrant rather that is guilty of sedition, since he encourages discord and sedition among his subjects, that he may lord over them more securely; for this is tyranny, being conducive to the private good of the ruler, and to the injury of the multitude."[172]

This last argument, found in the last lines of Aquinas's reply on the question of sedition, seems to clarify all questions that yet hang in the air. Clearly, the Chief "encourages discord and sedition among his subjects," a discord found both among those who serve him in the Fellowship's absence, and between the Fellowship and the servants of the Chief. This divided body politic may not be "easier" to rule, but it creates a condition wherein the Chief may "lord over them more securely," a phenomenon that is evident in that, as Robin Smallburrow says, "[The Chief] sends [his men] round everywhere, and if any of us small folk stand up for our rights, they drag him off to the Lockholes. They took old Flourdumpling, old Will Whitfoot the Mayor, first, and they've taken a lot more."[173] This passage reveals both that there has been a sizeable population of discontented hobbits before the Fellowship's return, but it also reveals that the very *power* of the Chief likely lacks authority. Jacques Maritain helpfully notes that, "to separate power and authority is to separate force and justice."[174] In the case of the Chief, we see the face of force without justice, particularly in that Will Whitfoot, the legitimate Mayor, is compulsorily dragged to jail. Lotho, or perhaps we should address him by his more dignified name, Pimple, moves beyond merely establishing a business monopoly. "Old Will the Mayor set off for Bag End to protest" the expanding pillaging that Lotho's property-grab incites, "but he never got there. Ruffians laid hands on him and took and locked him up in a hole in Michel Delving, and there he is now. And after that, it would be soon after New Year, there wasn't no more Mayor, and Pimple called himself Chief Shirriff, or just Chief, and did as he liked; and if anyone got 'uppish' as they called it, they followed Will."[175] Here we witness a clear shift from

171. Tolkien, *The Lord of the Rings*, 1000.
172. Aquinas, *Summa Theologiae*, II-II, Q.42.
173. Tolkien, *The Lord of the Rings*, 1002.
174. Maritain, *Scholasticism and Politics*, 94.
175. Tolkien, *The Lord of the Rings*, 1012.

authority (Will Whitfoot) to sheer *power* (Lotho), articulated most plainly in the shift from "Mayor" to "Chief Shirriff," captured also in the actions of each: Mayor Whitfoot uses his authority to protest on behalf of those whose property is damaged, while Pimple uses his power to do "as he [likes]," that is, to do what, in Aquinas's words, is "conducive to the private good of the ruler, and to the injury of the multitude." Of course, before his captivity, the Mayor's "only [notable] duty was to preside at banquets, given on the Shire-holidays, which occurred at frequent intervals." When we consult Aquinas' analysis of tyranny, however, we find that this seemingly petty political office, like the seemingly petty hobbits of Tolkien's *legendarium*, shows itself to be unexpectedly consequential; Aquinas cites Aristotle's *Politics,* wherein we find that tyrants "prohibit those things which create fellowship among men, such as wedding-feasts and banquets and other such things by which familiarity and trust are usually produced among men."[176]

We see, then, that the Shire did contain a political office before the War of the Ring, that the political dimension of hobbit existence remained a potency awaiting fulfillment. In *The Politics* Aristotle describes the family as "established by nature for the supply of men's everyday wants." In the "Prologue," we read that "'The Shire' at this time had hardly any 'government.' Families for the most part managed their own affairs."[177] Tolkien goes on to describe Shire life as predominantly agrarian, so that a more profound political dimension is lacking largely because "growing food and eating it occupied most of their time."[178] Apparently this was not always the case, as there remains an ancient tradition concerning the high king at Fornost. Although the ruins of the kings are covered with grass, the hobbits still hold these kings in reverence, for "they attributed to the king of old all their essential laws; and usually they kept the laws of free will, because they were The Rules (as they said) both ancient and just."[179] It is apparent, then, that the current period of withered political reality is held together not merely in some small farm anarchism, but rather through the perseverance of a set of laws that could only have been forged through the establishment of a kingship. The hobbits echo Aristotle in their consideration of these kings as great benefactors, and in their determination that "wild folk and wicked things (such as trolls)" are those who "had not heard of the king."[180] They also recognize that without such a benefactor beings are also "separated

176. Aristotle, *Politics.*
177. Tolkien, *The Lord of the Rings*, 9.
178. Tolkien, *The Lord of the Rings*, 9.
179. Tolkien, *The Lord of the Rings*, 9.
180. Tolkien, *The Lord of the Rings*, 9.

from law and justice," which makes them "worst of all; since armed injustice is the more dangerous . . . [whereas] "justice is the bond of men in states, for the administration of justice, which is the determination of what is just, is the principle order in political society."[181] Without the laws laid down by ancient kings, the Shire would lack the necessary means for the administration of justice.

Although a major part of what the hobbits come to recognize is the relative smallness of even their greatest goods when considered in the context of Middle-earth, they must also come to recognize the relative flimsiness of a sheer agrarian life that lacks both sufficient laws and the virtues which those laws should aim to inculcate. We know that the Shire folk have not completely forgotten the nobility that the laws—that the measure of justice—call them to in that the descendants of the kings, the Took family, of which Pippin is a part, are shown respect on account of their liability to "produce in every generation strong characters of peculiar habits and adventurous temperament."[182]

Nicomachean Hobbits

By introducing the language of "habit," Tolkien partakes of the language of Aristotelian ethics, and it seems clear, from this vantage point, that Pippin needed to partake in Frodo's quest not merely because Frodo needed friendship, but also so that the Took could develop those habits the capacity for which remained sunk under the Shire's stupor. At the beginning of the quest, Pippin demonstrates several characteristic Aristotelian vices. In *The Nicomachean Ethics* Aristotle argues that the sanguine person cannot acquire the virtue of courage because thoroughgoing optimists "are confident in danger," to the point that they are blind to reality, believing that all will turn out well, and will likely undertake various "hardships" without an accurate understanding of their difficulty and without a right motive.[183] In this sense, Aristotle notes, optimists are like drunkards, a point to which we will return momentarily. Pippin's excessive sanguinity comes forth when, after learning that the Council of Elrond culminates with Sam's being given leave to travel with Frodo, he proclaims this to be "most unfair" insisting that a more appropriate award for Sam's cheek would have been clapping him in chains. To this Frodo declares that he "can't imagine a more severe punishment. You are not thinking what you are saying: condemned to go

181. Aristotle, *Politics*.
182. Tolkien, *The Lord of the Rings*, 9.
183. Aristotle, *Nicomachean Ethics*, 54.

on this hopeless journey, a reward?"[184] True, Pippin goes on to clarify that he mostly was arguing that the Fellowship should "stick together" on the next leg of the quest. And yet he immediately goes on to quip that the party needs "someone with intelligence," which prompts Gandalf to indicate that such would exclude Pippin.[185] It initially seems, then, that Pippin's poor character, his inability to read reality rightly, should forbid him from the quest. And yet, when Elrond assembles the Fellowship one final time before their departure, and Pippin becomes aware that the Elf considers the Took unfit because he "[does] not understand and cannot imagine what lies ahead," Gandalf's response is at first unexpected: "'Neither does Frodo,' said Gandalf, unexpectedly supporting Pippin. 'Nor do any of us see clearly. It is true that if these hobbits understood the danger, they would not dare to go. But they would still wish to go, or wish that they dared, and be shamed and unhappy.'"[186]

Gandalf contends that Pippin's characterological state is not permanent. Given his careful study of Hobbiton, he likely understands that the apolitical culture has left its mark on the youngest member of the Fellowship. And yet the wizard's reading seems to snuff out prudence, given Pippin's actions at the Prancing Pony. Surely someone who had even the slightest grasp of the gravity of the quest, and its connection with the nature of the Ring, would not permit himself to the drunken dissemination of Bilbo's birthday story, a profoundly imprudent act that endangers the entire company, given that Frodo has to intervene with reckless abandon if he is to divert attention from his cousin's reckless disclosure, an intervention that ultimately ends with another conspicuous disappearance that, happening as it does in the common room, almost costs the Fellowship their lives.

Here, however, we witness the preeminence of friendship in Tolkien's economy of the virtues. Pippin may be guilty of the excess of "ready wit," in that he carries "humor to excess," and is thus a "vulgar buffoon, striving after humour at all costs, and aiming rather at raising a laugh than saying what is becoming."[187] Elrond may be correct in his reading of Pippin's cluelessness and malnourished political imagination. But Gandalf here finds company with Aristotle, who notes that although justice is the "greatest of all virtues . . . [for] in justice is every virtue comprehended"; indeed, even though justice is "the actual exercise of complete virtue" on account

184. Tolkien, *The Lord of the Rings*, 272.
185. Tolkien, *The Lord of the Rings*, 272.
186. Tolkien, *The Lord of the Rings*, 277.
187. Aristotle, *Nicomachean Ethics*, 77.

of its being exercised on behalf of others,[188] nevertheless "friendship seems to hold states together, and lawgivers to care more for it than for justice . . . and when men are friends they have no need of justice."[189] Friendship, Aristotle goes on to write, is not merely necessary, but also noble. Gandalf sees this nobility of friendship, and advances it in spite of all vices that need overcoming. Whereas Aristotle at times seems to conclude that persons must become virtuous in order to make friends who are virtuous, Gandalf seems to conclude that at times persons must persist in friendship in order to develop the virtues.

Pippin's vices are not merely papered over by some sentimental appeal to, and portrait of, friendship. This "Fool of a Took," as Gandalf calls him, does not merely persist in friendship; he also persists in foolishness. Upon arrival at Minas Tirith, in spite of Gandalf's advice that Pippin "be careful of your words . . . this is no time for hobbit pertness,"[190] Pippin quickly unveils much that Denethor wishes to know.

Their conversation inevitably turns to Boromir's death, of which Gandalf warned Pippin not to make mention when he indicated that Denethor loved Boromir "greatly: too much perhaps, and the more so because they were unlike."[191] Denethor despises the very name of "Halfling," considering hobbits those that "drew away [his] son on the wild errand to his death."[192] Gandalf cautions him to "[b]e not unjust in your grief," insisting that Boromir claimed the errand voluntarily, which thus at least mitigates the Halflings' part in his son's death.[193] Still, Pippin openly acknowledges that Boromir "[died] to save us."[194] It is at this point that Pippin, moved in part by Boromir's sacrifice on his behalf, and in part by Denethor's unnerving coldness, offers his service "in payment of my debt."[195] We might question the substance of this debt, but Pippin himself here recognizes the common good to be at stake, particularly in the form of the virtue of justice. Aquinas argues that restitution is an act of commutative justice, "and thus demands a certain equality."[196] Restitution denotes the return of the very thing that was taken, but concedes that "when it is impossible to repay the equivalent,

188. Aristotle, *Nicomachean Ethics*, 828.

189. Aristotle, *Nicomachean Ethics*, 142.

190. Tolkien, *The Lord of the Rings*, 753.

191. Tolkien, *The Lord of the Rings*, 753.

192. Tolkien, *The Lord of the Rings*, 755.

193. Tolkien, *The Lord of the Rings*, 755.

194. Tolkien, *The Lord of the Rings*, 755.

195. Tolkien, *The Lord of the Rings*, 756.

196. Aquinas, *Summa Theologiae*, II-II, Q.62.

it suffices to repay what one can, as in the case of honor due to God and our parents."[197] If a limb be taken, Aquinas continues, perhaps money, or perhaps honor, could meet the demands of commutative justice; particular judgments must be made by "a good man." It is possible to read Pippin as overly scrupulous, as offering restitution beyond that which justice demands. And yet, even if this were the case, his act contributes toward "unity," which is one of the great Thomistic political goods.

Pippin assumes the highly-public office of "Guard of the Citadel," swearing fealty and service to Gondor. Denethor invites and accepts Pippin's service because "[he is] not daunted by words, and [he has] courteous speech . . . and we shall have need of all folk of courtesy, great or small, in the days to come."[198] True as it is that Denethor succeeds in his suicidal pyre, Pippin's service at the very least works to ameliorate Denethor's despair; at Minas Tirith his wit comes closest to serving a common good that transcends his own excessive passion for buffoonery. Pippin, for all the differences that separate him from Boromir, is at least like Boromir in relation to Denethor in that, as Gandalf says of the latter, his father's fondness for him is premised in part upon their dissimilarity. Simply put, Denethor is more than melancholic, is despairing with the sickness unto death, while Pippin is sanguine.

It is necessary to note that Gandalf accuses Denethor of using his grief over his dead son Boromir "as a cloak."[199] This deep grief allows Denethor to cultivate a corrupted, narrow vision of the good. Such a small-minded "good" excludes that common good which everyone—from Elves, to hobbits, to the Riders of Rohan—has been brought to share. Wounded by his son's death, and given to consult the Palantir as a means of maintaining Minas Tirith, Denethor rejects Gandalf's counsel on the grounds that the wizard is doling "out such gifts according to your own designs. Yet the Lord of Gondor is not to be made the tool of other men's purposes, however worthy. And to him there is no purpose higher in the world as it now stands than the good of Gondor."[200] The Shirefolk's excessive envelopment in the good of the Shire blinds them to the broader and greater goods that are more common in nature, but they are largely unconscious of this narrowness. Denethor's declaration reveals a conscious rejection of the common good in favor of his own articulation of the good of Gondor, which, as his plan to kill both himself and Faramir on the pyre reveals, is actually his own

197. Aquinas, *Summa Theologiae*, II-II, Q.62.
198. Tolkien, *The Lord of the Rings*, 756.
199. Tolkien, *The Lord of the Rings*, 758.
200. Tolkien, *The Lord of the Rings*, 758.

perverse privatization of the good of Gondor masking as a public good. Gandalf tries to counter Denethor's excess by insisting that he also is a steward, even though "the rule of no realm is mine, neither of Gondor nor any other . . . but all worthy things that are in peril as the world now stands, those are in my care,"[201] but Denethor seems beyond persuasion. Indeed, whether because he considers Boromir to have been used as an instrument in someone else's quest, or whether familiarity with the Palantir has inculcated in him the Enemy's disposition toward instrumentalist exploitation, Denethor has reached a point wherein he can conceive of Sauron's use of "others as weapons" as a sign of "wisdom."[202] All of this is exacerbated by a paranoia that leads him to suspect Gandalf of hoping "to rule in my stead, to stand behind every throne . . . ."[203]

After taking Pippin into his service as a substitute for the steward's esquire, Denethor asks whether he is able to sing. "Yes," Pippin remarks, "well, yes, well enough for my own people. But we have no songs fit for great halls and evil times, lord . . . most of my songs are about things that make us laugh . . . ."[204] Denethor presses the hobbit, indicating that "[w]e who have long lived under the Shadow may surely listen to echoes from a land untroubled by it."[205] This encounter is interesting on a number of levels. First, we see that the wittiness and joviality of the Shire, which Pippin has on many occasions carried to an excess, is here framed as a good which can serve a part of Middle-earth long burdened by gloom. Aquinas himself indicates that theatre, in part as it provides reprieve from the rigors of everydayness, contributes to the common good. More importantly, though, Pippin's response to Denethor's request indicates a degree of interiority that he has thus far lacked. His heart sinks. He does not "relish the idea of singing any songs of the Shire to the Lord of Minas Tirith, certainly not the comic ones that he knew best; they were too, well, rustic for such an occasion."[206] That he can even gauge the discrepancy between these Shire songs and the occasion at hand indicates increased prudence.

Further, when Denethor dismisses Pippin and orders him to obtain proper livery, the political role that Pippin has assumed shifts his interior disposition even further. He at last can see the Shire from a politically realistic precipice: "Already it seemed years to Pippin since he had sat there

201. Tolkien, *The Lord of the Rings*, 758.
202. Tolkien, *The Lord of the Rings*, 818.
203. Tolkien, *The Lord of the Rings*, 853.
204. Tolkien, *The Lord of the Rings*, 807.
205. Tolkien, *The Lord of the Rings*, 807.
206. Tolkien, *The Lord of the Rings*, 807.

before in some half-forgotten time when he had still been a hobbit, a light-hearted wanderer touched little by the perils he had passed through. Now he was one small soldier in a city preparing for a great assault, clad in the proud but somber manner of the Tower of the Guard."[207] In addition to this existential sea change, he learns to wait on others while they eat. He begins to grapple with the meaning of honor, instead of grappling with the various goods provided by food and drink. He learns public-spiritedness from his tutelage under Beregond, of the Third Company of the Citadel, whose very life demonstrates what goods can come when goodness takes the shape of a city and not merely of a man.

At the same time, one cannot underestimate the profound crisis resultant from Pippin's first political office under Denethor, one so obsessed with private goods that when Gondor fails he believes that the "West has failed . . . it shall go up in a great fire."[208] A better way of reading this is perhaps that he interprets the limited evil of Gondor's destruction as equal to the destruction of the whole West. Subjection to, affiliation with, a man capable of muddling private and public seems to produce a keener discernment in him. It is not unreasonable to see this increased keenness operative in his insistence, upon finding out that there is a shortage of pipe-weed in the Shire, that "Lotho will be at the bottom of it: you can be sure of that."[209] Capacity to read the (shortage of tobacco) leaves may be a small matter, and Gandalf chastens this judgment by indicating that Lotho is "[d]eep in, but not at the bottom," but the wizard clearly reads the hobbits as, at last, politically capable, enough that he departs from them at this very point: "You must settle [the Shire's] affairs yourselves; that is what you have been trained for."[210] It is important not to understate this point: the quest has as its teleological end not merely the negative good of the Ring's destruction. Beyond this, the members of the Fellowship are made to develop the virtues necessary for them to participate in the good life.

Still, the destruction of the Ring is *not* the end of the novel, and upon their arrival home the Fellowship soon finds the aforementioned proliferation of Rules. Pippin, perhaps in part because service under Denethor sensitized him to the chasm that can sometimes separate official rule from natural law, tears down the list of Rules that awaits them upon arrival at the inn. Later, when one of Saruman-Lotho's ruffians mocks Frodo, snapping his fingers in the Ringbearer's face, Pippin proclaims that "You are speaking

207. Tolkien, *The Lord of the Rings*, 808.
208. Tolkien, *The Lord of the Rings*, 852.
209. Tolkien, *The Lord of the Rings*, 995.
210. Tolkien, *The Lord of the Rings*, 996.

to the King's friend, and one of the most renowned in all the lands of the West. You are a ruffian and a fool. Down on your knees in the road and ask pardon, or I will set this troll's bane in you!"[211] Here Pippin yet again shows his keen capacity to aspire after restitution, toward commutative justice. Aquinas numbers defamation and taking away another's good name among the wrongs that demand restitution, which the defamer can accomplish by "showing . . . deference to undo its effect, viz. the lowering of the other man's personal dignity in the opinion of other men."[212] Pippin doesn't ultimately enforce justice to the degree that the ruffians flee in fear, but he at least ameliorates the wrong done to him who carried an incalculable burden on behalf of the Shire and all of Middle-earth.

Pippin, again hungering after justice, insists that Lotho should be destroyed. Here he echoes the language of Frodo, who contended that Bilbo should have killed Sméagol, and of Sam that Frodo should have killed Sméagol. Frodo once again must perfect justice with mercy; he notes that "Lotho never meant things to come to this pass."[213] Again, although his passions are not initially aligned with the idea that rescuing Lotho-Pimple could somehow be a good, he concedes to Frodo, thereby at least acknowledging the authoritative weight of his friend's *misericordia*.

Still, it is Pippin's penchant for justice that we see most fulfilled at the end of *The Lord of the Rings*. In the last scenes wherein we see him play a significant role, he rounds up the Tooks for rebellion, and, with Merry, rounds up all ruffians and rids the Shire of their presence. These last deeds, combining as they do the martial spirit and its attendant virtue of courage with justice, crown his preparation for the office of Thain of the Shire, he who oversees the military forces in emergencies.

As Thain, though, Pippin reaches beyond even the martial and political virtues in collecting a library of historical information relating to Númenor and Elendil's heirs. In this way, Pippin has moved, perhaps imperfectly, but perhaps as profoundly as a hobbit of his sort can, through Aristotle's three categories or ways of life: the life of pleasure, which he inhabits both poignantly and painfully at the novel's start; the political life, or life concerned with honor, which begins in earnest with his service to Denethor and culminates in his service as Thain; and the life of contemplation, which finds articulation in his establishing a library and contemplating the past. Given our own access to the tales of Númenor, these do not lack philosophic content, and they often contain a contemplative character. Thus

211. Tolkien, *The Lord of the Rings*, 1005.
212. Aquinas, *Summa Theologiae*, II-II, Q. 62.
213. Tolkien, *The Lord of the Rings*, 1006.

we see Aristotle's assessment come to fruition in Pippin's life: "For . . . the just man needs people towards whom and with whom he shall act justly, and the temperate man, the brave man, and each of the others is in the same case, but the philosopher, even when by himself, can contemplate truth, and the better the wiser he is."[214]

Frodo, also, moves toward this good "self-sufficiency." We find that, upon his return to the Shire, in spite of the initial defamation the ruffians snapped in his face, Frodo eventually finds that "he was more lucky himself; for there was not a hobbit in the Shire that was looked after with such care. When the labours of repair had all been planned and set going he took to a quiet life, writing a great deal and going through all his notes."[215] The text here parallels the progression Aristotle outlines in *Politics:* "When several villages are united in a single complete community, large enough to be near-ly or quite self-sufficing, the state comes into existence, originating in the bare needs of life, and continuing in existence for the sake of a good life."[216]

When the repair is finished, and the bare needs of life met by various villages of hobbits all united in their care for Frodo, he is at last able to live a life of leisured contemplation. Although Sam is "pained to notice how little honor he had in his own country," Frodo himself, who has "dropped quietly out of all the doings of the Shire," seems to have moved beyond the economy of honor. He is too much devoted to writing to be troubled by the goods—but the lesser goods—of political life.

Still more, Frodo has "been too deeply hurt" to remain in the Shire. He has tried to save the Shire, he says, "and it has been saved, but not for me."[217] In this sense, Frodo passes out of an Aristotelian economy altogether and more closely approximates the *kenosis* of Christ. And yet he is just now departing to the Undying Lands, to that pace of pure being untainted by becoming; that *being qua being* which the Númenorians had tried to take by force so long ago will now be the culmination of his life. But beyond this he has left with Sam the Red Book which he took over from Bilbo, and which he tasks Sam with reading "so that people will remember the Great Danger and so love their beloved land all the more. And that will keep you as busy and as happy as anyone can be, as long as your part of the Story goes on."[218] Frodo's parting words reveal, further, the way that the life of lei-sure, contemplation, and writing, finds its fruits in a political aim—that the

214. Aristotle, *Nicomachean Ethics*, 194.

215. Tolkien, *The Lord of the Rings*, 1025.

216. Aristotle, *Politics*.

217. Tolkien, *The Lord of the Rings*, 1029.

218. Tolkien, *The Lord of the Rings*, 1029.

people who listen to the tales will *love their beloved land all the more.* This dynamic illuminates De Koninck's argument that the practical happiness of the community is not ordered to the speculative happiness of the singular person, "but to the person considered as a member of the community."[219] Still, for Aristotle, as for Aquinas, even this right understanding of the relation between speculative happiness and community does not complete the end of speculative life. Contemplation leads to "the highest beatitude, which consists in the vision of God," which is "essentially a common good." In "The Grey Havens," in Tolkien's narration of an entire company departs for the Undying Lands to behold *being qua being,* we see that "the independence of persons from each other in the vision itself does not prevent the object from having that universality which means, for any created intellect, essential communicability to many."[220]

It is only right that a that a book aiming to draw out the Thomistic in Tolkien leaves the last word on the common good not to Aquinas, but to Augustine, even if we leave the last word itself in the language in which Aquinas thought and wrote. Hannah Arendt argues that through his *De Civitate Dei*, among other writings, Augustine was able to deliver Christianity from politically-phobic paralysis, and this in part through the Latin language itself. In Latin, the word, "'to live' had always coincided with *inter homines esse*, 'to be in the company of men,' so that an everlasting life in Roman interpretation was bound to mean that no man would ever have to part from human company," even after death.[221] Augustine summarized this sense that alongside the city of man's politics of *libido dominandi* the saints themselves inhabit a political life. Augustine's insistence that the political is not merely a part of the city of man which we must endure as a necessity, but that it is in fact a common good, both in this life and in the eternal city, is articulated in a single sentence from *De Civitate Dei*: "*Socialis est vita sanctorum.*"[222] Such—translated into Elvish, of course—could be the motto of the ship departing for the Grey Havens.

219. De Koninck, "On the Primacy of the Common Good."

220. De Koninck, "On the Primacy of the Common Good."

221. Arendt, *Between Past and Future*, 73.

222. Even the life of the saints is a life together with other men. Arendt, *Between Past and Future*, 72.

Epilogue

From Apocalypse to Eucatastrophe:
"The End of History," Happy Endings,
and the Politics of Narrative Form

In "The End" of *The Sense of an Ending*, Frank Kermode argues that when tales previously recognized as fictions warp into myths people begin to "live by that which was designed to know by."[1] Thus, we could argue, Fascism is an instance of a political movement justifying and *verifying* fictions by their practical incarnations and effects. In political life the myths of apocalyptic bloodshed and "demonic hosts" infesting a pure people are played out. The Emperor of the Last Days, a stock figure of the apocalyptic genre, turns up as Hitler. After this Last Emperor commits suicide, the faithful consult their stars, searching for possible miscalculation. Others, such as Joseph Pieper, will not likely "be scorned for saying that many have indeed been Antichrist, or types of him, so that Nazism is a 'milder preliminary form of the state of Antichrist.'"[2] For Kermode, we who live after the end of Nazism, even if we would have rejected both Pieper's analysis and any temptation to see Hitler as the Emperor of the Last Days, nevertheless are shaped by the "apocalyptic types—empire, decadence and renovation, progress and catastrophe," all of which "are fed by history and underlie our ways of making sense of the world from where we stand, in the middest."[3]

---

1. Kermode, *Sense of an Ending*, 112.
2. Kermode, *Sense of an Ending*, 26.
3. Kermode, *Sense of an Ending*, 29.

Some think and live in an eminently apocalyptic mode, "totally end-directed," a way of being that profoundly influences the shape of a life in that "the end which [we] imagine will reflect [our] irreducibly intermediary preoccupations."[4] Many of us, who "claim to live now in a period of perpetual transition," have merely "elevated the interstitial period" of the apocalypse "into an 'age' or *saeculum* in its own right, and the age of perpetual transition in technological and artistic matters is understandably an age of perpetual crisis in morals and politics."[5] Whereas an apocalyptic thinker such as Joachim of Fiora would have situated the "transition" or "interstitial period" as that time of crisis that directly precedes the final end, we preserve the transition, but turn it from a preparatory period into a sort of perpetual end in itself. Others "project [themselves]—a small, humble elect, perhaps—past the End, so as to see the structure whole, a thing we cannot do from our spot of time in the middle."[6] For still others, life lived under the auspices of an apocalyptic form plays out in such a way that they "refuse to be dejected by discomfirmed predictions" concerning various apocalyptic contents, thereby "asserting a permanent need to live by the pattern rather than the fact, as indeed we must."[7] *Must* is a strong word. Kermode means it. Through his hospitality toward even the most conspiratorial cases of apocalyptic narrative we sometimes see him sneering at what he calls "naïve apocalyptism," an "eschatological despair" which comes from fanatically fixating on the end, and frantically calculating and recalculating its contents. But all of us, Kermode contends, at least those of us who have been sufficiently steeped in the forms of the West, "under varying existential pressures," imagine the end—the end of the world, and our own ends within it. And yet, while the influence of apocalyptic form and content, of the apocalyptic narrative, should not lightly be cast aside, Tolkien provides us with a slight modification of the apocalyptic form in the *eucatastrophe,* and it is worth asking whether the possibility of an ethical-political "eucatastrophe" might make the recovery of, say, virtue ethics, or the common good, less apocalyptic.

Frodo's words, spoken just after Gollum's theft and subsequent gloating seal the destruction of the Ring of Power, are nothing if not apocalyptic: "I am glad you are here with me. Here at the end of all things, Sam."[8] After an interlude among the Eagles, several pages later Tolkien gives us

4. Kermode, *Sense of an Ending,* 7.

5. Kermode, *Sense of an Ending,* 28.

6. Kermode, *Sense of an Ending,* 8.

7. Kermode, *Sense of an Ending,* 13.

8. Tolkien, *The Lord of the Rings,* 947.

almost the exact same admission from Frodo: "'I am glad that you are here with me,' said Frodo. 'Here at the end of all things, Sam.'"[9] Sam confirms his presence, pressing Frodo's wounded hand to his breast. But Sam resists the end, resists the sense of an ending that Frodo reads in their destined abandonment at the Crack of Doom. "After coming all that way," he says, "I don't want to give up yet. It's not like me, somehow, if you understand."[10] Frodo consents to move a bit further from the Crack itself, even as he contends that "[i]t's like things are in the world. Hopes fail. And end comes. We have only a little time to wait now. We are lost in ruin and downfall, and there is no escape"[11] We might see Sam as stubbornly sanguine in spite of the Facts, Frodo as the realist. But of course an end does not come; escape does, as Gandalf proclaims from the carnage-covered field of Cormallen: "the Eagles are coming!" coming to carry them to safety. Upon awakening after the rescue, Sam says that he "thought I was dead myself. Is everything sad going to come untrue? What's happened to the world?,"[12] and Gandalf explains that a "great Shadow has departed." Remember that Tolkien defines "eucatastrophe" as:

> The consolation of fairy-stories, the joy of the happy ending: or more correctly of the good catastrophe, the sudden joyous "turn" (for there is no true end to any fairy-tale): this joy, which is one of the things which fairy-stories can produce supremely well, is not essentially 'escapist,' nor 'fugitive.'[13]

It is not escapist in part because it does not deny the possibility of *dycatastrophe*—of sorrow and failure—rather, it is premised upon the reality of these. What it does deny is "universal final defeat, containing as it does a fleeting glimpse" of "Joy beyond the walls of this world, poignant as grief."[14] This Joy is able to break into the Story as grace breaks into the Primary World. "The Birth of Christ is the eucatastrophe of Man's history.

9. Tolkien, *The Lord of the Rings*, 950.

10. Tolkien, *The Lord of the Rings*, 950.

11. Tolkien, *The Lord of the Rings*, 950.

12. Tolkien, *The Lord of the Rings*, 951.

13. Tolkien goes on:
In its fairy-tale—or otherworld—setting, it is a sudden and miraculous grace: never to be counted on to recur. It does not deny the existence of dyscatastrophe, of sorrow and failure: the possibility of these is necessary to the joy of deliverance; it denies (in the face of much evidence, if you will) universal final defeat and in so far is evangelium, giving a fleeting glimpse of Joy, Joy beyond the walls of the world, poignant as grief. Tolkien, "On Fairy Stories," 384.

14. Tolkien, "On Fairy Stories," 384.

The Resurrection is the eucatastrophe of the story of the Incarnation."[15] At least in "On Fairy-Stories," Tolkien's sense of eucatastrophe is incarnational and Christological more than it is eschatological, but it does, after all, have an end.

Formally, the eucatastrophe is close kin to the *deus ex machina* of ancient Greek drama, and in this sense can leave unresolved much that seems to need resolution. As Alasdair MacIntyre observes:

> In the conflicts of Sophoclean tragedy . . . the attempt at resolution unsurprisingly invokes an appeal to and a verdict by some god. But the divine verdict always ends rather than resolves the conflict. It leaves unbridged the gap between the acknowledgment of authority, of a cosmic order and of the claims to truth involved in the recognition of the virtues on the one hand, and our particular perceptions and judgments in particular situations on the other . . .[16]

In *The Lord of the Rings*, though, the eucatastrophe moves beyond *deus ex machina* in that it brings characters not merely beyond "ruin and downfall," beyond the seemingly insurmountable Doom, but also beyond the point of crisis and onto a new "plain" from which to work out various new conflicts. Further, as this book has hopefully demonstrated, it brings them to ethical and political and contemplative ends that embody a Thomistic sense of the common good.

What exactly is the "ruin and downfall" from which the characters are rescued? While it is possible to read the hobbits at the start of the *legendarium* as typically bourgeois, it is also fairly easy to see in the Shirefolk the type of "last man" whom Alexander Kojève sees as inhabiting what Hegel called "the end of history." It may be fruitful for us to read the Shirefolk before the War of the Ring as Tolkien's mythical treatment of the Hegelian "last man" who lives at "the end of history." The end of history signals a world defined by the equal recognitions of all individuals, a near or total abolition of "masters" and "slaves," leaving only free human beings who recognize one another's freedom. In such a scenario, Kojève claims:

> Man remains alive as animal, with the specification that "what disappears is Man properly so-called, yet one cannot say that "all the rest can be preserved indefinitely: art, love, play, etc." If Man becomes an animal again, his arts, his loves, and his play must also become purely "natural" again. Hence it would have to be admitted that after the end of History, men would construct

their edifices and works of art as birds build their nests and spiders spin their webs, would perform musical concerts after the fashion of frogs and cicada, would play like young animals, and would indulge in love like adult bees. But one cannot then say that all this "makes Man happy." One would have to say that post-historical animals of the species homo sapiens (which will live amidst abundance and complete security) will be content as a result of their artistic, erotic and playful behavior, inasmuch as, by definition, they will be contented with it.[17]

Tolkien indicates that hobbits "are examples of natural philosophy and natural religion,"[18] and yet they do seem more *natural* than naturally philosophical or religious, something Chance observes when she notes that "[t] he hobbits relish what is natural for them, which involves physical activities, living close to nature—dwelling in holes, eating, smoking tobacco. To do otherwise is unhobbitlike."[19] The hobbits are contented with it. And so contented, they, like Hegel's last man, witness the disappearance of philosophy, of the love of wisdom, of the understanding of self and world—of, we might add to the list Kojève enumerates—ethics, and politics, and contemplation. And yet, again, as this book has hopefully demonstrated, even though the hobbits at the novel's start seem like mythical incarnations of the failure of "man" to embody that rationality and that striving after wisdom and the common good upon which his humanness is premised, and even though their near-animal states seem permanent, the political eucatastrophe of a common project emerges, thereby piercing Middle-earth with that joy which comes from knowing the common good.

Still, here at the end, I cannot help but sense that I am overstating the case. Kermode's underlying argument concerns the importance of narrative to the creation of human meaning, and even the creation or corruption of human moral and political life. Alasdair MacIntyre shares this concern, but his argument concerning narrative is more compelling in that he demonstrates the relations between a broader range of narrative forms and their corresponding social structures. "The narrative form of epic or saga," he writes, is "a form embodied in the moral life of individuals and in the collective social structure. Heroic social structure is enacted epic narrative."[20] Insofar as *The Lord of the Rings* is an epic narrative, though, this narrative

17. Kojeve, *Introduction to the Reading of Hegel*, 159.

18. Quoted in Chance, *Mythology of Power*, 28.

19. Quoted in Chance, *Mythology of Power*, 28.

20. MacIntyre, *After Virtue*, 129.

form would seem impossible to enact in a social structure that is definitively bourgeois. For MacIntyre, this dilemma is acute enough that he asks:

> in the context of forms of complexity quite alien to heroic society whether it can remain true that a human life as a whole can be envisaged as a victory or a defeat and what winning and losing really consist in and amount to. And they will press upon us the question as to whether the narrative forms of the heroic age are not mere childlike storytelling, so that moral discourse while it may use fables and parables as aids to the halting moral imagination ought in its serious adult moments aim for a more discursive style and genre.[21]

In the context of our own consideration of the pertinence of Tolkien's *legendarium* to serious ethical-political reflection and action, I would respond to MacIntyre's important question with two remarks, remarks which will at last bring this study to an end. First, as we have witnessed in manifold ways, Tolkien's myth is, if a continuation of the epic form, markedly modern, not least in its mythologization of the machine, and thus time spent in his Secondary World is not by necessity an escape into mere childlike storytelling. Second, the capacity of the human mind for analogy allows us to find parallels and patterns, and, importantly, *virtues* and *forms of our relation to the common good* in the narrative which we can transpose into our own social structures, even those wherein (is it not at times also so in the *legendarium*?) "the substance of morality is increasingly elusive."[22]

Finally, though, we must turn to MacIntyre's own capitulation to that form of fantasy we sometimes call "utopia," which, among all political "stories" or "forms," is most subject to the critique of "primary color painting." At the end of *Dependent Rational Animals,* having laid out the political and social structures of the common good, MacIntyre admits that such Utopian standards are scarcely realized beyond utopia. However, he continues, "trying to live by Utopian standards is not Utopian although it does involve a rejection of the economic goals of advanced capitalism."[23] Such a rejection is necessary in that, in spite of the differences marking the economically various institutional forms that promote the common good, they have in common one thing:

> They do not promote economic growth and they require some significant protection from the forces generated by outside

---

21. MacIntyre, *After Virtue*, 148.

22. MacIntyre, *After Virtue*, 243.

23. MacIntyre, *Dependent Rational Animals*, 145.

markets. Most importantly, such a society will be inimical to and in conflict with the goals of a consumer society. But to take note of this directs our attention to the extent to which these norms are sometimes already accepted in a variety of settings—households, workplaces, schools, parishes—in which resistance to the goals and norms of a consumer society is recurrently generated.[24]

Tolkien's *legendarium* is eminently able to incite our development—within smaller communities and groups—of virtues which conform to the primacy of the common good, be they some form of the economy of gift or the demonstration of *misericordia*.

This being said, the communitarian, subsidiarity solution is never sufficient. Progressive and traditionalist thinkers alike have rejected communitarian politics out of concern that it will simply be absorbed into multiculturalism as one more relativistic expression abiding by a "politics of side-by-side development in which members of distinct cultures preserve their own cultures against the incursions of other cultures."[25] Some, Richard Rorty among them, go so far as to advocate the federal implementation of a combination of indefinite growth of the welfare state and political correctness, reducing the influence of local communities, which, Rorty claims, tend toward racism, sexism, homophobia, and nativism, and reforming them—in part through State education—by means of a progressive correctness of ordinary language until what he considers "cruel otherness" disappears from language, thought, and culture, and the homogeneous American citizen alone remains.

From my own vantage point within the vein of virtue ethics, it is not that various justifications for a communitarian or subsidiarity politics lack rational justification. Consider Aquinas's analysis of both subsidiarity and the vices born of excess trade resultant from a departure from communitarian structure: "Now the city which is supplied by the surrounding country with all its vital needs is more self-sufficient than another which must obtain those supplies by trade."[26] Further, "if the citizens themselves devote their life to matters of trade, the way will be opened to many vices. Since the foremost tendency of tradesmen is to make money, greed is awakened in the hearts of the citizens through the pursuit of trade. The result is that everything in the city will become venal."[27] Good faith will be whittled away, and

24. MacIntyre, *Dependent Rational Animals*, 145.
25. Rorty, *Achieving Our Country*, 24.
26. Aquinas, *De Regno*, 51-52.
27. Aquinas, *De Regno*, 51.

trickery will increase. Finally, "each one will work only for his own profit, despising the public good; the cultivation of virtue will fail since honour, virtue's reward, will be bestowed upon the rich. Thus, in such a city, civic life will necessarily be corrupted."

Other examples abound. Consider E.F. Schumacher's articulation in *Small is Beautiful*:

> The higher level must not absorb the functions of a lower one, on the assumption that, being higher, it will automatically be wiser and fulfill them more efficiently. Loyalty can only grow from the smaller units to the larger (and higher) ones, not the other way around—and loyalty is an essential element in the health of any organization . . . The burden of proof always lies on those who want to deprive a lower level of its functions and thereby its freedom and responsibility in that respect; *they* have to prove that the lower level is incapable of fulfilling this function satisfactorily.[28]

The problem with Schumacher's and Aquinas's otherwise cogent defenses of communitarian politics is that we live in a world wherein the "higher levels" of so many organizations operate as though there is no need to proffer a "burden of proof," be it because eternal growth is posited as a sufficient logic for every decision or because power exerts itself from behind a screen that implies it needs not offer rationale for action. Though in truth "human power for which no one is answerable simply does not exist," nevertheless "the bearers of power have become increasingly anonymous," so that "there may be no appealable will at all, no person answerable for power, only an anonymous organization, each department of which transfers its authority to the next, thus leaving each—seemingly—exempt from responsibility."[29] However, even in the face of this power, these powers, common projects are decidedly *not* as utopian as MacIntyre's self-criticism suggests. Utopia, as Ernst Bloch defines it, encapsulates the "all-surpassing *summum bonum*,"[30] of which we all dream, a utopia actualized in Hegel's "beautiful soul," that soul who dodges the harshness of political responsibility, with all of its contingency, in order to preserve a sense of absolute moral purity. A recovery of the primacy of the common good, achieved both imaginatively and intellectually, and by its attendant political articulation in a common project, is *not* utopian: it avoids the pitfalls of those Western Marxists who continue to dream like "beautiful souls" of a purist communist state in spite of so-many

28. Schumacher, *Small is Beautiful*, 244.

29. Guardini, *End of the Modern World*, 123–24.

30. Bloch, *The Principle of Hope*, 305.

realists holding armfuls of evidence demonstrating the "inhuman violence as well as the pitiless statecraft practiced by the leaders of really existing socialist regimes."[31] Perhaps the scale of such modes and aims of recovery remains, like the hobbits, "bourgeois," betraying a "crushing dread at the prospect of sweeping, coercive change"; but perhaps those who undertake such projects, embarked upon with the same small-mindedness with which the hobbits operated at the start of their quest, will find that their work on behalf of the common good will expand through the common good's own superabundance.

In the meantime, we must live by an ethics that is premised upon the primacy of the common good. That is, engaging in deliberative reasoning with others, depending upon and being depended on in a manner akin to the cast of Tolkien's *legendarium,* we will be forced to reckon with the political-metaphysical fact that we are ultimately never actually autonomous "individuals." In fellowship, our positions as always only a part of the whole are made more obvious. Taking our cue from Beregond of Gondor, when we inevitably encounter "the doings at Isengard" that shake us out of our little communities, we will already be prepared for a state in which we may be "caught now in a great net and strategy," knowing that "we are but one piece in it, whatever pride may say."[32] What better way to live as we await The Return of the King?

31. Paik, *Utopia to Apocalypse,* 8.
32. Tolkien, *The Lord of the Rings,* 766.

Bibliography

Aquinas, Thomas. *De Regno.* 1267. In *Aquinas: Political Writings,* Edited by R. W. Dyson. 5–45. Cambridge: Cambridge University Press, 2002.

———. *Summa Theologiae.* Latin-English Edition, Secunda Secundae, Q. 57–140, Volume VI. San Bernardino, CA: NovAntiqua, 2013.

Arendt, Hannah. *Between Past and Future.* New York, NY: Penguin, 1977.

Aristotle. *Nicomachean Ethics.* New York, NY: Oxford University Press, 2009.

———. *Politics.* MIT Classics. http://classics.mit.edu/Aristotle/politics.1.one.html

Augustine. *City of God.* New York, NY: Image, 1958.

Barnett, Malcolm Joel. "The Politics of Middle Earth (Book Review)." *Polity* 1, no. 3 (1969) 383–87.

Basney, Lionel. "Tolkien and the Ethical Function of Escape." *Mosaic* 13, no. 2 (1980) 23–36.

Bergolio, Jorge. *Laudato Si'.* Encyclical letter on Care for Our Common Home. Vatican Web site. May 24, 2015. http://w2.vatican.va/content/francesco/en/encyclicals/documents/papa-francesco_20150524_enciclica-laudato-si.html.

Birzer, Bradley J. *J.R.R. Tolkien's Sanctifying Myth: Understanding Middle-Earth.* Wilmington, DE: ISI, 2002.

Blamires, Cyprian. *World Fascism: A Historical Encyclopedia, Volume 1.* Edited by Cyprian Blamires and Paul Jackson. Santa Barbara: ABC-CLIO, 2006.

Bloch, Ernst. *The Principle of Hope.* Charlottesville: University of Virginia Press, 2010.

Boyle, Nicholas. *Sacred and Secular Scriptures: A Catholic Approach To Literature.* London, UK: Darton Longman & Todd, 2004.

Brogan, Joseph. "Tolkien on Res Publica." Presentation at the Annual Meeting of the Political Science Association. Philadelphia Marriott Hotel, Philadelphia. Aug 27, 2003.

Caldecott, Stratford. *The Power of the Ring: the Spiritual Vision Behind the Lord of the Rings and the Hobbit.* New York: Crossroads, 2012.

Carpenter, Humphrey. *J. R. R. Tolkien: a Biography.* Boston: Houghton Mifflin, 2000.

Chance, Jane. *The Lord of the Rings: The Mythology of Power.* Lexington: University Press of Kentucky, 1992.

———. *Tolkien's Art: a Mythology for England.* Lexington: University Press of Kentucky, 2001.

Colebatch, Hal. *Return of the Heroes: The Lord of the Rings, Star Wars, Harry Potter, and Social Conflict.* 2nd ed. Christchurch, NZ: Cybereditions, 2003.

Curry, Patrick. *Defending Middle Earth: Tolkien, Myth and Modernity.* New York: St. Martin's, 1997.

Dadlez, E. M. *Mirrors to One Another: Emotion and Value in Jane Austen and David Hume.* Chichester, UK: Wiley-Blackwell, 2009.

Dawson, Christopher. "Catholicism and the Bourgeois Mind." https://www.catholicculture.org/culture/library/view.cfm?recnum=2580.

———. "New Leviathan." In *Enquiries into Religion and Culture (The Works of Christopher Dawson),* 3–16. Washington DC: CUA Press, 2009.

———. *Religion And the Rise of Western Culture.* New York, NY: Sheed & Ward, 1950.

De Koninck, Charles. "On the Primacy of the Common Good: Against the Personalists." Idataworks. http://ldataworks.com/aqr/V4_BC_text.html.

Donelly, Colleen. "Feudal Values, Vassalage, and Fealty in *The Lord of the Rings.*" *Mythlore: A Journal of J. R. R. Tolkien, C. S. Lewis, Charles Williams, and Mythopoeic Literature* 25 (April 2007) 17–28.

Dumouchel, Paul. *The Ambivalence of Scarcity and Other Essays.* East Lansing: Michigan State University Press, 2014.

———. "Revenge or Justice?: Obama Gets Osama." *Contagion: Journal of Violence, Mimesis, and Culture,* no. 19 (2012) 9–17.

Du Pont, Yves. *Catholic Prophecy.* Charlotte, NC: TAN, 1994.

Dyzenhaus, David. "Introduction." *Law as Politics: Carl Schmitt's Critique of Liberalism,* edited by David Dyzenhaus, 1–22. Durham, NC: Duke University Press, 1998.

Emerson, Ralph Waldo. *The Essay on Self-Reliance.* East Aurora, NY: Roycrofter's, 1908.

Euben, Peter J. *The Tragedy of Political Theory: The Road not Taken.* Princeton: Princeton University Press, 1990.

Evola, Julius. *Revolt Against the Modern World.* Translated by Guido Stucco. Rochester, VT: Inner Traditions International, 1995.

Fanfani, Amintore. *Catholicism, Protestantism, and Capitalism.* Norfolk, VA: HIS Press, 2002.

Flieger, Verlyn. *Splintered Light: Logos and Language in Tolkien's World.* Kent: Kent State University Press, 2002.

Foucault, Michael. *Discipline and Punish: The Birth of the Prison.* New York, NY: Vintage. 1995.

———. *Power/Knowledge: Selected Interviews and Other Writings, 1972–1977.* Edited by Colin Gordon. New York, NY: Pantheon, 1980.

Garth, John. *Tolkien and the Great War: The Threshold of Middle-Earth.* New York, NY: Mariner, 2005.

Gillespie, Michael. *Death and Desire: War and Bourgeoisification in the Thought of Hegel.* In *Understanding the Political Spirit: Philosophical Investigations from Socrates to Nietzche.* New Haven, CT: Yale University Press, 1988.

Girard, Rene. *To Double Business Bound.* Baltimore, MD: JHU Press, 1988.

———. *Sacrifice.* Translated by Matthew Pattillo and David Dawson. East Lansing, MI: Michigan State University Press, 2011.

Guardini, Romano. *The Death of Socrates: An Interprettion of the Platonic Dialogues, Euthyphro, Apology, Crito and Phaedo.* Whitefish, MT: Literary Licensing LLC, 2013.

———. *The End of the Modern World.* Wilmington, DE: ISI Books, 1998.

Head, Hayden. "Imitative Desire in Tolkien's Mythology: A Girardian Perspective." *Mythlore: A Journal of J. R. R. Tolkien, C. S. Lewis, Charles Williams, and Mythopoeic Literature* 26, no. 1, 2 (2007) 137–48.

Hegel, G.F.W. *Elements of the Philosophy of Right.* Edited by Allen W. Wood. Translated by H. B. Nisbet, Cambridge: Cambridge University Press, 1991.

Heidegger, Martin. "The Question Concerning Technology." *The Question Concerning Technology, and Other Essays*, 3–35. New York, NY: Harper & Row, 1977.

Hobbes, Thomas. *Leviathan.* Oxford: Clarendon, 1909.

Hobsbawm, Eric. "The Bourgeois World." *The Age of Capital*, 230–50. New York, NY: Vintage, 1975.

Horkheimer, Max, and Theodore W. Adorno. *Dialectic of Enlightenment.* New York, NY: Herder and Herder, 1972.

Kermode, Frank. *Sense of an Ending: Studies in the Theory of Fiction.* New York, NY: Oxford University Press, 2000.

Kirwan, Michael. *Discovering Girard.* London, UK: Darton, Longman & Todd, 2004.

Kojeve, Alexandre. *Introduction to the Reading of Hegel.* Ithaca, NY: Agora, 1980.

Koselleck, Reinhardt. *Critique and Crisis: Enlightenment and the Parthenogenesis of Modern Society.* Cambridge, MA: MIT Press, 2000.

Landa, Ishay. "Slaves of the Ring: Tolkien's Political Unconscious." *Historical Materialism* 10, no. 4 (2002) 113–33.

Leo XIII. *Aeterni Patris.* Encyclical Letter on the Restoration of Christian Philosophy. Vatican Web site, June 26, 1879. http://w2.vatican.va/content/leo-xiii/en/encyclicals/documents/hf_l-xiii_enc_04081879_aeterni-patris.html.

McIntosh, Jonathan. "The Flame Imperishable: Tolkien, St. Thomas, and the Metaphysics of Faerie." PhD diss., University of Dallas, 2009.

MacIntyre, Alasdair C. *After Virtue: A Study in Moral Theory.* Notre Dame, IN: University of Notre Dame Press, 1984.

———. *Dependent Rational Animals.* La Salle, IL: Open Court Publishing, 1999.

Manent, Pierre. *An Intellectual History of Liberalism.* New French Thought. Translated by Rebecca Balinski, Princeton, NJ: Princeton University Press, 1994.

———. *Seeing Things Politically.* Translated by Ralph C. Hancock. South Bend, IN: St. Augustine's Press, 2015.

———. *A World Beyond Politics? A Defense of the Nation-State.* Princeton, NJ: Princeton University Press, 2006.

Manni, Franco. *Tolkien and Philosophy.* Edited by Roberto Arduini and Claudio A. Testi. Zollikofen, Switzerland: Walking Tree, 2014.

Marcel, Gabriel. *Man Against Mass Society.* South Bend, IN: St. Augustine's Press, 2008.

Maritain, Jacques. *Scholasticism and Politics.* New York, NY: Image, 1960.

Marx, Karl. *The Communist Manifesto.* New York, NY: Simon and Schuster, 2013.

Mauss, Marcel. *The Gift: The Form and Reason for Exchange in Archaic Societies.* Translated by W.D. Halls. New York, NY: Routledge, 2002.

Medaille, John C. *The Vocation of Business: Social Justice in the Marketplace.* New York, NY: Continuum, 2007.

Milbank, Alison. *Chesterton and Tolkien as Theologians: The Fantasy of the Real.* New York, NY: T&T Clark, 2007.

———. "'My Precious': Tolkien's Fetishized Ring." In *The Lord of the Rings and Philosophy.* Edited by Gregory Bassham, and Eric Bronson, 33–46. La Salle, IL: Open Court, 2013.

Mouffe, Chantal. *On the Political.* London, UK: Routledge, 2005.

Nardi, Dominic J., Jr. "Political Institutions in J.R.R. Tolkien's Middle-earth: Or, How I Learned to Stop Worrying about the Lack of Democracy." *Mythlore: A Journal of J. R. R. Tolkien, C. S. Lewis, Charles Williams, and Mythopoeic Literature* 33, no. 1 (2014) 101–23.

Nietzsche, Friederich. *The Gay Science.* Edited by Bernard Williams, Josefine Nauckhoff, and Adrian Del Caro. Translated by Josefine Nauckhoff, and Adrian Del Caro. Cambridge: Cambridge University Press, 2001.

Novak, Michael. *The Spirit of Democratic Capitalism.* Lanham, MD: Madison Books, 1990.

Paik, Peter Yoonsuk. *From Utopia to Apocalypse: Science Fiction and the Politics of Catastrophe.* Minneapolis, MN: University of Minnesota Press, 2010.

Palaver, Wolfgang. "Rene Girard's Mimetic Theory." *Studies In Violence, Mimesis, and Culture.* East Lansing, MI: MSU Press, 2013.

Peterson, Erik. "Monotheism as a Political Problem." In *Theological Tractates.* Translated by Michael J. Hollerich, 68–105. Redwood City, CA: Stanford University Press, 2011.

Pius XI. *Quadragesimo Anno.* Encyclical Letter on Reconstruction of the Social Order. Vatican Web site. May 15, 1931. http://w2.vatican.va/content/pius-xi/en/encyclicals/documents/hf_p-xi_enc_19310515_quadragesimo-anno.html

Plato. *Timaeus and Critias.* Oxford Classics Edition. Translated by Robin Waterfield. New York, NY: Oxford University Press, 2008.

Rorty, Richard. *Achieving Our Country: Leftist Thought in Twentieth-century America.* Cambridge, MA: Harvard University Press, 1998.

Rosen, Stanley. *Hermeneutics as Politics.* New Haven, CT: Yale University Press, 2003.

Rosenberg, Alfred. *The Myth of the 20th Century.* Sussex, England: Historical Review Press, 2004.

Rossi, Lee D. *The Politics of Fantasy: C. S. Lewis and J. R. R. Tolkien.* Ann Arbor MI: UMI Research Press, 1984.

Scarf, Christopher. *The Ideal of Kingship in the Writings of Charles Williams, C. S. Lewis, and J. R. R. Tolkien: Divine Kingship Is Reflected in Middle Earth.* Cambridge: James & Clarke, 2013.

Schmitt, Carl. *The Concept of the Political.* Chicago, IL: University of Chicago Press, 2007.

———. *Leviathan in the State Theory of Thomas Hobbes: Meaning and Failure of a Political Symbol.* In *Contributions in Political Science.* No. 374. Translated by George Schwab and Erna Hilfstein. Chicago, IL: University of Chicago Press, 1996.

Schumacher, E. F. *Small is Beautiful.* New York, NY: Harper Perennial, 1989.

Schumpeter, Joseph A. *Capitalism, Socialism, and Democracy.* New York, NY: Routledge, 2003.

Sebo, Erin. "'Sacred and of Immense Antiquity': Tolkien's Use of Riddles in the Hobbit." In *Tolkien: The Forest and the City.* 133–143. Dublin, Ireland: Four Courts, 2013.

Shippey, Tom. *Author of the Century.* New York, NY: Houghton Mifflin Harcourt, 2014.

———. *The Road to Middle-Earth: How J.R.R. Tolkien Created a New Mythology.* New York, NY: Mariner, 2003.

Silva, Cherylynn. "One Ring to Rule Them All: Power and Surveillance in the Film Adaptation of The Lord of the Rings." *Bridegwater State University Undergraduate Review* vol. 2, (2006) 15–20.

Simpson Nikakis, Karen. "Sacral Kingship: Aragorn as the Rightful and Sacrificial King in The Lord of the Rings." *Mythlore: A Journal of J. R. R. Tolkien, C. S. Lewis, Charles Williams, and Mythopoeic Literature* 26, no. 1–2 (2007) 83–90.

Sinex, Margaret. "'Monsterized Saracens': Tolkien's Haradrim and other Medieval 'Fantasy Products'." *Tolkien Studies: An Annual Scholarly Review* (2010) 175–96.

Sirico, Fr. Robert A. "Creative Destruction" *The Acton Institute*. http://www.acton.org/pub/religion-liberty/volume-23-number-2/creative-destruction.

Sombart, Werner. *The Quintessence of Capitalism*. Translated by M. Epstein. New York, NY: E.P. Dutton & Company, 1915.

Stackpole, Gregory. "Charles Taylor On Disenchantment." Into the Clarities. August 23rd, 2014. https://intotheclarities.com/2014/08/23/charles-taylor-on-disenchantment/#_ftn1.

Strauss, Leo. *On Tyranny*. Chicago, IL: University of Chicago Press, 2000.

———. "What is Political Theory." In *The Review of Politics,* 343–68. Notre Dame, IN: University of Notre Dame Press, 2007.

Tally, Jr., Robert T. "Let Us Now Praise Famous Orcs: Simple Humanity in Tolkien's Inhuman Creatures," *Mythlore: A Journal of J.R.R. Tolkien, C.S. Lewis, Charles Williams, and Mythopoeic Literature*: Vol. 29 : No. 1 , Article 3 (2010).

Tolkien, J. R. R. "Appendix A." In *The Lord of the Rings*. New York, NY: Houghton Mifflin Company, 1994.

———. *The Hobbit*. New York, NY: Ballantine Books, 1986.

———. "On Fairy Stories." In *Tales from the Perilous Realm*, 315–400. New York, NY: Houghton Mifflin Harcourt, 2008.

———. *The Lord of the Rings*. New York, NY: Houghton Mifflin Company, 1994.

———. *The Lost Road and Other* Writings. New York, NY: Ballantine, 1996.

———. *Monsters and the Critics and Other Essays*. New York, NY: HarperCollins, 1997.

———. *Morgoth's Ring*. Edited by Christopher Tolkien, New York, NY: Ballantine, 1996.

———. "The Notion Club Papers (Part Two)." In *Sauron Defeated*. Edited by Christopher Tolkien, 145–318. Boston, MA: Houghton Mifflin Harcourt, 1992.

———. *The Silmarillion*. New York, NY: Ballantine, 2002.

———. *Unfinished Tales of Númenor and Middle Earth*. New York, NY: Houghton Mifflin Harcourt, 2012.

Tolkien, J. R. R., Humphrey Carpenter, and Christopher Tolkien. *The Letters of J.R.R. Tolkien*. Boston, MA: Houghton Mifflin, 1981.

Voegelin, Eric, Gebhardt, Jurgen, and Hollweck, Thomas. *Collected Works of Eric Voegelin, Volume 25: History of Political Ideas, Volume 7: New Order and Last Orientation*. Columbia, MO: University of Missouri Press, 1999.

———. "On Hegel: A Study in Sorcery." In *Published Essays, 1966- 1985*. Edited by Ellis Sandoz, 213–255, Columbia, MO: University of Missouri Press, 1990.

———. "*Timaeus* and *Critias*." In *Order and History Volume III: Plato and Aristotle*. Edited by Dante L. Germino, 224–68. Columbia, MO: University of Missouri Press, 2000.

———. *Science, Politics, and Gnosticism*. Washington, D.C.: Regenery, 2012.

Vries, Hent De., and Lawrence Eugene Sullivan. *Political Theologies: Public Religions in a Post-secular World*. Edited by Hent De Vries and Lawrence E. Sullivan. New York, NY: Fordham University Press, 2006.

Watson, Ben. "Fantasy And Judgement: Adorno, Tolkien, Burroughs." *Historical Materialism* 10.4 (2002) 213.

Werber, Niels. "Geo- and Biopolitics of Middle-Earth: A German Reading of Tolkien's 'The Lord of the Rings.'" *New Literary History* 36, no. 2 (2005) 227–46.

Winslow, Matthew Scott. "Two On Tolkien by Jane Chance." *The Green Man Review.* http://th egreenmanreview.com/gmr/book/book_chance_twoontolkien.html.

Witt, Jonathan, and Jay Richards. *The Hobbit Party: The Vision of Freedom That Tolkien Got and the West Forgot.* San Francisco: Ignatius, 2014.

Yates, Jessica. "Tolkien the Anti-Totalitarian." In *Proceedings of the J.R.R. Tolkien Centenary* Conference. Edited by Patricia Reynolds and Glen H. Goodknight. 233–45. Keble College, Oxford, 1992. Altadena, CA: Mythopeic, 1995.

Index